# Contents

PENGUIN BOOKS

# MATERNAL DEPRIVATION REASSESSED

*Editor*: B. M. Foss

Professor Michael Rutter completed his basic medical education at the University of Birmingham, qualifying in 1955. After taking residencies in internal medicine, neurology and paediatrics, he proceeded to the Maudsley Hospital, London, for training in general psychiatry and then child psychiatry. He spent the 1961–2 year on a research fellowship studying child development at the Department of Pediatrics, Albert Einstein College of Medicine, New York, returning then to work in the Medical Research Council Social Psychiatry Research Unit. In 1965 he took an academic position at the University of London's Institute of Psychiatry, where he became Professor and Head of the Department of Child and Adolescent Psychiatry in 1973, a post he still holds. During the academic year 1979–80 he was a Fellow at the Center for Advanced Study in the Behavioral Sciences, Stanford, California. His research interests include stress resistance in children, psychosocial development in an ecological context, schools as social institutions, reading difficulties, interviewing skills, neuro-psychiatry, infantile autism and psychiatric epidemiology. His published work includes many books and scores of scientific papers. *Helping Troubled Children*, *Juvenile Delinquency* (written with Henri Giller) and *Personal Development* (with Marjorie Rutter) have also been published in Penguin.

Michael Rutter

# Maternal Deprivation Reassessed

## Second Edition

Penguin Books

PENGUIN BOOKS

Published by the Penguin Group
Penguin Books Ltd, 27 Wrights Lane, London W8 5TZ, England
Penguin Books USA Inc., 375 Hudson Street, New York, New York 10014, USA
Penguin Books Australia Ltd, Ringwood, Victoria, Australia
Penguin Books Canada Ltd, 10 Alcorn Avenue, Toronto, Ontario, Canada M4V 3B2
Penguin Books (NZ) Ltd, 182–190 Wairau Road, Auckland 10, New Zealand

Penguin Books Ltd, Registered Offices: Harmondsworth, Middlesex, England

First published 1972
Second edition 1981
Reprinted in Pelican Books 1986
Published in Penguin Books 1991
10 9 8 7 6 5 4 3 2

Printed in England by Clays Ltd, St Ives plc
Set in Linotype Times

# Editorial Foreword to the First Edition

More than twenty years ago John Bowlby began to publish the results of his research on maternal deprivation, considering both its short-term effects on the child, and long-term effects in the development of pathological or deviant personality. The work has had a remarkable influence. It has led to a considerable amount of experiment, in animals and humans; it has resulted in practical changes concerned with the hospitalization of children; it has affected psychological theorizing, and drawn attention to the need to explain the characteristics of the child's bond with his mother; and, as might be expected, it has given rise to strongly held attitudes, often polarized, regarding methods of rearing children. Bowlby's approach to the topic was influenced by a psychoanalytic background and also by the early work of the animal ethologists. Michael Rutter, on the other hand, has the approach of a 'hard-headed experimentalist'. Considering these differences it is remarkable that their conclusions have so much in common: but of course there are differences.

In this book, Michael Rutter reviews the research and the theorizing, surveying a large amount of published work. He confines himself to the short-term and long-term effects of maternal deprivation in childhood only, and analyses carefully the various kinds of deprivation, and what is meant by quality of mothering. From his analysis he finds it necessary to distinguish between a failure to make bonds of affection, and deprivation after such bonds have been made. He is also careful to distinguish between various kinds of deprivation.

As well as discussing separation and deprivation, Dr Rutter asks whether or not there is something special about the bond of affection with the mother, or mother substitute.

He concludes that it may be stronger than other bonds, but not different in kind. However, there are adults who would say that irreconcilable grief, for them, would be the result of the death of one particular person, and one only. If Dr Rutter is right, it looks as though some people become increasingly 'monotropic' between childhood and adulthood. Possibly there are big differences between different children, in that some develop several bonds and others only one, even when given the choice. There is indeed already evidence suggesting this.

Dr Rutter brings to his task a disciplined mind, a great deal of practical experience, and an obvious warm concern for the welfare of children. Research continues. Its outcome will be of theoretical interest, but also of great practical importance for our future.

B.M.F.

# Acknowledgements for the First Edition

The ideas expressed in this book have developed through the course of many discussions with colleagues and friends over the last few years and to all of them I express my thanks. I am particularly indebted to Robert Hinde who has done much to clarify my ideas on 'maternal deprivation' and whose rigorous constructive criticism of an earlier draft of the manuscript eliminated many inconsistencies and faults of logic. Those that remain are mine alone. Many of my thoughts stem from my research collaboration over the last ten years with Jack Tizard and Philip Graham, to both of whom I owe a great deal. Their detailed criticism of the manuscript led to many improvements. I also received much help from others who have read and commented on the text – M. Berger, L. Hersov, R. Maliphant, James and Joyce Robertson, Barbara Tizard, W. Yule and a number of other colleagues. The original stimulus came from the results of studies into the effects on children of separation experiences and marital discord. My thinking on 'maternal deprivation' was much influenced by discussions with my colleagues on this project, whom I thank. I am also grateful to the Association for the Aid of Crippled Children (New York) for a generous grant which made the research possible. Like all other writers on 'maternal deprivation', I am indebted to John Bowlby, whose books and papers first opened up the subject and whose work has done so much to provide a stimulus on this topic. I am also most grateful to him for his helpful comments on a paper which formed the basis of sections of the book. Finally, I would like to express my gratitude to Catherine Greenwood and June Rice for the care given in the preparation of the manuscript and for help in checking references and proofs.

# Preface to the Second Edition

Since the publication of the first edition of this book in 1972 there has been a continuing growth of knowledge on the various ways in which children may be affected by acute and chronic stresses and by different patterns of upbringing. Much of the research into these issues has not directly utilized the term 'maternal deprivation' but, in spite of differences in terminology, it is easy to see that the origins of the work lie in the ideas first introduced through that concept. There has been an increasing emphasis on the mechanisms involved and on the links with the process of normal development. To that extent there are clear continuities with the issues discussed in the first edition. However, to a considerable extent the recent research has opened up new ideas and new concepts. It builds on the earlier work but it takes for granted the resolution of many of the controversies of earlier years. Most of the suggestions put forward in the first edition have proved valid but new issues and new controversies have emerged. As a result it has seemed appropriate to leave the six chapters of the first edition unaltered; their arguments still stand and the discussions there of the possible mechanisms involved in the various outcomes of 'maternal deprivation' experiences remain theoretically and practically pertinent. However, four short further chapters have been added bringing the findings, concepts and approaches up to date. The first briefly reviews the new evidence on the topics discussed in the first six chapters, and the last three are concerned with a discussion of the meaning and the practical implications of the findings on new topics only just touched on in the first edition. These include the development of social relationships and the process of bonding, the social/emotional consequences of day care, 'critical periods' of development and the long-term effects of experiences in infancy, influences on parenting, and the possible reasons why so many children do *not* succumb to deprivation or disadvantage.

Michael Rutter
May, 1980

# Acknowledgements for the Second Edition

The postscript for this second edition was prepared while I was a Fellow at the Center for Advanced Study in the Behavioral Sciences. I am grateful for the financial support provided by the Grant Foundation, the Foundation for Child Development, the Spencer Foundation and the National Science Foundation (B N S 78–24671); and especially for the stimulation, ideas and criticism from my colleagues at the Center. The postscript chapters are largely based on four articles: 'Maternal deprivation, 1972–1978: new findings, new concepts, new approaches', published in *Child Development*, June 1979; 'Separation experiences: a new look at an old topic' published in the *Journal of Pediatrics*, April 1979; 'The long-term effects of early experience', published in *Developmental Medicine and Child Neurology*, in 1980; and 'Social/emotional consequences of day care for pre-school children', published in 1981 in the *American Journal of Orthopsychiatry* (copyright American Orthopsychiatric Association, Inc.). I am indebted to the publishers of all four journals for permission to reprint portions of the articles. Lastly, I would like to express my thanks to Joy Maxwell who gave invaluable help in preparing the index and in checking the text and references.

# 1. Introduction

No area of controversy in psychology has given rise to such widely differing assertions as the topic of 'maternal deprivation'. Thus in 1951, Bowlby concluded that '... mother love in infancy and childhood is as important for mental health as are vitamins and proteins for physical health'. In sharp contrast, Casler, reviewing the same field in 1968, concluded that '... the human organism does not need maternal love in order to function normally'. Or again, more recently, Bowlby (1969) has gone so far as to suggest that individuals suffering from any type of psychiatric disorder *always* show an impairment of the capacity for affectional bonding and that frequently it is a disturbance of bonding in childhood which has caused the later psychiatric disorder. He suggests that this view provides guidelines for the day-to-day management of psychiatric patients. Conversely, O'Connor and Franks (1960) judged that the maternal deprivation hypothesis has not been experimentally confirmed to a degree which would warrant its acceptance as a guide to action.

Despite severe methodological and other criticisms (Casler, 1961; O'Connor, 1956, 1968; Orlansky, 1949; Wootton, 1959; Yarrow, 1961), the concept of 'maternal deprivation' has gained very wide currency and it has been held to be the cause of conditions as diverse as mental subnormality, delinquency, depression, dwarfism, acute distress and affectionless psychopathy (Ainsworth, 1962; Bowlby, 1951). While it has been recognized that the experiences subsumed under 'maternal deprivation' are complex, there has been a tendency to regard both the experiences and the outcomes as a syndrome which can be discussed as a whole (Jessor and Richardson, 1968). That different types of deprivation (perceptual, social, biological and psychological) tend to accompany one another is certainly true. However, as Yarrow (1961) emphasized, little progress is likely to occur until the basic variables indiscriminately combined under the term 'maternal deprivation' are differentiated and the separate effects of each determined. His thoughtful review suggested that different psychological mechanisms may account for different types of outcome. The present book seeks to explore this possibility in the light of the available evidence from research. No attempt will be made to criticize defects of design in individual studies, as this has been done in several previous reviews (see references above). Readers are referred to these and to other summaries of findings (Clarke, 1968; Dinnage and Pringle, 1967a, 1967b; Thompson and Grusec, 1970; Yarrow, 1964) to appraise the strengths and weaknesses of the raw material upon which this discussion is based. Rather, the data will be discussed in terms of their implications for concepts of deprivation, and deficiencies of the work will be touched on only very briefly when this is necessary to make sense of the findings. There is one further restriction in coverage – outcome will be considered only in terms of childhood and no reference will be made to the associations between childhood experiences and adult psychiatric disorder.

It will be appreciated that most psychiatric disorders have multiple causes. Quite apart from the effects of different types of 'maternal deprivation', there is good evidence that hereditary factors and organic damage or dysfunction of the brain play an important part in the genesis of emotional and behavioural disorders (see e.g. Rutter, Graham and Yule, 1970). The question of the relative influence of genetic, biological and psychosocial factors in particular psychiatric disorders will not be considered here. Rather, *within* that part of the variance which can be attributed to 'maternal deprivation', attention will be directed to which psychological mechanisms are concerned.

The material is organized in three parts. The first deals with the qualities of mothering considered necessary for normal development, the second with the short-term effects of 'deprivation' and the third with long-term consequences.

# 2. Qualities of Mothering Needed for Normal Development

Any discussion of mothering must rely heavily on Bowlby's writings, as his contributions over the last twenty years, ranging from his World Health Organization monograph in 1951 to his very important account of attachment behaviour in 1969, have been by far and away the most influential on this topic. In 1951 he stated that it was essential for mental health that the infant and young child should experience a warm, intimate and continuous relationship with his mother. He laid particular stress on the need for continuity and was explicit that this could not be provided by a roster. Nevertheless, while Bowlby (1969), in pointing to the importance of the mother–child *bond*, still regards an attachment to *one* mother-figure as crucial, he has always been explicit that 'it is an excellent plan to accustom babies and small children to being cared for now and then by someone else' (Bowlby, 1958b). Only in this way can mothers have the freedom to have some time released from child care to shop in peace or be with friends. He emphasized that particular care needs to be taken to ensure that alternative arrangements for mothering have regularity and continuity if mother goes out to work, but given this it may work out all right.

On the other hand, Bowlby's writings have often been misinterpreted and wrongly used to support the notion that only twenty-four hours' care day in and day out, by the same person, is good enough. Thus, it has been claimed that proper mothering is only possible if the mother does not go out to work (Baers, 1954) and that the use of day nurseries and crèches has a particularly serious and permanent deleterious effect (W H O Expert Committee on Mental Health, 1951).

The importance of a stimulating interaction with the child

has been emphasized by others (e.g. Casler, 1961, 1968). To these workers mothering consists of the supply of 'essential' stimuli which must be discriminable, functional and provide effective contingencies with the child's behaviour (Gewirtz, 1968, 1969).

Putting together these and other statements in the literature, six characteristics have usually been said to be necessary for adequate mothering: a loving relationship, which leads to attachment, which is unbroken, which provides adequate stimulation, in which the mothering is provided by one person, and which occurs in the child's own family. The evidence for each will be considered in turn in order to establish which features of 'mothering' appear important for development and which might be affected by 'deprivation'. The effects of 'deprivation' will be discussed in later chapters.

### A loving relationship

'Love' is difficult to define and many writers have rejected this aspect of mothering as introducing mystical and immeasurable elements. However, characteristics of interpersonal interaction, as covered by terms such as 'warmth', 'hostility' and the like, have been shown to be susceptible to reliable measurement which can predict how family members will behave towards one another in other situations (Brown and Rutter, 1966; Rutter and Brown, 1966). In fact, the quality of family relationships has been found to be strongly associated with the nature of the child's psychological development in both cross-sectional and longitudinal studies (Craig and Glick, 1965; McCord and McCord, 1959; Rutter, 1971a; Tait and Hodges, 1962; West, 1969). Where warmth in the family is lacking, the child is more likely to develop deviant behaviour, particularly of an antisocial type. Thus, there is a good prima facie case for regarding 'love' as a necessary part of mothering. It should be added that the same evidence suggests that warmth is an equally important factor in parent–parent and father–child relationships with respect to their influence on children's development. This implies that, while warmth is a necessary part of mothering, it is not specific to mothering. Rather, it appears that warmth is a vital element in all kinds of family (and perhaps also extrafamilial) relationships. That warmth between parents (as well as between parent and child) may also influence the child suggests that it is not only as a factor leading to parent–child attachment that 'love' is important.

## Attachment

There is good evidence that most children develop strong attachments to their parents (Ainsworth, 1963, 1964; Schaffer and Emerson, 1964). In his extensive review of the topic, Bowlby (1969) points to the universal occurrence of attachment behaviour in both man and subhuman primates. It may be accepted that this is a fundamental characteristic of the mother–child relationship. However, it is equally clear that there is great individual variation in the strength and distribution of attachments; the main bond is not always with the mother and bonds are often multiple. Thus, Schaffer and Emerson (1964) found that the sole principal attachment was to the mother in only half of the eighteen-month-old children they studied and in nearly a third of cases the main attachment was to the father. Although there was usually one particularly strong attachment, the majority of the children showed multiple attachments of varying intensity. It may be concluded that attachment is an important, perhaps crucial, aspect of the mother–child relationship, but equally it is a characteristic shared with other relationships.

Bowlby (1969) has argued that there is a bias for a child to attach himself especially to *one* figure (a characteristic he has called 'monotropy') and that this main attachment differs in kind from attachments to other subsidiary figures. However, there is a lack of supporting evidence for this claim; Schaffer (1971) has concluded that Bowlby's view is not borne out by the facts and that the breadth of attachments is largely determined by the social setting. The issue remains unsettled and requires further study.

If it is accepted that attachments are an important feature, it is necessary to proceed to the issue of what circumstances are required for their development. This is a question on which there are few facts in spite of an abundance of theories (Ainsworth, 1969; Bowlby, 1969; Cairns, 1966b; Gewirtz, 1969; Maccoby and Masters, 1970; Walters and Parke, 1965). The available evidence has been well reviewed by both Bowlby (1969) and Schaffer (1971). In this connection it is evident that proximity seeking and attachment to *specific* figures must be differentiated from dependency and attention-getting as a *general* characteristic. Bond formation is only concerned with the former (although non-specific attachment behaviour can lead to specific attachments).

If specific attachments are to develop with respect to individual persons it appears, although evidence on the point is lacking, that the *same* person must have contact with the child over a prolonged period on the grounds that attachments take time to develop. At least above a certain level, the absolute amount of time spent in the company of the child does not seem to affect the development of attachment, but the *intensity* of the parental interaction with the child probably is important (Schaffer and Emerson, 1964). Mothers who play with their child and give him a great deal of attention have a more strongly attached child than those who interact with the child only when giving routine care. Similarly, when a relatively unstimulating mother is found in conjunction with an extremely attentive father, the latter is likely to head the infant's hierarchy of attachment objects, despite the mother's greater availability (Schaffer, 1971). That intensity, rather than duration of interaction, is the crucial feature, is also suggested by anecdotal studies of kibbutzim children (Bowlby, 1969), who seem to be more often attached to their mothers (whom they see for short periods of intensive interaction) than to the metapelet who cares for them all day (but less intensively and as one of several children).

Schaffer and Emerson (1964) also showed that maternal responsiveness was associated with the strength of attachments. In cases where mothers responded regularly and quickly whenever their infants cried, attachments were strongest. Ainsworth (Ainsworth and Bell, 1969; Ainsworth and Wittig, 1969), on the basis of her observations of mother–infant interaction, also concluded that a key feature was the mother's sensitivity to her baby's signals. Attachments probably develop most readily to persons who can adapt their behaviour to the specific requirements of the individual infant, by taking into account the infant's individuality and by learning to recognize his particular signals (Schaffer, 1971).

Anxiety and fear, as well as illness and fatigue, tend to increase attachment behaviour (Bowlby, 1969; Maccoby and Masters, 1970). How this influences bond formation remains uncertain but it is probable that bonds are most likely to develop to the familiar person who is present, and so able to provide comfort, at times of distress. When a person is associated with relief of anxiety, an attachment is fostered. Whether the person is associated with anxiety or relief of anxiety obviously will depend on the circumstances. Children do not usually become attached to the dental nurse or the family doctor who gives them injections! Yet, under some conditions, they may actually develop attachments to people or objects who cause them distress. This has been shown experimentally in animals (Bowlby, 1969), but clinical experience suggests that the same may occur in man. Occasional parental rejection may actually increase attachment behaviour (in spite of the bond being less secure). It is parental apathy and lack of response which appear more important as inhibitors of the child's attachment.

The number of caretakers does not seem to be a major variable if other factors are held constant, but there is some suggestion that attachments may be stronger when the child has few caretakers (Caldwell, 1962; Schaffer and Emerson, 1964).

The content of the interaction appears largely irrelevant, and neither feeding nor caretaking are essential features – though they may facilitate the development of attachments (Schaffer, 1971). Attachments may develop to brothers or sisters (Schaffer and Emerson, 1964), and the presence of a child's even very young sibs may serve to reduce his anxiety in stress situations (Heinicke and Westheimer, 1965). Attachments may be formed to individuals who play with the child but do not feed him, and Schaffer and Emerson (1964) found that a third of children were mainly attached to someone who was *not* their principal caretaker.

It is uncertain whether the factors that aid attachment in animals are similar to those in man, but it seems that to the rhesus monkey body-contact comfort is more important than feeding (Harlow and Zimmermann, 1959) and that the type of surface contacted is relevant (Furchner and Harlow, 1969). However, if 'comfort' is held constant, both in that species (Harlow, 1961) and in dogs (Igel and Calvin, 1960), a lactating surrogate is preferred to one which is non-lactating. Little is known about the effects of facial appearance. However, a preliminary study (Gardner and Gardner, 1970) on just two monkeys suggested that this may also influence monkey preferences for different surrogates – although it is clear that this is at most a very subsidiary factor. Cairns (1966a, 1966b) reported that lambs can form attachments to animals they can see (through a glass panel) but not contact, showing that direct interaction is not essential. Mason's work (1968) implies that moving dummies may be preferable to stationary devices. All these experiments are useful in pointing to possible factors which may influence the development of attachments. However, it is clear from long-term studies of the rhesus monkey that, in spite of inducing attachments, surrogates of all types are almost totally ineffective as mothers so far as preventing the ill-effects of isolation is concerned (Harlow and Harlow, 1969, 1970). They provide immediate comfort in frightening situations, but in the long term they are only marginally better than no surrogate and are very much worse than a monkey mother. Mothering requires a *reciprocal* interaction and so consists of far more than the passive reception of attachment behaviour (see accounts of the development of maternal behaviour in different species in Rheingold, 1963). This is well shown by Hinde and Spencer-Booth's (1971a) recent analysis of the dynamics of the developing mother–infant relationship in group-reared rhesus monkeys. It is also illustrated by the differences in mother–infant interaction in group- and cage-reared animals (Hinde and Spencer-Booth, 1967; Wolfheim, Jensen and Bobbitt, 1970).

In humans, there are variables not present in subhuman primates which also play a part. Language is the most important of these. This is influential both as a means of conveying feelings and emotions and through its role in thought processes enabling the infant to retain a concept of the mother when she is away from him. As well as factors directly concerned with mother–infant interaction, human studies suggest that the total amount of social stimulation provided may also influence the propensity to form attachments (although this possibility requires further study). Rheingold (1956) showed that extra mothering of six-month-old institutionalized infants led to an increase in their social responsiveness. Also, Schaffer (1963), in a comparison of infants in hospital with those in a baby home, found that the first group (which had received less social stimulation) were slower to form attachments on their return home.

It should be added that the infants' own characteristics influence the development of attachment behaviour (Schaffer and Emerson, 1964) as they do other aspects of the mother–infant relationship (Bell, 1971; Harper, 1971). Moss (1967) found sex differences in early interaction; Prechtl (1963) and Ucko (1965) have shown how damage arising in the womb or soon after birth can influence the child's behaviour in ways that may influence the mother's response to him; and Freedman (1965) showed a genetic component in infants' early social responses. The behaviour of a neonate helps shape the response of his mother during feeding (Bell, 1964; Levy, 1958), and Yarrow (1963) showed that foster parents were influenced in their behaviour by the characteristics of their foster children. The child's contribution to parent–child interaction is a most important but much neglected subject.

The development of bonds in man has often been likened to the acquisition of a following response in nidifugous birds – a process known as 'imprinting'. Imprinting was originally regarded as a unique phenomenon which could develop only during a very short critical period in early infancy and which was irreversible once it had developed (Lorenz, 1935). Accordingly, it was once thought that the development of human attachments, too, might be restricted to a very narrow age period. It is now quite clear that this early view of imprinting was incorrect. There is no reason for thinking that imprinting is fundamentally different from other forms of learning; the period of its acquisition is influenced by environmental circumstances and is not rigidly fixed, and the following response is not irreversible (Bateson, 1966; Hinde, 1970). Nevertheless, the phenomenon is an important and interesting one and it remains true that it can only develop during a 'sensitive' period in early infancy (although this period is less clearly defined than first thought). To what extent the development of a mother–infant attachment in humans is similarly restricted to a particular phase of development remains quite uncertain (Schaffer, 1971). Undoubtedly, attachments can develop up to the age of one year (Schaffer, 1963) and often up to two years (Tizard and Tizard, 1972), but it is not known how long the readiness to develop an attachment can be maintained or what environmental circumstances are necessary for the readiness to persist. It is also quite unknown whether an attachment that develops late is as strong, stable and secure as one that develops early (Bowlby, 1969). These are important questions but ones to which no answers are yet available.

### An unbroken relationship

The main reasons for regarding continuity as an essential requisite of mothering are the well-established associations between 'broken homes' and delinquency (see page 65), and the short-term disturbance which often follows a young child's separation from his parents (Yarrow, 1964). Both of these findings suggest that breaks in the parent–child relationship *may* have adverse effects, but as breaks are frequently associated with other adverse factors it remains to be established whether it is the separation as such which is the deleterious influence (this issue is discussed further in later chapters).

That transient separations are not necessarily a bad thing is evident from the high rate of separations in normal individuals. Douglas, Ross and Simpson (1968), in a national sample of some five thousand children, showed that by four and a half years of age, a third of children had been separated from their mother for at least one week. Furthermore, they showed that there was only a weak association between brief separations and delinquency (forty-one per cent separations in delinquents as against thirty-two per cent in controls). Of course, all children must separate from their parents sometime if they are to develop independent personalities, so the question is not *whether* children should separate from their mothers but rather *when* and *how* separations should occur. The finding that certain sorts of happy separation may actually protect young children from the adverse effects of later stressful separation (Stacey, Dearden, Pill and Robinson, 1970) also emphasizes the importance of considering the circumstances of a separation when deciding whether it is likely to be beneficial or harmful.

Perhaps an even more crucial point is the equation of 'separation' with 'discontinuity' in a relationship. In his 1951 monograph, Bowlby argued that the young pre-school child is unable to maintain a relationship with a person in their absence and that for this reason even brief separations disrupt a relationship. Experience with normal children suggests that this is not always so, at least in favourable circumstances. Of course, young children do find it more difficult, but it seems probable that environmental conditions as well as age influence a child's ability to maintain a bond during a person's absence. As the point is vital to the whole argument on continuity it deserves greater attention than it has received. The implications are discussed further in later chapters.

## A 'stimulating' interaction

Different writers have varied greatly in the emphasis placed on 'stimulation' in mothering and on perceptual lack in 'maternal deprivation'. Some (e.g. Casler, 1968) have considered perceptual factors the most important influence, whereas others (e.g. Ainsworth, 1962) have regarded them as of only minor significance. Institutions have been used in many studies as an example of a deprivation situation and it is clear from several independent investigations that the sheer amount of adult–child interaction is one of the biggest differences between institutions and families (David and Appell, 1961; King, Raynes and Tizard, 1971; Provence and Lipton, 1962; Rheingold, 1960). On this basis it would be reasonable to include 'stimulation' as one of the hypothesized necessary elements in mothering, particularly as there is evidence that this is a necessary element in the development of language and intelligence (Haywood, 1967; Rutter and Mittler, 1972). However, it should be noted that 'stimulation' is a most unsatisfactory blanket term which means little unless further defined. Furthermore, although institutions may lack certain forms of stimulation, they differ from normal family life in many complex ways and it remains to be determined which differences lead to which effects. These issues are considered in more detail in chapters 4 and 5.

### Relationship with one person

The suggested requirement that the mothering should be provided by one person is more controversial and not one given much emphasis by Bowlby (1951) in his WHO report. Although he expressed reservations about kibbutzim where mothering is shared between parents and metapelet (p. 43), he suggested (p. 72) that large multiple-generation family groups had certain advantages in that there were always relatives at hand to take over the maternal role in an emergency. On the other hand, he has always (Bowlby, 1969) laid great emphasis on the hypothesized need for a child to attach himself specifically to just *one* person. Presumably if 'multiple mothering' did not allow this a child would be expected to suffer.

Actually there are several quite different situations included under 'multiple mothering', as Ainsworth (1962) has pointed out. First, there is the case where one major mother-figure shares mothering with a variety of mother-surrogates.

This is exemplified by what happens when the mother goes out to work and in this situation there is good evidence that the children do not suffer provided stable relationships and good care are provided by the mother-surrogates (Rutter, 1971a; Yudkin and Holme, 1963).* Secondly, there is the dispersal of responsibility among several (but not many) figures who have a high degree of continuity, as in the Israeli kibbutzim (Miller, 1969) or in societies with extended family systems (Mead, 1962). Again, although the evidence is quite weak, there is no reason to suppose that children suffer from this arrangement. Thirdly, multiple mothering may be associated with discontinuity and/or inadequate interaction, as in many long-stay institutions or residential nurseries. It is in these circumstances that children may suffer. While it is true that the number of mother-figures in institutions (sometimes a hundred plus) is usually also very much larger than is the case with either working mothers or kibbutzim, in practice a very large number of mother-figures virtually never occurs without there also being either discontinuity of relationships or inadequate interaction. It may be concluded that it is *not* necessary for mothering to be provided by only one person. In practice there is a strong tendency for situations involving very many mother-figures to be unsatisfactory in many other ways. Nevertheless, the very limited available evidence suggests that, if the mothering is of high quality and is provided by figures who remain the same during the child's early life, then (at least up to four or five mother-figures) multiple mothering need have no adverse effects. As this point is very pertinent to Bowlby's views on 'monotropy', well-controlled systematic studies are much needed to confirm or refute this very tentative conclusion.

## Mothering in the child's own home

Finally, it has been suggested that mothering must be provided in the child's own home. Thus, Bowlby in his 1951 monograph maintained that children thrive better in bad homes than in good institutions and that a residential

* But see also chapter 8.

nursery cannot provide a satisfactory emotional environment for infants and young children. His more recent writings have shown that he is well aware of the complexities of the situation and of the dangers of comparisons of this sort. Nevertheless his early dictum was widely accepted and led to a very marked reluctance by some Children's Officers to remove children from even appalling home circumstances. It also led to foster homes being preferred as a placement over children's homes in spite of the fact that discontinuity of mothering is often just as great in foster homes (Dinnage and Pringle, 1967a, 1967b). Actually, there is no satisfactory evidence in support of the dictum 'better a bad family than a good institution'. Taken at its face value it seems to imply some mystical quality present in the family and suggests that the quality of mothering provided is irrelevant. This is such an obvious nonsense (and certainly not intended by Bowlby) that it scarcely warrants serious consideration. The development of children is so bad in the worst families – such as those where baby battering occurs (Helfer and Kempe, 1968; Skinner and Castle, 1969), where there is chronic discord and lack of affection between two psychopathic parents (Rutter, 1971a), or where parental social adjustment is at its worst (West, 1969) – that even an institutional upbringing may be preferable. The outcome for children reared in institutions is certainly worse than that of the general population (Ferguson, 1966), but the outcome for many children from the best institutions is reasonably satisfactory (Conway, 1957; Tizard, Cooperman, Joseph and Tizard, 1972). The frequency of deviant behaviour in institutional children is well above population norms (Yule and Raynes, 1972), but equally it is below that of children in the most disturbed and loveless homes (Rutter, 1971a). The generally good adjustment of kibbutzim children (noted above) who sleep and spend their day in an institution (although remaining in contact with their parents) also argues against the suggestion that mothering must take place in the child's own home.

Nevertheless, there is something in the dictum in that it is clear that the quality and amount of maternal care provided in the *average* institution is much worse than the *average* family. Furthermore, the care in even the best institutions often falls well short of the average home although it is superior to the worst homes. As Bowlby (1951) rightly noted, it does seem peculiarly difficult for an institution to provide parental care of the quality and quantity expected in a family setting. The observation undoubtedly means that the greatest caution should be exercised in placing a child in long-term institutional care, but equally a bad home should not be automatically preferred to a good institution. It is necessary in each case to examine the quality of parental care provided (including its stability).

## Other features

In the discussion up to this point, attention has been focused on those aspects of the relationship which have been emphasized in the scientific literature as supposedly specific to mothering. However, it is important to note that mothers fulfil many roles in the family and have an important influence on their children's development in a myriad of ways not so far discussed.

Obviously, the young child needs care and protection to ensure that he comes to no harm. As he grows older discipline and guidance are necessary. Food is essential to life and when young the infant cannot feed himself. In all these circumstances the mother is often a dominant influence in the home. Throughout childhood and adolescence both parents constitute models of behaviour for the child to follow (or reject). Play has a crucial function in psychological development (Millar, 1968) and although much play is with other children, play with parents is also influential in many ways. Some of the class-related differences between parents in their view of the use of toys may be important for children's later development (Bernstein and Young, 1967). Especially following Bernstein's theoretical papers (1961, 1965), people have become increasingly aware of the influence of parent–child communication on cognitive development, with particular respect to language functions (e.g. Bernstein, 1972; Hess and Shipman, 1967; Lawton,

1968). In all these (and other) different respects, parents are important. To what extent these variables determine the effects of 'maternal deprivation' will be considered in later chapters.

## Conclusions

Mothering is a rather general term which includes a wide range of activities. Love, the development of enduring bonds, a stable but not necessarily unbroken relationship, and a 'stimulating' interaction are all necessary qualities, but there are many more. Children also need food, care and protection, discipline, models of behaviour, play and conversation. It seems unlikely that all of these have the same role in a child's psychological development and one of the main tasks of later chapters will be to identify the separate consequences of different types of 'maternal deprivation'. It is also evident that many of the qualities required for good mothering also apply to other relationships experienced by the child. It is perhaps preferable to concentrate on the various requirements for normal development rather than to attempt any rather artificial separation of functions which are specifically those of the mother.

# 3. Short-Term Effects of 'Maternal Deprivation'

There can be no clear-cut demarcation between short-term and long-term effects of 'maternal deprivation', as they blend into one another. Nevertheless, it is useful for the purposes of discussion to consider consequences in this way. The effects will be considered 'short-term' when they refer to the immediate response to a depriving experience and to the behaviour shown over the next few months. 'Long-term' will be primarily used to refer to the effects seen some years later, either following a brief period of deprivation or after continuous and prolonged privation. Intermediate effects will not be considered separately but will be mentioned in either context when they throw light on the psychological mechanisms involved.

Before turning to a discussion of possible variables and mechanisms it is necessary to consider what short-term effects have been attributed to 'deprivation'. As the literature has been previously well reviewed from several different viewpoints and as, for the most part, the observations (as distinct from the interpretations) are not in dispute, this introduction will be quite brief.

Short-term effects have been most studied with respect to children admitted to hospital or to a residential nursery (Vernon, Foley, Sipowicz and Schulman, 1965; Yarrow, 1964). There is good evidence that many (but not all) young children show an immediate reaction of acute distress and crying (what has been called the period of 'protest'), followed by misery and apathy (the phase of 'despair'), and finally there may be a stage when the child becomes apparently contented and seems to lose interest in his parents ('detachment' in Robertson's and Bowlby's terms) (Bowlby, 1958a, 1962, 1968; Robertson and Bowlby, 1952). That these reactions occur is well established. What remains controversial is their clinical significance and the psychological mechanisms involved.

The other syndrome seen as an early response to 'maternal deprivation' is developmental retardation (Provence and Lipton, 1962). There may be a global impairment of developmental progress but language and social responsiveness are usually most affected.

The psychological processes involved in these reactions will be considered by first examining the factors which modify the reactions and then discussing the possible mechanisms involved.

## Modifying factors
### Age of child
Systematic observations of children admitted to hospital have shown that emotional distress is most marked in children aged six months to four years, but even in this age group it occurs in only some children (Illingworth and Holt, 1955; Prugh, Staub, Sands, Kirschbaum and Lenihan, 1953; Schaffer and Callender, 1959). Distress does occur in some older children admitted to hospital but it tends to be less severe, less prolonged and it occurs in a lower proportion of children. Under the age of about six months there is usually *no* distress associated with admission to hospital.

The effect of age on developmental retardation associated with institutional care is quite different, suggesting that different psychological mechanisms are involved. Infants under the age of six months in hospitals, or other institutions where there is little stimulation, vocalize little and become socially unresponsive (Brodbeck and Irwin, 1946; Provence and Lipton, 1962; Schaffer and Callender, 1959). Deviations in language, social and motor development have been reported as early as the second month. However, there is no particular upper age restriction on this reaction, which also occurs in older children.

### Sex of child
The findings on sex differences are somewhat contradictory

and no differences have been found in many studies (Vernon *et al.*, 1965), but where there has been a sex difference, both in young subhuman primates and in children, the male has usually been found to be the more vulnerable to the adverse effects of separation experiences (Sackett, 1968; Spencer-Booth and Hinde, 1971a; Stacey *et al.*, 1970). If this tentative finding is confirmed it would be in keeping with the evidence suggesting that young males may be generally more susceptible than females to psychological stress, as certainly they are to biological stress (Rutter, 1970b).

## Temperament of child

There is ample evidence that individuals differ strikingly in their behaviour and responsiveness from early infancy (Berger and Passingham, 1972). A variety of studies have shown that infants differ in their psychophysiological characteristics (Steinschneider, 1967), response to stimulation (Bridger and Birns, 1968), oral activity (Korner, Chuck and Dontchos, 1968), behavioural style and response to new situations (Thomas, Chess and Birch, 1968; Thomas, Chess, Birch, Hertzig and Korn, 1963). The determinants of these individual differences are not fully understood, but sex-linked factors (Berger and Passingham, 1972), genetic mechanisms (Freedman and Keller, 1963), perinatal trauma (Ucko, 1965) and environmental influences (Zigler, 1966) probably all play a part. The importance of these individual differences has been shown by their association with the child's later behavioural disturbance (Rutter, Birch, Thomas and Chess, 1964; Thomas, Chess and Birch, 1968) and educational performance (Kagan, 1965).

Until very recently, however, there has been little investigation of temperamental differences in relation to children's responses to hospital admission or other forms of separation. The studies already mentioned suggest the importance of temperamental attributes and one of the most striking features of all investigations of 'deprivation' has been the enormous variation in the way individuals have reacted. A pilot study by Stacey and her colleagues (1970) has now shown that part of this individual variation can be accounted for in terms of what the children were like prior to the separation experience. Those who were said to make poor relationships with adults and other children, and to be socially inhibited, uncommunicative and aggressive, were the ones most likely to be disturbed by admission to hospital. Temperamental differences have also been found to be important with respect to the developmental retardation shown by infants in a depriving environment. In a study of infants under six months of age, the most active infants were the ones who showed the least drop in developmental quotient (Schaffer, 1966).

### Previous mother–child relationship

The fact that distress following separation does not usually occur in infants under the age of six months has already been mentioned. As this is about the age that maternal attachment becomes firm (Schaffer and Emerson, 1964), it may be accepted as circumstantial evidence that the child probably needs to have developed a relationship before he can show emotional distress with a separation experience. Apart from this well-established finding, the human evidence on the importance, or otherwise, of the child's previous relationship with his mother is extremely weak. On the whole it appears that short-term distress is less if the child had a good relationship before separation (Vernon *et al.*, 1965). It has also been suggested that disturbance is less likely to occur where the child has had more caretakers and therefore less intense and less exclusive attachments (Mead, 1962), but the evidence for this is anecdotal.

The most impressive evidence on the importance of mother–child relationships in response to separation comes from animal work: a series of very important investigations by Hinde and his colleagues has thrown much-needed new light on the question. In a longitudinal study of the effects of a short period of separation on young rhesus monkeys, they found that the infants who showed the greatest disturbance following separation were those who had shown the most 'tension' in their relationship with their mother prior to separation (Hinde and Spencer-Booth, 1970). 'Tension' was operationally defined in terms of the frequency of maternal rejections and the role of the infant in maintaining proximity to his mother. While results from animal work cannot be directly applied to humans, these findings strongly suggest that the area requires further exploration in children.

The differences in separation response between different species of monkey are also relevant in this context (Kaufman and Rosenblum, 1969a, 1969b). Pigtail macaques have been found to exhibit greater distress on separation than do bonnet macaques and it has been suggested that this is explicable in terms of differences in the mother–infant relationship between the two species. Bonnet macaques are normally less dependent on their mothers than are pigtails; they spend more time in social play, more often approach other members of the group and leave their mothers for longer periods, going longer distances. In the same way, bonnet mothers are more permissive than pigtail mothers. As a result of this, during the period of separation the bonnet infants are more likely to achieve an association with another adult who thereby produces substitute mothering. In contrast pigtails become withdrawn and isolated following the first acute distress and do not attach to other adults. This difference seems to be due to the previous interactional experiences in the two species rather than to any general differences in maternal solicitude.

## Previous separation experiences

It is generally supposed that children who have experienced separation once become sensitized so that later similar experiences are likely to be especially traumatic for them (Ainsworth, 1962), but there is remarkably little evidence on this point. Spencer-Booth and Hinde (1971a) found that infant rhesus monkeys separated for the second time responded in much the same way as those separated for the first time at the same age. In humans, too, there is surprisingly little to support the notion of a sensitizing effect. What little evidence there is suggests that whether this happens depends greatly on the nature of the first separation. Where children have had a previously unhappy experience of separation there is some suggestion that they are more likely to respond adversely to hospital admission than are children without such a previous stress (Vernon *et al.*, 1965). On the other hand, it appears that if the separations have been happy ones, there may be the reverse effect. Thus Stacey *et al.* (1970) found that children who were undisturbed by hospital admission were more likely than the distressed children to have had *more* 'normal' separation experiences such as staying overnight with friends or relatives, having baby-sitters, attending nursery school and being left all day with a familiar person. There is too little evidence to be dogmatic on the matter and further research on the issue should be rewarding, but it seems that a child's response to a separation experience may be influenced for the better or worse by the nature of previous separations.

## Duration of separation/deprivation

Even with short-term responses to separation/deprivation it seems that distress may be greater the longer that the experience lasts, although not much is known on this point. Heinicke and Westheimer (1965), in a study of ten children placed in a residential nursery, found more disturbance at the end of the separation period in the four children separated for seven to twenty-one weeks than in the six children separated for less than three weeks. Similarly in a study of rhesus monkeys, Hinde and Spencer-Booth (1971b) found that distress was greater following a thirteen-day separation than that after a six-day separation.

## Different effect of separation and strange environment

Douglas and Blomfield (1958) found that long-term ill-effects generally followed separation *only* when separation was accompanied by change of environment. This finding, and the fact that most studies of the short-term effects of separation concern children in strange environments such as a hospital, has led to the suggestion that the distress may be due to the environment rather than the separation as such.

To examine this question it is necessary to determine what happens when a child is present in a strange setting *with* his mother and conversely what happens if he is left at home without his mother. Rheingold (1969) has examined the first question with respect to the immediate responses of ten-month-old infants. She found very little distress when infants were placed in a strange environment *with* their mother, but considerable distress when placed there on their own or with a stranger. Similar results were reported by Ainsworth and Wittig (1969) in a study of twelve-month-old infants. Many (but not all) infants showed some distress when their mothers left them in a room which they had entered together a few moments previously. Morgan and Ricciuti (1969) found that over a third of ten- to twelve-month-old infants reacted negatively to strangers even when sitting on their mother's lap but that a negative reaction was much more likely if the infant was across the room from his mother. Negative reactions also occurred more often when the stranger touched the baby than when he made a 'peek-a-boo'-like head movement without approaching. It may be concluded that strange persons and strange environments are fear-provoking stimuli for infants, but that the presence of the mother goes a long way to reducing or eliminating the distress in a novel setting.

These findings all apply to distress during separations of a few minutes. Less is known about longer separations but the findings seem to be similar. Children's disturbance during hospital admission is greatly reduced if they are admitted together with their mother or if there is daily visiting by parents (Faust, Jackson, Cermak, Burtt and Winkley, 1952; Illingworth and Holt, 1955; Prugh *et al.*, 1953). Unfortunately, it is not possible from these studies to determine how much reduction in distress was due to the mother's presence and how much to other factors, as the experimental programmes included many features such as special play facilities, careful preparation of the children for admission and the reduction of potentially traumatic procedures such as venipunctures and enemas.

There are several descriptions suggesting that the presence

of the child's mother is the crucial variable (MacCarthy, Lindsay and Morris, 1962; Mićić, 1962; Robertson, 1958, 1962) but only two studies which have isolated this factor in a systematic fashion. Fagin (1966), in a comparison of two groups of thirty children, one admitted to hospital alone and one with their mothers, found distress almost entirely eliminated when the mothers were there. In contrast, Vernon, Foley and Schulman (1967) found only a small (but significant) difference due to the mother's presence, suggesting that other factors designed to reduce the stress of hospital admission were of considerable importance.

Bowlby (1969) has pointed out that the anecdotal evidence on how young children behave during family holidays also suggests that infants in a strange environment *with* their parents usually show little distress. Although a few young children may be upset in such conditions, prolonged or marked disturbance is quite uncommon.

There is also extensive evidence from animal studies that mothers, or even mother-surrogates (such as a cloth figure), have a marked effect in imparting security to infants placed in a strange or frightening situation. This has been well shown for rhesus monkeys by Harlow and his colleagues (e.g. Harlow and Harlow, 1965) and has been noted in goats by Liddell (1950).

On the second question – how infants react when left by their mothers while remaining in a familiar situation – there are anecdotal reports of the occurrence of distress following loss of the mother-figure occurring in infants who remained in their home environment (Deutsch, 1919; Spiro, 1958). On the other hand, the Robertsons (see page 46) have found that distress need not occur in this situation. Systematic studies are needed but pose difficulties in that, at least for longer separations, the children would have to be left with someone and if the setting were to be familiar the person would likely be known to the child. As discussed below, the presence of a familiar person has similiar stress-reducing properties to the mother's presence.

However, the question has been studied in subhuman primates reared in a group setting (Kaufman and Rosenblum, 1969a, 1969b; Spencer-Booth and Hinde, 1971a, 1971b). It is clear from these studies that infant monkeys show acute distress when their mothers are taken away, the infants remaining in their usual environment.

The extent to which the sequence of protest, despair and detachment is separation-specific is a matter of some interest. It seems that the protest state of acute distress and clinging is non-specific. Mason (1967) has found similar effects in chimpanzees following restraint, noise and stimulant drugs. Evidence is lacking but the stages of despair and detachment *might* be more specific to separation experiences.

In summary, both separation and a strange environment occurring individually may produce distress in infants, but distress is most marked when both occur together. The effects of a strange environment are less consistent and it seems that it is the nature of the strangeness as well as the presence of a novel stimulus which is important. Indeed, some novel stimuli may be pleasurable to the child. Nevertheless, on the whole, it appears that separations may be less stressful if the infant remains in a familiar environment. Conversely, strange environments are much less stressful if the infant is present with his mother. The fact that this effect is more marked and more consistent than the ameliorating effect of a familiar environment during separations suggests that separation may be of more basic importance. However, it is not possible meaningfully to compare separation and strangeness without further specification. Clearly, the relative importance of each will vary with the environmental circumstances.

## Presence of persons other than the mother

One of the problems in comparing the effects of separation and a strange environment has been the confounding effect of the presence of other persons. Several studies have shown that familiar people, other than the mother, also reduce children's distress in strange situations. In 1943, Arsenian demonstrated that children from a residential nursery showed distress when introduced to a strange situation but that this was often less when they were accompanied by one of the nursery helpers with whom they were familiar. With 'dependent' children the presence of a substitute mother was not as effective as that of the true mother. In young adults, too, the presence of a friend (but not a stranger) reduced autonomic disturbance in a stress situation (Kissel, 1965).

In their study of children admitted to a residential nursery, Heinicke and Westheimer (1965) found that distress was much reduced in those children admitted with a sib. This was so in spite of the fact that the sibs were too young to take on a caretaking role.

Animal work leads to similar conclusions. The short-term effects of infant–infant separation in rhesus monkeys reared apart from their mothers seem similar to the effects of mother–infant separation (Suomi, Harlow and Domek, 1970). Also, the presence of another monkey of the same age tends to reduce the emotional disturbance of young rhesus monkeys in a strange situation (Mason, 1960).

As already noted, children form attachments with many people other than their mother and it is evident that the presence of familiar persons acts to reduce stress in a strange situation just as the presence of the mother does. It is important to note in this connection that bonds form with people who have no caretaking role towards the child and the presence of a peer or sib reduces stress in similar fashion to the presence of a parent-surrogate. On the whole children are less distressed with their mother than with some other person so that it would be wrong to conclude that any individual does equally well. But there is no evidence that it is being a mother that is important. On the basis of the very scanty available evidence it seems more likely that the stress-reducing properties of the accompanying person are related to the strength of bond formation. It may be hypothesized that where the bond is strongest with the mother she will have the greatest stress-reducing properties; where bonds are stronger with someone else she will not.

### Nature of circumstances during separation/deprivation

The beneficial effect of improved hospital conditions in reducing children's distress following admission has already been mentioned (Faust *et al.*, 1952; Prugh *et al.*, 1953). Emotional disturbance is far from universal in children admitted to hospital (Davenport and Werry, 1970). It is quite evident that the circumstances experienced by an infant during separation or institutional care make a major difference to the infant's emotional response, but which environmental factors are the most important in this connection is largely unknown. Since Burlingham and Freud's (1942, 1944) important early studies at the Hampstead Nursery, much emphasis has been placed on the provision of high-quality substitute maternal care involving stability, affection and active involvement. In hospital, careful attention has also been paid to the reduction of unpleasant procedures and the adequate preparation of the child for those which are unavoidable.

The provision of ample toys with play facilities supervised by trained workers has been advocated by paediatricians (Jolly, 1969) on the grounds that boredom leads to distress. A recent experimental investigation of ten-month-old infants by Rheingold and Samuels (1969) has now provided support for this view. Not surprisingly, children with their mothers but without toys fussed and fretted more than children who had both their mothers present and toys to play with. Nevertheless, it should be noted that this study did not show whether or not toys will reduce distress in children *without* their mothers.

The importance of environmental stimulation in counteracting developmental retardation has been shown in several studies. Rheingold (1956) showed that institutional infants became more socially responsive when provided with extra individual attention and communication. In a later study she showed that the vocalizations of three-month-old infants can be increased by smiling, speaking to them and touching them (Rheingold, Gewirtz, and Ross, 1959). Casler (1965) found that daily tactile stimulation diminished the degree of retardation in institutional children. White (1967, 1971) has shown that the onset of hand regard, visually directed reaching and the growth of visual attentiveness in human infants are significantly improved by providing extra handling, placing the infant so he can look around better, putting bright striped mittens on his hands to attract his attention, and by making sure that there are plenty of mobiles and other interesting things for him to watch. The difficulty of determining exactly which experience had which effect is illustrated by Korner and Grobstein's (1966) finding that picking up tearful infants not only soothed them but also led to increased visual alertness and scanning of the environment.

Sayegh and Dennis (1965) showed a gain in developmental quotient as a result of giving institutional infants an hour's extra attention per day. Schaffer has shown similar effects. He found that eleven- to fourteen-week-old infants in a baby home with a high degree of measured social stimulation showed no developmental retardation, whereas those in a hospital with a low degree of stimulation were retarded (Schaffer, 1965). In both cases the children were admitted for only short periods and following discharge the developmental quotients in the two groups were comparable. This showed that the retardation was a function of the institution and not the type of children admitted. A further study of twenty-four-week-old infants showed that the developmental quotient could be immediately raised following a period of stimulation, suggesting that the retardation was a function of the environmental situation rather than a measure of reduced organismic capacity (Schaffer and Emerson, 1968). Of course, if non-stimulating conditions were to continue for long enough a true reduction in capacity might occur, but the experiment was solely concerned with short-term effects.

## Possible mechanisms

As evident from the findings already discussed, the factors modifying the two main short-term effects of deprivation (distress and retardation) are rather different. This suggests that different psychological mechanisms may be involved and possible explanations will have to be considered separately for each.

*Separation or a strange environment?*

This question has already been discussed in connection with modifying factors. Physical illness or unpleasant medical (and surgical) procedures may be stressful experiences to young children, but the fact that the adverse effects of admission to a residential nursery are so similar to those following admission to hospital argues against this being the main factor in the distress associated with separation. Experimental studies on the beneficial effect of toys and on the results of measures designed to make hospital admission less traumatic certainly suggest that environmental factors other than separation may sometimes play an important part in the production of the acute distress associated with hospital admission. The finding that distress is much less common in some hospitals than in others supports the same conclusion.

Nevertheless, the evidence already discussed suggests that separation from family members is probably a more basic cause of emotional distress. When the parents, young children may even find a strange environment interesting and altogether a positive experience. However, much depends on what sort of strange environment it is and some can be quite frightening to young children.

The finding that the developmental retardation of children in hospital can be reversed without altering the strangeness of the environment suggests that strangeness is not an important factor in causing retardation.

*Separation or disturbed mother–infant relationship?*

The analysis of just what it is in a separation experience which makes it have adverse effects (or conversely which prevents it having such effects) provides many methodological problems, not the least of which is the great difficulty of isolating each of the elements. This is most readily done in an experimental design and ethical considerations mean that we have to turn to animal studies for an answer.

This question has been investigated by Hinde and his co-workers in a carefully controlled set of studies of rhesus monkeys (Hinde and Davies, 1972; Hinde and Spencer-Booth, 1970). There are three main findings which are relevant in this connection. Firstly, as noted above, infants' distress following separation is a function of both the pre-separation and the contemporaneous mother–infant relationship. Secondly, changes in mother–infant interaction from day to day after reunion largely depend on the mother. Thirdly, infants showed much *less* post-separation distress and more *normal* mother–infant interaction when they themselves were removed to a strange place for thirteen days and then restored to their mother than when the mothers were removed to a strange place for a similar period. In other words the monkey equivalent of 'mother goes to hospital' led to *more* disturbance than did the monkey equivalent of 'baby goes to hospital'. These are important and striking findings, particularly as the third observation runs counter to what one might expect. Hinde has argued convincingly that the probable explanation is that the infants' post-separation distress is not primarily due to the separation as such but rather to the consequent disturbance in maternal behaviour. Where separation leads to distortions in the mother's interaction with the infant, the infant suffers. Where separation does *not* affect the mother's behaviour, the distress in the infant is very much less.

As Hinde has been most careful to point out, it is necessary to be cautious in generalizing the finding to other species and it is important to draw parallels at the right level. For example, it may well be that in humans the infant's role in determining mother–infant interaction is greater than in the rhesus monkey. Nevertheless, it seems reasonable to suggest that if a disturbed mother–infant interaction is the mediating factor in separation distress in rhesus monkeys then it may also be so in humans, as the reactions to separation appear so similar in other respects in the two species. Hinde's hypothesis is most important in both its theoretical and practical implications; human research into the question is urgently called for. Some of the Robertsons' work is relevant here, but as it refers more directly to the effects of deprivation of maternal care it will be discussed in the next section.

## Separation or deprivation of maternal care?

Most human studies of distress following separation have been concerned with children admitted to hospital or to a residential nursery, confounding the effects of separation and of deprivation of maternal care. In this context, 'separation' is used to refer to the physical loss of the mother-figure but not necessarily of mothering. 'Deprivation' refers to the loss of maternal care but not necessarily of the mother-figure (Howells, 1970). There is ample evidence that even in good institutions the maternal care provided differs in both quantity and quality from that experienced in a family setting (David and Appell, 1961; King, Raynes and Tizard, 1971; Rheingold, 1960; Tizard and Tizard, 1971).

The question, then, is whether separation from a *person* to whom bonds of attachment have developed (in this case the mother) can lead to distress even though there is a normal provision of good maternal care and no other environmental stress. Bowlby (1961, 1968, 1969; Bowlby and Parkes, 1970) has argued over many years that it can. In short, he suggests that separation constitutes a *grief* reaction or a response to bereavement. It is the loss of a *person* which is crucial, not just the loss of maternal care (although he has always emphasized that the damage is much greater when both occur together). This is an important question, the answer to which has far-reaching implications concerning the avoidance of distress during separation experiences.

There cannot be much animal evidence on this point in that separation from mother in most animal species almost inevitably leads to some deprivation of maternal care. In humans, however, this need not be the case. The mother may be absent but yet perfectly adequate care be provided by other people. It will not, of course, be quite the *same* as that given by the mother in that the personal style of interaction will differ, but it may easily be of similar quality and quantity.

Perhaps the most convincing evidence that separation is a key variable is the finding that the presence of sibs or other familiar persons greatly ameliorates children's distress following admission or in some other stress situation. Distress seems to be less even though the accompanying person neither provides nor improves maternal care.

Investigations of children separated from familiar persons but remaining in a small family group would help clarify the situation. In this connection, the Robertsons' valuable films of children in brief separation are most informative (Robertson and Robertson, 1967, 1968a, 1968b). The film showing the response of a two-year-old to admission to hospital (Robertson, 1952) and the short stay of a seventeen-month-old boy in a residential nursery (Robertson and Robertson, 1968b) clearly illustrated the acute distress which often occurs when children are separated *and* in a strange and potentially stressful situation. They have also made two films of what happens when children of a similar age are separated from their parents but remain in a small family setting (the Robertsons' home). Both the children they studied showed signs of mild stress or insecurity, but basically they maintained developmental progress and adapted to the change. While there was evidence of the tension implicit in the separation experience, their reactions were vastly different to the marked psychological disturbance shown by the children admitted to hospital or to a residential nursery. With the fact of separation held constant, distress could be very greatly ameliorated by improving maternal care *during* the separation. Although the Robertsons' study design was quite different to that used with rhesus monkeys by Hinde it should be noted that the conclusions are similar; namely that it is not separation as such which is the key factor but rather the accompanying distortion of the mother-child relationship. Controlled comparisons of larger numbers of children are obviously needed but the available findings suggest that although separation from mother may induce some stress, the disturbance which follows this alone is very much less than that which occurs when separation is accompanied by deprivation of maternal care.

However, before concluding that it is the deprivation of maternal care which leads to the distress, it is necessary to emphasize again that separation and bond disruption cannot be equated. Was there anything in the Robertsons' foster-home situation which was *not* present in the residential nursery or hospital and which may have enabled the children to maintain bonds during separation? In this connection, one difference stands out. Whereas none of the adults in the nursery was known to John (the seventeen-month-old admitted for nine days to a residential nursery), Kate and Jane, the two children fostered by the Robertsons, had both met them *before* the separation. The presence of a familiar adult may have helped the children maintain bonds. If this is so, only brief acquaintance may be sufficient for the adult to be regarded as 'familiar'. The children had only been introduced to the Robertsons for the first time in the few weeks prior to separation.

There was one other difference relevant to the maintenance of bonds. The Robertsons took special care to talk to the children about their mothers and so keep alive memories during the separation. For the same reasons they endeavoured to follow the children's known daily routines and to keep to the overall pattern of discipline and child-rearing to which they were accustomed. This was not possible to the same extent in the residential nursery where the staff knew little about the children and their patterns of family life.

In short, the findings are entirely compatible with a hypothesis that bond disruption is the key variable, so long as it is recognized that this is not a necessary consequence of separation. The extensive evidence already discussed, of the marked comforting effect of a familiar figure during a stress situation (even though maternal care is not altered), also provides support for this view and argues against deprivation of maternal care being accepted as a sufficient explanation.

On the other hand, there were differences between the care provided by the Robertsons and that given in hospital or the residential nursery. As no systematic measures of care were recorded, it is only possible to speculate on the differences using what is known about hospital and nursery care and what is shown in the Robertsons' films. The nursery in which John showed such severe distress was well staffed with trained people and there was ample provision of toys. While a general reduction in perceptual stimulation or in the range of daily life experiences may well play an important part in the genesis of distress in *other* situations, it is very unlikely that this was the case with John. If this is so, it means that there must be some other crucial ingredient in maternal care which is needed to prevent the distress seen in many children admitted to hospital or to a residential nursery.

It is likely that this ingredient is the opportunity for a continuing intense personal interaction with the same individual or individuals over time. This did not occur in the nursery where care was on a work-assignment basis, with nurses turning to whatever task came to hand with whichever children were concerned. This, together with the organization of off-duty times, meant that John had to interact with a varying group of adults, none of whom was specifically allocated to look after him, and in a situation where it was unpredictable (to him) who would be available to deal with him at different times. In contrast, in the Robertsons' home the children had only two adults looking after them and one of these was always present and available to provide care, comfort or play as was required. This is a situation which allows attachments to develop and in fact the children *did* develop attachments to the Robertsons during their brief spell with them. This did not occur with John in the residential nursery. If this emphasis is correct, then the necessary ingredient in maternal care (to prevent distress during separation) is a personal and continuing interaction with the child which can provide a basis for bond formation.

The available evidence does not allow a choice between the two explanations for the distress so often seen during separation experiences – namely bond disruption and impairment of attachment behaviour (in general rather than to the person who is absent). However, in both cases it appears that separation *per se* is not the key factor, but that some distortion or disruption of the bonding process is crucial. From the rather slender circumstantial evidence which is available it would seem likely that both factors probably play an important part in the genesis of distress. Which factor makes the most difference is not known (in any case this is likely to vary with individual circumstances). Indeed, further study is required to determine whether the two hypothesized factors are actually the relevant ones. Whereas the evidence seems to point to their influence, the relevant data are weak.

The explanation for developmental retardation must be quite different, because severe retardation has been found in children born in, or admitted to, institutions in the first month of life at a time when they have yet to develop any attachments and have a very limited ability to differentiate between the adults providing care (Dennis, 1960), and the retardation is reversible simply by increasing stimulation without altering the separation situation. Also, again separation as such cannot be the explanation because some studies of institutional children have failed to find any retardation in spite of the fact that all have experienced separation from parents.

The findings are reasonably clear-cut that some form of privation of stimulation rather than any type of separation is responsible for the retardation. What remains uncertain is the relative importance for each type of developmental retardation (the retardation may affect a variety of different developmental functions, such as speech, motor coordination and bladder control) of different types of stimulation – social, perceptual, motor, experiential and linguistic. It is highly likely that different developmental functions require different forms of stimulation for their development, but the point has been little investigated.

## Deprivation or privation?

The above evidence also makes it clear that the retardation

is due to a *lack* of stimulation and not to the *loss* of stimulation. Accordingly, privation is a more correct description than deprivation.

Again the situation is different for the syndrome of distress. Children who have never developed attachments seem *not* to show this syndrome of distress (although they have other disturbances – see chapters 4 and 5 on long-term consequences of deprivation). Accordingly, the distress syndrome is probably due to 'deprivation', not to privation. Whether the 'deprivation' involves disruption of a bond or the loss of attachment opportunities is considered below. Very little is known about the emotional consequences of loss other than in the context of separation from a familiar person.

*Separation from mother*
*or separation from a familiar person?*

The evidence that distress is much reduced by the presence of a brother or sister or a friend even when the mother remains absent strongly suggests that there is nothing specific about mother separation. Indeed it is most curious that studies of children in hospital or a residential nursery are nearly always considered as examples of separation from mother when in fact they consist of separation from mother *and* father *and* sibs *and* the home environment. There are no studies of the short-term effects of paternal absence and the influence of the father has been greatly neglected. The author's unsystematic observations of young children in families where the father spends occasional periods away from home suggest that in many families this is as likely to lead to emotional distress as is the absence of the mother. Whether or not this is so, and if it is *why*, requires investigation.

Amelioration of distress during maternal absence does not occur if the person with the child is unfamiliar, and the degree of amelioration varies greatly according to which family member or friend is present. This is not a function of a mothering role because distress is reduced even with younger sibs of two or three years. The available evidence suggests that the relevant variable is the strength of the child's attachment to the person. The most parsimonious explanation of the research findings suggests that a child needs to have the presence of a person to whom he is attached but it is irrelevant whether or not this person is his mother. He also needs to have adequate maternal care and if this is not provided he suffers. But it appears that this need not be given by the person to whom he is most attached. If this hypothesis is correct (and it requires rigorous testing) then the emphasis on attachment behaviour and bonding by Bowlby (1968, 1969) and others is correct, but its linking with maternal care is misleading. The implications for practical policy are also different from an exclusive maternal attachment view. If it is bond formation which is important (rather than mother–child bond formation), it is in a child's interest to encourage attachment to several people, not just one, so that if one person is away another is present. Furthermore, from this point of view separation should not be regarded as synonymous with bond disruption. If a child is used to short stays with friends and relatives in happy circumstances he is more likely to learn that separations are temporary and can be pleasant. Accordingly, later unavoidable separations of an unhappy kind (such as hospitalization of parent or child) are likely to be less traumatic.

So far as can be determined, developmental retardation is not due to bond disruption of any type but rather to privation of some type of care or stimulation.

### Disruption of all bonds or disruption of one of several bonds?

The argument above rather depends on the assumption that disruption of one bond is less traumatic if other bonds exist than if that is the only bond. It might seem obvious that this should be the case but evidence in support is largely lacking. Rosenblum (1971a) has some preliminary evidence that distress following mother–infant separation in squirrel monkeys is less when other adult monkeys ('aunts') have also mothered the infant and remain available during the separation. The Robertsons' film on Jane, the seventeen-month-old child they fostered for ten days, showed that there was some mild tension associated with the child's separation from

the Robertsons at the time of the mother's return home
(Robertson and Robertson, 1968a). This and other observations in the literature suggest that there can be *some* stress
associated with even the disruption of one of many bonds.
However, the same observations suggest that the stress is
very much less than in the case of the disruption of a solitary
bond. The matter needs systematic study.

### Disruption of bonds or loss of bonding behaviour?

It has already been noted that the distress associated with
admission to a strange residential nursery involves *both*
separation from all familiar people *and* care which lacks
intensity and individuality so that the attachments the child
is accustomed to cannot redevelop. Which is more important? Again evidence is largely lacking, although once more
the Robertsons' films provide a lead. The children they
fostered had known them only a few weeks before the
separation experience so that prior bonds with the children
were probably quite weak. But they were familiar to the
children and the children's father continued to visit, so the
break was only partial.

On the extremely slender anecdotal evidence available it
might be hypothesized that either separation from all
familiar people *or* care which did not allow attachments
are likely to be stressful to a young child, and that both are
influential. The issue requires investigation. It should be
noted in passing that substitute care for children separated
from their families frequently involves deprivation of both.

### Discussion

The evidence strongly points to the operation of quite
different psychological mechanisms in the genesis of acute
distress and of developmental retardation as short-term responses to 'deprivation'. The retardation appears explicable
in terms of a privation or lack (rather than loss) of environmental 'stimulation'. It remains uncertain whether social
stimulation as provided by interaction with people, perceptual
and motor stimulation as provided by play, experiences and
activities, or linguistic stimulation as provided by conversa-

tion and meaningful talk on an individual basis is most important. Probably all three are needed but for rather different aspects of development.

In contrast the syndrome of distress (as shown by the sequence of protest, despair and detachment) is probably due to deprivation (i.e. loss rather than lack) of some aspect of bonding or attachment behaviour. Whether the loss of a particular person to whom the child is attached or rather the general loss of any opportunity to develop attachments is the more important remains uncertain. Whereas these consequences may occur, and perhaps particularly occur, with separation from the mother, it should be noted that there is nothing to suggest that her role is a specific one in this connection, and a good deal of evidence to suggest that it is not. The mother is usually the person who has done most for the child, is most familiar to the child and has given most comfort. For all these reasons her presence is likely to be more important than anyone else's. But her importance stems from her contact with the child, and her relative importance compared with other family members will depend on the constellation of relationships in each particular family. In the writer's view, theories of mothering have frequently been too mechanical in equating separation with bond disruption, too restricted in regarding the mother as the only person important in a child's life, and too narrow in considering love as the only important element in maternal care.

This review has been concerned with the psychological mechanisms involved in the short-term effects of deprivation on the child. However, it is vital not to overlook the important evidence (briefly noted above) that children vary greatly in their response to separation and deprivation. Parent–child interaction is an active ongoing two-way process with the child's own attributes being an important determinant of how the interaction develops (Bell, 1968). Study of this rather neglected side of the dyad is likely to prove rewarding.

## Conclusions

Evidence on the factors modifying or influencing children's

responses to short-term separation or deprivation has been reviewed and possible psychological mechanisms have been considered. It is concluded that the syndrome of distress (protest, despair, detachment) is probably due to a disruption or distortion of the bonding process (not necessarily with the mother), and that the syndrome of developmental retardation is probably due to a privation of social, perceptual and linguistic stimulation.

# 4. Long-Term Consequences: Modifying Factors

The initial case for regarding 'maternal deprivation' as the cause of long-term disturbance rests largely on clinical studies. Bender (1947), Bowlby (1946) and others (reviewed in Bowlby, 1951) noted the frequency with which both delinquency and affectionless psychopathy were associated with multiple separation experiences and institutional care. A variety of investigations have found an association between delinquency and broken homes (see reviews by Wootton, 1959, and Yarrow, 1961). Studies of children reared in institutions have also shown a high level of language retardation and mental subnormality (Goldfarb, 1945a, 1945b; Pringle and Tanner, 1958; Provence and Lipton, 1962). Children already handicapped by organic brain impairment such as in Down's syndrome ('mongolism') make less progress in institutions than they do at home (Francis, 1971; Lyle, 1959, 1960; Stedman and Eichorn, 1964). Following on early paediatric observations that institutional children often fail to gain weight properly (Bakwin, 1949), more recent investigations have shown a connection between dwarfism and growth failure on the one hand and a history of maternal rejection and lack of warmth on the other (Patton and Gardner, 1963). The evidence linking maternal deprivation with depression mostly concerns adult patients (Rutter, 1971a) but family disruption has also been found in association with depression in children (Caplan and Douglas, 1969).

It may be concluded that disorders of conduct, personality, language, cognition and physical growth have all been found to occur in children with serious disturbances in their early family life, which have been included under the rather loose general heading of 'maternal deprivation'. However, the early family disturbances reported, as well as the later outcomes, are rather heterogeneous and, as with short-term effects, it remains to be determined which type of 'deprivation' has which long-term consequence.

## Long-term effects of early life experiences

As it is sometimes claimed that psychological development is genetically determined to an extent which leaves little room for environmental influences to have any significant effects, it may be useful to consider some of the evidence that early life experiences can have a major impact on later functioning.

The most convincing evidence comes from experimental animal work where it is possible to control the relevant variables in a fashion that allows the effects of each to be measured. There are numerous studies which show quite clearly that environmental manipulations can have a very fundamental and long-lasting effect on development. They also demonstrate that experimental manipulations of one sort of behaviour may influence the development of an apparently different sort of behaviour.

The animal evidence in support of these statements is so extensive (Hinde, 1970; Sluckin, 1970; Thompson and Grusec, 1970) that only a small number of examples can be included to illustrate the wide range of such effects on development of early life experiences and to note the wide range of species in which the effects have been shown. Perhaps the best known example of early learning with a persisting influence into adult life is the phenomenon of 'imprinting' (Hinde, 1970). During a short sensitive period in early infancy nidifugous birds will follow a wide range of moving objects. The objects they learn to follow during this sensitive phase are the ones to which attachments develop and the birds will continue to exhibit following behaviour to matchboxes, men or whatever other objects upon which they become imprinted. Conversely they will *not* follow objects upon which they have *not* been imprinted – thus they will not follow their own mother if she was not present during the 'imprinting' phase. A similar phenomenon (but less consistent and arising slightly later) influences adult choice of sexual object (Fabricius, 1962). Birds which learn to follow humans in early life will on reaching maturity often also exhibit sexual behaviour towards humans. The effects of early experience on the stimuli eliciting later social or reproductive behaviour have also been shown in fish, mice, lambs, guinea pigs, indeed in almost all vertebrate groups (Hinde, 1970).

A wide range of studies (e.g. Bronfenbrenner, 1968; McCandless, 1964) have shown the cognitive and perceptual deficiencies which follow early stimulus deprivation. For example, it has been found that patterned visual stimulation is important in the development of visually guided behaviour (Riesen, 1965). Held and his colleagues (Hein and Held, 1967; Held and Bauer, 1967; Held and Hein, 1963) have gone further and demonstrated with both cats and monkeys that *active*, as distinct from passive, visual experience was necessary. Animals whose visual experience was the result of their own active movements showed superior judgement of distance and space (as judged by paw placing and the visual cliff experiment) to those whose visual experience was the result of their being passively transported. A simple apparatus which allowed only progressive movement around a circular box controlled the amount of visual experience in the two cases.

Levine (1962) and others have shown the far-reaching psychological and physical effects (in rats) of quite minor stimulation in early infancy. Stimulated rats showed early eye opening, less 'emotionality', greater weight gain and early maturation of certain glandular functions associated with response to stress. There are some inter-species differences in the effects of stimulation and the mechanisms are ill-understood. Some of the changes evidently result from the direct action on the young, but some seem to be due to changes in the behaviour of the mother towards her offspring (Barnett and Burn, 1967).

The sometimes long-term effects of brief periods of separation in infancy in rhesus monkeys has been observed by Hinde and Spencer-Booth (1971b; Spencer-Booth and Hinde, 1971b). Five months after the separation experience, although their behaviour lay within normal limits, the separated infants approached and interacted with strange objects in a strange situation less readily than did the controls. Some of these differences still persisted as long as two years after separation.

The much more severe ill effects of total isolation (a very unbiological form of treatment) have been shown by Harlow and his co-workers (Harlow, 1958; Harlow and Griffin, 1965; Harlow and Harlow, 1969, 1970). Infant rhesus monkeys isolated for six months in early life showed gross and persistent disorders of social and sexual behaviour in adult life. These findings have been confirmed by other workers (Mason, 1960; Missakian, 1969).

Emotional behaviour is also markedly influenced by early isolation. Harlow's monkeys showed gross fear responses when first removed from isolation, and chimpanzees reared in a restricted environment showed avoidance of novel objects (Menzel, 1964). Dogs given restricted rearing exhibited increased activity and arousal and were slow to learn how to avoid painful stimuli, such as burns and electric shock (Melzack and Scott, 1957; Thompson and Melzack, 1956). To what extent the restricted rearing led to *deviant* behaviour rather than just impaired learning is uncertain. Melzack (1965) has suggested that restriction has the effect of increasing the novelty of cues in any testing situation (because of the restriction, stimuli which would be familiar to a normal animal are strange to a restricted one) and that this accounts for some of the apparently abnormal behaviour.

One important feature of restricted rearing procedures is the complexity of the resulting defects, so that it may be quite difficult to disentangle which element of restriction leads to which outcome by which mechanism. This is well demonstrated by the experiments on the effects of rearing animals (mainly cats) in darkness or in the absence of patterned vision (Ganz, 1968; Lindsley and Riesen, 1968; Riesen, 1965). This results in increased fear of new situations, deficiency in problem solving and other 'intellectual' tasks, perceptual deficits, retinal defects and dysfunction of the visual cortex.

These studies emphasize that not only is 'behaviour' dependent upon experience for its development, but also that sensory stimulation influences neural growth. It has been well shown that neural metabolism varies with the rate of stimulation and recent work has demonstrated ganglionic atrophy and a reduction in dendritic growth following light privation during the stage of active cell growth. Preliminary findings of experiments with rats suggest that, conversely, stimulation in infancy may lead to changes in brain chemistry and an increase in cortical weight (Rosenzweig, Bennett and Diamond, 1967; Rosenzweig, Krech, Bennett and Diamond, 1968).

The cortical dysfunction following visual privation probably stems from *disorganization* of function, as well as from disuse. Thus, Hubel and Wiesel (1965) found that effects similar to those obtained from eye-lid closure followed the production of an artificial squint. The same workers (Wiesel and Hubel, 1965a) also showed that in some respects the effects on kittens of binocular privation of vision were less severe than those of monocular visual privation. It was as if the ill-effects of closing one eye could be averted by closing the other.

There is ample evidence from animal studies that in certain circumstances early life experiences *can* have far-reaching effects. The findings are sufficiently striking to make it well worthwhile to search for the possible long-term consequences of 'maternal deprivation' in man.

Drawing on the findings of his own studies in rats, Denenberg (1969) has summarized the effects of early life experiences in terms of five principles: genetically based characters may be drastically modified by early experiences; early experiences have long-term consequences; early experiences are one major cause of individual differences; early experiences have multiple effects; and the age when stimulation is administered is critical.

These statements appear well based and probably apply generally, not just to rats. However there is also the other side of the coin. It could equally well (and rightly) be claimed that an individual's mode of response to the environment is greatly influenced by his genetic make-up. Children respond selectively to stimuli in terms of their idiosyncratic and developmental characteristics – they are not passive recipients of stimuli. Rather, they *elicit* responses from other people (Bell, 1971; Yarrow, 1968). Children's characteristics help determine how their parents respond to them (Bell, 1964, 1968, 1971; Cummings, Bayley and Rie, 1966; Levy, 1958; Yarrow, 1963) and to some extent it may be that one child in a family is deprived whereas others are not, just because of his particular personality attributes. As Berger and Passingham (1972) have recently pointed out in a thoughtful review of the topic, the importance of individual differences in response to deprivation has been widely under-estimated and neglected.

### The special importance of infancy

It is frequently thought that the infancy period has a special signficance in development so that environmental influences in early life have an overriding effect on what happens later, regardless of later experiences. This claim has been disputed in several reviews and actually there is no evidence that environmental factors can *only* have a decisive influence in early childhood (Clarke, 1968; Stein and Susser, 1970; Stevenson, 1957).

Two issues arise in this connection: whether there are 'sensitive' periods during which the individual is more susceptible to a particular life experience and whether the effects of infantile experiences always predominate over the effects of experiences in later life.

The existence of 'sensitive' periods has been shown for a wide range of functions in many different animal species. The example of 'imprinting' in birds, already mentioned, is of course well known but there are many others. The effects of infantile 'stimulation' in rats and mice vary according to the age when stimulation is administered (Bell and Denenberg, 1963; Henderson, 1964; Levine, 1962); the cortical dysfunction following visual restriction in infancy does not occur following similar restriction in adult life (Wiesel and Hubel, 1963); social isolation of older chimpanzees does not have the devastating effect it does on infants (Davenport, Menzel and Rogers, 1966), and the disturbance following social isolation in dogs is greatest when isolation occurs during the four- to fourteen-week period (Scott and Fuller, 1965). The presence of similar 'sensitive' periods in man has not been shown but it may be accepted that they are likely to occur.

However, it is important to note that these periods are not innately fixed and absolute (hence the modern preference for the adjective 'sensitive' rather than 'critical'). The influence of environmental variables on the timing of the period for 'imprinting' has already been mentioned – similar effects may be seen with other 'sensitive' periods. For example, the influence of age on the response to infantile stimulation in rats is dependent on the intensity of stimulation (Denenberg and Kline, 1964; Nyman, 1967). It should be added that the existence of a 'sensitive' period may depend as much on age-related differences in general attributes, such as emotional responsivity, as on any specific tendency to respond to a particular stimulus (Fox and Stelzner, 1966).

With regard to the overriding importance of infantile experience, it is certainly true that *some* effects of early privation are extremely persistent and resistant to later influences. For example, cats subjected to early visual privation show little recovery later (Wiesel and Hubel, 1965b), and chimpanzees show only limited improvement after early social isolation (Turner, Davenport and Rogers, 1969). Nevertheless, it would be wrong to suppose that this is a general characteristic. The relative importance of early and of later influences depends on the type and severity of the life experience at each age, on the developmental function concerned and on the animal species. In many cases later experiences can have a marked effect.

The importance of experience in adolescence is perhaps most convincingly demonstrated with 'imprinting' in domestic birds – as this is the phenomenon classically (though misleadingly) associated with permanent and irreversible effects. For example, Guiton (1966) reared domestic cocks in isolation from one another for the first forty-seven days of life and compared their development with that of communally reared cocks. Many of the isolated birds when first tested attempted to copulate with a stuffed yellow rubber glove rather than with another bird (the cocks had been fed during the imprinting period by an experimenter who always wore yellow rubber gloves), whereas the communally reared birds copulated with birds rather than gloves. Both groups were then reared in pens with females until adult and tested again. Now both groups copulated only with hens. Apparently the isolated birds, following their adolescent experience with other birds, lost their reaction to man, and more specifically to the yellow glove, and exhibited normal heterosexual behaviour.

Similarly, Klinghammer (1967; Klinghammer and Hess, 1964) found that doves if raised individually by people became attached to them and when adult would choose human beings as their sexual partners. Yet this preference gradually waned following contact with other doves and after some years other doves, rather than people, were chosen as mates. This reversibility of early sexual imprinting does not apply to all species – in some cases later experience seems to have little effect (Hinde, 1970). Although early life experiences *may* have a permanent influence, in some circumstances the results may be overruled by the effects of adolescent experience. There is no experimental evidence for the unique importance of early experience in determining later choice of a sex partner, as was claimed by Lorenz.

There are age-specific effects, and early learning will influence later learning. Because of its primacy early learning may in some ways disproportionately influence development. Yet it is essentially reversible and in some cases the effects of later experience will predominate. There can be no general rule. Whether or not 'maternal deprivation' in infancy has a long-term effect depends in large part on environmental conditions in later childhood.

## Factors modifying long-term effects
### Separation from parents
For simplicity, separation experiences can be considered under three headings: very brief separations as a consequence of maternal care being provided by several or many mother-figures, transient separations lasting at least several weeks and permanent separations.

*Very brief associations associated with multiple mothering.* In spite of claims in the past that the children of working mothers are likely to become delinquent or show psychiatric disorder, there is abundant evidence from numerous studies that this is not so (Burchinal and Rossman, 1961; Cartwright and Jefferys, 1958; Douglas, Ross and Simpson, 1968; Hoffman, 1963; Rutter, Tizard and Whitmore, 1970; Siegel and Haas, 1963; Stolz, 1960; West, 1969; Yarrow, 1961; Yudkin and Holme, 1963). Children do not suffer from having several mother-figures so long as stable relationships and good care are provided by each. Indeed some studies have shown that children of working mothers may even be *less* likely to become delinquent than children whose mothers stay at home. In these circumstances it seemed that the mother going out to work was a reflection of a generally high standard of family responsibility and care. Two provisos need to be made with respect to these studies. First, there has been little investigation of the effects of mothers starting work while their children are still infants, although such data as are available do not suggest any ill-effects. Second, a situation in which mother-figures keep changing so that the child does not have the opportunity of forming a relationship with any of them may well be harmful. Such unstable arrangements usually occur in association with poor-quality maternal care, so that it has not been possible to examine the effects of each independently (Moore, 1963, 1964).

Much the same can be said about the effects of day nurseries and crèches (as particular forms of care often used when mothers go out to work). Assertions in official reports (W H O Expert Committee on Mental Health, 1951) concerning their permanent ill-effects are quite unjustified. Day care need not necessarily interfere with the normal mother–child attachment (Caldwell, Wright, Honig and Tannenbaum, 1970) and the available evidence gives no reason to suppose that the use of day nurseries has any long-term psychological or physical ill-effects (Yudkin and Holme, 1963).* The one disadvantage of day-nursery care for very young children is that they get more of the common childish infectious diseases, presumably through their greater contact with other children, and they tend to have more hospital care (Douglas and Blomfield, 1958).

As has already been discussed so far as is known, there are no adverse psychological *sequelae* associated with upbringing in the Israeli kibbutzim, where children are raised in residential nurseries but still retain strong links with their parents (Irvine, 1966; Miller, 1969). Not only is their emotional development satisfactory but also the children do not appear to have the linguistic handicaps often associated with institutional care (Kohen-Raz, 1968). Anecdotal evidence has suggested that delinquency may actually be less frequent in kibbutzniks but enuresis may be more prevalent. Both these observations require systematic study before they can be accepted.

*Transient separations.* Several investigations of short-term separations (usually a month or more) in early childhood have shown little in the way of cognitive, emotional or behavioural ill-effects (Andry, 1960; Bowlby, Ainsworth, Boston and Rosenbluth, 1956; Douglas, Ross and Simpson, 1968; Naess, 1959, 1962) and rates of separation in child-guidance-clinic patients differ little from control populations (Howells and Layng, 1955). On the other hand, most studies have shown that children who experience separation from their parents for at least a month in the early years of life do have a very slightly increased risk of later psychological disturbance, particularly of an antisocial type (Ainsworth, 1962). The interpretation of this observation is bedevilled by the fact that in most studies widely differing

* But see also chapter 8.

types of separation experience have been pooled and in many cases the separation has also involved considerable deprivation or stress (Yarrow, 1964). Also, the children's subsequent experiences have frequently been atypical. Recent findings from our own studies show that separation is associated with antisocial disorder only when it occurs as a result of family stress or discord (Rutter, 1971a). Thus, children admitted for short periods into the care of a local authority show much deviance and disorder. But this is a group of children who have been at a social and biological disadvantage from birth (Mapstone, 1969), and their transient separation from home is but a minor episode in a long history of disturbing life experiences. Separations for other reasons (such as a holiday or admission to hospital) had no measurable ill-effects in our studies (Rutter, 1971a).

These studies have all been concerned with the emergence of *deviant* behaviour following separation and not with variations within the normal range. Evidence on lesser changes of a persistent kind following separation experiences is, however, available from Hinde's studies of rhesus monkeys. As already described, monkeys separated from their mothers for one week in infancy still showed more apprehension two years later in a strange situation than did non-separated controls. Although the behaviour of the two groups in a familiar setting showed no differences, this persisting difference in response to strange objects may well be of some importance. Whether or not similar changes may follow separation in humans is not known, but clinical anecdota suggest that *some* children may remain apprehensive of new situations for a while following an unpleasant separation experience. How often this occurs and how long it persists when it occurs is quite unknown.

Language retardation and intellectual impairment have not been a feature of separated children in any of the studies.

*Prolonged or permanent separations.* Similar problems arise in the analysis of the effects of very long-term separations which may also occur for a diversity of reasons. Thus, there is a very extensive literature showing an association between 'broken homes' and delinquency (e.g. Wootton, 1959; Yarrow, 1961, 1964), but no association with neurosis (Rutter, 1970; Wardle, 1961). However, in some cases the break-up of the home is no more than a minor episode in a long history of family discord and disruption, and to differentiate the effects of separation as such it is necessary to consider 'broken homes' according to the various causes of break.

The most obvious distinction is between homes broken by death and those broken by divorce or separation. It is only the latter which show a strong association with delinquency (Douglas, Ross and Simpson, 1968; Gibson, 1969; Gregory, 1965). Parental death has been associated with only a very slight (and usually statistically insignificant) rise in delinquency rate. Even this slight rise may not be due to the death itself (Birtchnell, 1969). Chronic physical illness which often precedes death is itself a factor associated with child psychiatric disorder (Rutter, 1966). Grief in the surviving parent is often quite prolonged (Bowlby and Parkes, 1970; Marris, 1958) and this, too, may affect the child's adjustment. Death of the father is frequently followed by economic and social deterioration (Douglas, Ross and Simpson, 1968; Rowntree, 1955) and these may also constitute important adverse influences on the child. Douglas, Ross and Simpson (1968) found intellectual impairment in bereaved children only when the death followed a prolonged illness.

Which parent dies seems of possible importance, in that two studies have found ill-effects to be most marked following the death of the same-sexed parent (Gregory, 1965; Rutter, 1966). However, this has not been found in other studies.

Because of the almost exclusive concern with 'maternal deprivation' there has been little investigation of the consequences of loss of a father. However, there have been some studies of the effects of paternal absence due to the father being away at sea, serving in the armed forces or absent for other reasons (Bach, 1946; Lynn and Sawrey, 1959; Sears, Pintler and Sears, 1946; Stolz et al., 1954). The reports are few and the measures used were often weak, but it seems that serious disorders of behaviour were unusual. On the other hand it appears that in some cases the sexual identification of children is impaired by the continuous absence of their father (Biller, 1971).

## Types of child care

The type and quality of child care provided has been shown to be a crucial factor in a wide variety of studies of both family settings and institutions.

So far as private homes are concerned, the most important variable with regard to behavioural development has usually been the quality of family relationships (Jonsson, 1967; McCord and McCord, 1959; Oleinick, Bahn, Eisenberg, and Lilienfeld, 1966; Rutter, 1971a). Parental discord, disharmony and quarrelling have been found to be associated with antisocial and delinquent behaviour in the children. Affectional relationships with the children are equally important and the degree of supervision exercised also appears relevant (Craig and Glick, 1965; Glueck and Glueck, 1962). In contrast, the methods of early child care (Caldwell, 1964) and the technique of discipline employed (Becker, 1964) seem to be of very little importance, except that extremes of discipline and great inconsistency are also associated with antisocial behaviour. No consistent associations have been found between patterns of care and neurotic disorders in the children.

In innumerable investigations low social class has been associated with poor intellectual and educational achievement, which some studies have found becomes more marked as the children get older (Douglas, 1964; Ross and Simpson, 1971). Social class differences in patterns of communication have been found (Brandis and Henderson, 1970; Hess and Shipman, 1965; Robinson and Rackstraw, 1967), and it has been suggested that these are, at least in part, responsible for the poor cognitive performance of the children. However, so far, very little is known concerning parental influences on cognitive development (Freeberg and Payne, 1967). Brief programmes of pre-school compensatory education have led to limited intellectual gains (Eisenberg, 1967; Klaus and Gray, 1968; Starr, 1971), but the variables which have led to cognitive improvement are not known.

Whereas numerous studies have documented the impaired language, poor intelligence and disturbed behaviour which frequently occur in children who have been reared in institutions (Ainsworth, 1962; Bowlby, 1951; Ferguson, 1966; Yarrow, 1961), this is found in children coming from only some institutions. Thus, Garvin and Sacks (1963) found an average *gain* of nearly nine I Q points in children admitted to an institution for short-term care (a period of some months) and Skeels (1966; Skeels and Dye, 1939) found a marked *rise* in I Q in children transferred from a poor over-crowded orphanage to an institution for the mentally sub-normal where more personal care was possible. Gardner, Hawkes and Burchinal (1961) and Rheingold and Bayley (1959) found no emotional or cognitive deficits following institutional care. Du Pan and Roth (1955) and Klackenberg (1956) also found little intellectual deficit in young children in well-run institutions. These results stand in stark contrast to those of Dennis and Najarian (1957), Goldfarb (1943a and b), Pringle and Bossio (1958a, 1958b), Provence and Lipton (1962) and others who reported gross intellectual impairment in institutional children. Similarly, Tizard (1971) found that children in residential nurseries had a normal intellectual level whereas Roudinesco and Appell (1950, 1951) found intellectual retardation to be prevalent.

It could be argued that these differences merely reflect differences in admission policy were it not for systematic experimental studies which have shown that change in institutional care can lead to an improvement in cognitive (verbal) level (Kirk, 1958; Lyle, 1960; Skeels, 1942; Tizard, 1964). But as many changes were introduced it is not possible to be sure which were responsible for the rise in intellectual level. The lack of adult–child interaction in institutions has been systematically assessed by Rheingold (1961); Provence and Lipton (1962) noted the inflexibility of institutional care; and David and Appell (1961) observed the lack of communication and responsiveness to the infants' needs. More recently, Tizard and his colleagues have done much to demonstrate the crucial features of institutional life and the ways in which various sorts of institutions differ one from another (King and Raynes, 1968; King, Raynes and Tizard, 1971; Tizard, 1969).

Some clues on the features likely to lead to retardation are provided by the experimental studies of the short-term effects of different types of stimulation (see page 41). Dennis (1960), in a comparison of institutions which led and those which did not lead to retardation, suggested that, at least for infants, lack of handling of the children, absence of toys and lack of play opportunities may retard motor development. The studies noted above have all demonstrated the lack of sensory, social and linguistic stimulation in many (but not all) long-stay institutions. However, to a considerable extent the answer to the key question of *which* institutional features lead to language deficit, intellectual retardation and behavioural disturbance remains a matter for further research.

Nevertheless, important clues are provided by animal studies. Stimulated by Hebb's (1949) theorizing on the importance of a diversity of experiences for intellectual growth, there has been a host of studies examining the effects of sensory restriction in infancy on later cognitive performance. Investigations using rats (e.g. Hymovitch, 1952; Nyman, 1967; Woods, Ruckelshaus and Bowling, 1960), dogs (e.g. Thompson and Heron, 1954) and chimpanzees (Davenport and Rogers, 1968; Rogers and Davenport, 1971) have all shown that a restricted rearing leads to later intellectual impairment, although Harlow, Schlitz and Harlow (1969) were unable to show this in rhesus monkeys.

Some progress has been made in specifying the crucial elements in early experience. Hebb's (1949) original pilot study compared laboratory-reared rats with those reared in his own home as pets and showed that the pets scored more highly on 'intelligence' tests and seemed better able to profit by new experiences at maturity. He suggested that the important difference between the groups was the greater breadth of experience of the pets who had been allowed to run about the house. This view has been substantially confirmed by later experiments (Bingham and Griffiths, 1952;

Forgays and Forgays, 1952; Hymovitch, 1952). Rats reared in a 'free' environment giving access to a wide range of activities showed superior performance to those reared in individual cages. The importance of *breadth* of experience applies to sensory modalities as well as to range of activity. Thus, for example, Meier and McGee (1959) showed that rats reared with visual-tactile experiences showed superior perceptual abilities at maturity to rats reared with purely visual experiences. The same experiments have shown that it is indeed a range of perceptual and motor experiences which is crucial and not just the company of other rats. Thus, Hymovitch (1952) found that rats reared in individual mesh cages which were moved about the room from time to time were superior at problem solving to those reared in individual stove-pipe cages from which the animals could not see out. Similarly, Forgays and Forgays (1952) showed that among animals *all* of whom had been reared in a free environment with other animals, those brought up with playthings were better at problem solving than those brought up without playthings. Both seeing many things and doing many things had an important influence on intellectual growth.

While there are important differences with respect to the type of intellectual ability studied, it seems that for many skills active exploration of the environment influences development to a greater extent than purely passive exposure to sensory stimuli (see the experiments by Held and Hein discussed on page 57).

Although early life experiences may have a general effect on intellectual growth, the results of experiences in a particular modality are to some extent specific in nature. Accordingly, Forgus (1954) found that purely visual experiences in infancy were most important for later visual discrimination skills in rats, but that visuo-motor experiences were superior for the development of visuo-motor abilities (Forgus, 1955). Similarly, Nissen, Chow and Semmes (1951) showed that rearing a chimpanzee with its arms and legs enclosed in cardboard cylinders led to marked impairments in motor coordination and spatial orientation, but had no effect on visual discrimination. The specific effects on visual perception of early visual privation have already been described.

Human evidence is more limited, but what there is points in the same direction. White (1971) has found that providing babies with increased opportunities for touching things and looking at things led to an early maturation of certain visuo-motor skills. Starr (1971) reported an unpublished study by Saltz which showed that providing institutional children with a regular parent-surrogate aided their social adjustment, but did not influence intellectual development.

Undoubtedly the crucial difference between animals and man with respect to intellectual development is the influence of language on cognitive growth in humans. Verbal skills constitute a major part of intelligence in man and the presence of language aids intellectual growth in many ways (Rutter, 1972a). Here again specific influences are important (Rutter and Mittler, 1972) and the kinds of environmental conditions associated with the favourable development of verbal skills are not the same as those which foster perceptuo-motor development (Vernon, 1969). In short, although the evidence is incomplete and occasionally contra-dictory, it appears highly likely that different types of experience in early childhood are needed for different de-velopmental functions. It is not possible to say which is the most important feature in child rearing. Rather it is neces-sary to discuss which experiences are necessary for which type of skill.

Little is known about the factors in institutional life associated with a better or worse social adjustment. Both Conway (1957) and Pringle (Pringle and Bossio, 1960; Pringle and Clifford, 1962) found that a stable relationship with an adult (not necessarily the parent) led to better adjustment. Similarly, Wolkind (1971) found less behavioural disturbance in institutional children when they had been at least two years with the same house-mother. This appears to be an important factor but without more and better informa-tion on other aspects of the children's life it is not possible to determine how important this factor is or what others may also be influential.

*Duration of privation*

If attention is confined to studies of institutions in which the children show adverse *sequelae*, most (Goldfarb, 1943a and b, 1947; Roudinesco and Appell, 1951; Skeels, Updegraff, Wellman and Williams, 1938) but not all (Dennis and Najarian, 1957; Pringle and Bossio, 1958a, 1958b) have shown that the longer the stay in the institution the greater the cognitive deficit and the greater the emotional and behavioural disturbance. Where negative results have been found, the care of older children has probably been superior to that given to the younger ones. Several studies have suggested that the children of mentally retarded parents have higher I Qs if removed when young to a more intellectually stimulating home (e.g. McCandless, 1964). Not too much weight can be attached to any of the findings (positive or negative) in view of the uncertainties about the comparability of care at different ages and about the reasons why some children remained in care or with mentally retarded parents whereas others did not.

Nevertheless, it seems likely that the longer the privation persists the greater will be the psychological deficit in view of the similar findings from studies of children in their own homes (Gordon, 1923; Skeels and Fillmore, 1937; Wheeler, 1942). Older children in underprivileged homes were found to have lower I Qs than the younger children. Conversely, Lee (1951) found that the longer black migrants from the South had had schooling in the (less depriving) North of the U S A the higher was their I Q. There are important flaws in all of these studies either because the data are cross-sectional or because of the large number of children lost during follow-up. These flaws demand caution in accepting the results as they stand, but in the absence of better data it may be concluded that the weight of the evidence suggests that the longer the privation lasts the worse the effects.

Our own family studies (of children in their own homes) also provide circumstantial evidence in favour of this proposition (Rutter, 1971a). It was found that of children separated (temporarily) from their parents in early life because of family stress and discord, those who later were in a harmonious family setting were better adjusted than those who remained in a disturbed and quarrelsome home. Children whose parents had divorced or separated and whose *second* marriage was also disharmonious and unhappy more often showed antisocial behaviour than those whose parents were experiencing their *first* unsuccessful marriage. The presumption is that the marital discord had occupied more of the child's life in the former case.

## Presence of good relationships

Mention has already been made of the evidence from Conway and Pringle that institutional children who maintained a stable relationship with some adult were better adjusted than those who did not. Our own findings with regard to children in their own homes produced similar results (Rutter, 1971a). In homes all of which were characterized by severe marital discord, fewer children who had a good relationship with one parent were antisocial compared with those who had poor relationships with both the mother and the father.

## The opportunity to develop attachments with adults

Children admitted to institutions in infancy and who remain there until at least three years of age are in a situation less conducive to bond formation (see chapter 1) than are children in their own homes during this age period. Several studies have shown that the former is a group with a particularly poor outcome (Goldfarb, 1955; Pringle and Bossio, 1958a, 1958b). It also appears to be the group most likely to include children with the pattern of social disinhibition, indiscriminate friendships and an inability to form lasting relationships (Bowlby, 1946; Wolkind, 1971). In a study of foster care, Trasler (1960) found that prolonged institutional care in early life was the factor most likely to lead to subsequent breakdown of fostering. In keeping with the above suggestion, he also considered that this was the condition most likely to lead to affectionless detachment. The evidence on this issue is discussed in greater detail below when considering failure to develop bonds.

However, it should be added that institutional care at this age is perfectly compatible with a normal development of *language* and *intelligence* (Tizard, 1971).

## Age

Linguistic and intellectual retardation can arise with impaired life circumstances at any stage during the period of development, although the nature of the defects will vary with the child's age. Lack of vocalization, impaired responsiveness and developmental delay may be evident as early as the first few months of life in children reared in poor-quality institutions (Brodbeck and Irwin, 1946; Burlingham and Freud, 1944; Provence and Lipton, 1962). There is only very limited evidence on institutional effects on cognition and language in older children, but it appears that the older the child on admission the less the retardation (Pringle and Bossio, 1958a, 1958b). However, this finding is of little significance without evidence on the longitudinal course of cognitive development in children admitted to institutions at different ages – and this is still lacking. In view of the fact that post-natal brain growth is most rapid in the first two years of life (Marshall, 1968) and the probability that organisms are most susceptible to damage during periods of most rapid development (Dobbing, 1968), it is reasonable to suppose that the effects of privation might be most marked at this time. But evidence on this point is lacking. Furthermore, periods of susceptibility to damage should not be confused with periods when recovery can still occur (see page 77 for a discussion on this point).

There is some evidence that the long-term (delayed) effects of bereavement may be greatest in children whose parents die during the toddler age period (Rutter, 1966), but this point needs confirmation. There is also some suggestion that stress at this period may also be particularly likely to impair the acquisition of bladder control (Douglas and Turner, 1970). It is not known whether there is any period during the first five years when susceptibility to stress is particularly great.

Evidence on age differences in response to more long-standing influences such as parental discord or parental mental illness (Rutter, 1966, 1970, 1971a) is difficult to obtain just because the influences are chronic without any clear time demarcation. Nevertheless such information as is available suggests no particular age differences in susceptibility other than that young infants and older adolescents may be less often adversely affected.

Perhaps the one outcome which is crucially affected by age is the emergence of 'affectionless psychopathy', which appears to develop largely following lack of opportunities to form attachments during the first three years of life (this point is discussed in greater detail on pages 102 to 106).

## Sex of child

Surprisingly little attention has been paid to sex differences in long-term responses to deprivation. Recent studies of the effects of family discord and disharmony indicate that boys may be more vulnerable to their ill-effects and there is some suggestion that this may also apply to other forms of deprivation (Rutter, 1970). The matter requires further investigation before firm conclusions are possible.

## Temperament of child

The importance of individual differences was emphasized when considering the short-term effects of deprivation. Their relevance with respect to long-term effects can only be guessed at on the basis of their demonstrated influence in 'normal' children and in children whose parents have had some psychiatric disorder. The long-term consequences of temperamental differences in 'normal' children have been most systematically studied by Thomas and his associates in their New York sample of largely middle-class families (Thomas, Chess and Birch, 1968; Thomas et al., 1963). They measured the behavioural styles of infants and young children and related these attributes to the later development of mild behavioural disorders. Emotionally intense children slow to adapt to new situations, irregular in their sleeping, eating and bowel habits, who showed preponderantly negative mood were those most likely to develop behavioural disturbances a few years later (Rutter, Birch, Thomas and

Chess, 1964). A child's own characteristics influenced the development of emotional and behavioural disorders. Circumstantial evidence suggested that they probably did so through effects on parent–child interaction (Thomas, Chess and Birch, 1968).

Rather similar attributes have been found to influence children's responses to the stresses associated with discord in families with a mentally ill parent (Rutter, 1971a). Children whose behaviour was difficult to change, who did not mind messiness and disorder and who were markedly irregular in their eating and sleeping patterns were significantly more likely than other children to develop deviant behaviours. Whether temperamental attributes are equally important in other types of privation or deprivation has not yet been studied, but research on this point should be rewarding.

Two questions arise concerning the influence of temperamental attributes. Are the attributes themselves a result of environmental influences or do they have an important genetic component? In so far as the attributes lead to deviant behaviour do they do so directly or rather by influencing the child's interaction with his environment? Only limited information is available regarding the first issue. Genetic aspects of these temperamental features have been little investigated (Rutter, Korn and Birch, 1963), but the available genetic studies of such attributes in children suggest an important hereditary component (Freedman and Keller, 1963; Scarr, 1969).

However, it should not be thought that these temperamental attributes are either immutable or entirely hereditary. Although continuities in development are present, considerable modification of individual attributes by life experiences can occur (Hertzig, Birch, Thomas and Mendez, 1968; Yando and Kagan, 1968). Furthermore, some individual differences influencing a child's response to the environment may be largely experiential in origin. For example, Zigler (1966) has suggested that a major component in institutional retardates' style of response to learning tasks is determined by their previous experiences of social reinforcement.

On the second question of the manner in which temperamental attributes influence development, it appears highly likely that the mechanism concerns the way in which such attributes influence children's interaction with the environment (Rutter, 1971a; Rutter *et al.*, 1964; Thomas, Chess and Birch, 1968). This is true of genetic influences generally – only rarely is a child psychiatric disorder inherited as such. One of the most important effects of genetics on behavioural development is through its influence on an individual's adaptability and response to stress (Glass, 1954; McClearn, 1970; Thompson and Grusec, 1970). This has been most clearly demonstrated in animal experiments showing, for example, the interaction of genetic differences (in maze performance) with environmental restriction and enrichment (Cooper and Zubek, 1958); genetic effects with respect to the pre-natal administration of adrenaline (Thompson and Olian, 1961) or other stress conditions (DeFries, 1964); and breed differences in dogs' responses to 'indulgent' and 'strict' training regimens (Freedman, 1958). Genetic traits which give an advantage in one situation may lead to disadvantage in others (Searle, 1949).

## Reversibility

The extent to which the ill-effects of 'maternal deprivation' are irreversible has always been one of the chief points of controversy. Bowlby's (1951) initial conclusion that mothering is almost useless if delayed until after the age of two and a half years and useless for most children if delayed until after twelve months has not been supported by subsequent research. The question now is not whether the effects are irreversible, but rather how readily and how completely reversible are the effects with respect to each function impaired by deprivation (Ainsworth, 1962). Evidence on these points remains limited.

With regard to the cognitive ill-effects of deprivation in childhood, there is probably some tendency to minor and partial remission with age in the normal course of events. Thus, the intellectual handicap at five to six years shown by the institutional children studied by Dennis and Najarian

(1957) was less than the developmental retardation evident in the first year of life. However, this may be evidence that the circumstances were less depriving for older children than they were for infants. On the other hand, this could scarcely account for the IQ gains in adult life shown by the mildly retarded individuals from a socially deprived background studied by the Clarkes (Clarke, 1968) or those studied by Stein and Susser (1970). The observation that special training made little difference to the IQ gains (Clarke, Clarke and Reiman, 1958) suggests the operation of delayed maturation rather than a response to environmental change. These findings are of some interest, but it is important to recognize that the IQ gain with age was usually only moderate and fell very far short of reversing the early damage.

Considerable reversal of cognitive ill-effects is possible with a *complete and permanent change of environment*, provided that this occurs in infancy. This is clearly shown by the Iowa studies of children from very poor homes or inferior institutions who were adopted in the first two years of life (Skeels, 1966; Skeels and Harms, 1948; Skodak and Skeels, 1949). When tested in adolescence they had normal IQs which were some twenty or thirty points above that of their true parents. What is uncertain is the upper age limit beyond which complete reversal is not possible. Goldfarb (1955) found marked and persistent intellectual impairment in children transferred from a poor institution to a foster home at nearly four years. On the other hand, there is one well-documented case in the literature of a child reared in isolation with a mute mother in a dark attic up to the age of six years (Davis, 1947; Mason, 1942). When discovered she was severely retarded and without speech. Nevertheless, following intensive residential treatment she ultimately recovered to a remarkable extent, acquiring speech, gaining a normal intellectual level and achieving good social functioning. It may be concluded that extensive reversal is *usual* if the change of environment is complete and if it occurs during infancy. Reversal becomes less likely the longer the privation lasts and the older the child when removed from the privation. Even so, reversal may occasionally occur in older children.

These studies have sometimes led people to conclude that *partial and temporary changes of environment* might also have equally far-reaching effects, but the evidence shows that this is very far from the case. For example, the variety of studies of compensatory education for deprived pre-school children in the U S A have demonstrated only modest short-term benefits (Eisenberg, 1967; Jensen, 1969; Klaus and Gray, 1968). What is surprising is not that the beneficial effects of six weeks' environmental enrichment proved transitory but rather that anyone supposed it would be otherwise. It is encouraging that such brief and partial enrichment had any effect at all, but it is evident that the ill-effects of long-standing and persisting privation cannot be corrected by short-term environmental tinkering followed by the child's return to the depriving circumstances.

The rather banal conclusion is that the degree of reversibility depends on the duration and severity of the privation, the age of the child when privation ceases and how complete is the change of environment. More precise specifications regarding these variables are not yet possible.

Less is known about the reversibility of growth deficits following privation. In general, when malnutrition is corrected there is a rapid acceleration in growth which to a considerable extent compensates for the previous retardation. However, the compensation is not usually complete (Birch and Gussow, 1970). Whether it is very nearly so or whether considerable deficit remains depends on both the duration and severity of the malnutrition and on the child's age at the time. So far, most of the follow-up studies of 'deprivation dwarfism' (see page 94) have been fairly short-term, but the results appear closely similar: that is, compensation is rapid but often not quite complete.

Very little information is available on the reversibility of the affectionless psychopathy syndrome. Whereas complete reversal readily occurs if privation ceases during the infancy period (as shown by the adoptive studies already mentioned) it is quite uncertain whether reversal can occur after two or three years of age. Clinical accounts suggest that reversal occurs only partially and with great difficulty after the infancy period, but systematic studies to support or refute that conclusion are lacking.

The persistence of the severe social defects in monkeys subjected by Harlow to total social isolation for the first six months of life may be relevant in this connection. As already noted, these monkeys were sexually incompetent, socially deviant to a severe degree and grossly incompetent as mothers (so that several of the first batch of infants were killed). Some of these isolate mothers went on to have second and third babies and in a few cases mothering improved considerably (Harlow and Harlow, 1970). Harlow and Suomi (1971) have more recently tried to rehabilitate monkeys damaged by early total social isolation. Preliminary findings suggest that some of the damaged social capacities may improve appreciably given the appropriate social experiences after the infancy period. Even so, work with chimpanzees (Turner, Davenport and Rogers, 1969) suggests that the social abnormalities are modifiable only to a limited extent and then only with difficulty.

All in all, the scanty evidence available suggests that for affectionless psychopathy to be completely reversible, it is usually necessary for the child to have experienced normal relationships during early childhood. Data are lacking, but probably complete reversal is difficult after three years of age, although improvement may still occur later. Whereas antisocial disorder is certainly one of the most persistent of child psychiatric disorders (Robins, 1970), a change for the better in environmental circumstances during middle childhood was shown to be associated with a lower rate of disorder in our study of families showing discord and disharmony (Rutter, 1971a). Again, however, information is lacking on how early and how complete a change of environment is necessary for reversal to take place.

# 5. Long-Term Consequences: Possible Mechanisms

With respect to the long-term effects of 'maternal deprivation', mechanisms have to be determined for several distinct outcomes: mental retardation, dwarfism, delinquency, 'affectionless psychopathy' and possibly depression. It is clear from what has been said already that it is likely that the psychological processes involved in each of these are somewhat different.

### Disruption of bonds or change of environment?

Whether the adverse effects of 'maternal deprivation' were due to disruption of bonds or a change of environment was an important issue with regard to the short-term effects, as already discussed. However, it is of less importance in connection with long-term effects in that admission to hospital (the situation where the issue arises most clearly) is of less consequence for long-term development. There is little association with delinquency and antisocial behaviour (Rutter, 1971a), mental retardation (Rutter, Tizard and Whitmore, 1970), 'affectionless psychopathy' (Bowlby *et al.*, 1956) or dwarfism (Patton and Gardner, 1963).

However, enuresis may constitute an exception in that recurrent hospital admission in the first four years does seem to be a factor leading to an increased rate of persistent bed-wetting (Douglas and Turner, 1970). In this case, the limited evidence available suggests that neither bond disruption nor change of environment is the most important variable. Whereas repeated hospital admission was associated with a slight increase in enuresis, much the most marked effect was seen with children who have some surgical operation. Burns and fractures were also associated with an increased rate of enuresis. These findings from Douglas and his colleagues suggest that it is the presence of an unpleasant or stressful experience which is influential rather than the separation from family or the strange environment as such. They hypothesize that acute stress and anxiety during the first four years of life may interfere with the normal acquisition of bladder control. However, this may not be a sufficient explanation in that enuresis is also much commoner in children from families where the mother has died or where the parents have divorced (Douglas, 1970). The rate of enuresis is highest of all where the children are placed in foster homes or institutions. Numbers were small, but contrary to the earlier supposition, enuresis was most common when this occurred at four to six years rather than before four years (Douglas, 1973). To what extent the bed-wetting is a function of family discord that may precede institutional admission and to what extent a consequence of an institutional upbringing is uncertain. Douglas (1970) found that enuresis was just as common when the mother had died as when the parents had divorced or separated. This argues against the importance of family discord as the main factor.

Enuresis is quite common in children in many kinds of institutions (Stein and Susser, 1966, 1967). The evidence on this occurrence suggests that enuresis is partly a result of the stresses that led to institutional placement, but the finding that enuresis among children in care is significantly commoner in those in children's homes than in those in foster homes suggests that the qualities of institutional life may themselves be important (although selective biases could also be operative).

The one long-term outcome which may be associated with disruption of bonds is depression (Rutter, 1971a). The evidence is somewhat contradictory but it appears that depressive disorders during adult life may be particularly common when a parent has died during the person's adolescence. This finding, if substantiated, refers of course to adult psychiatric disorder, which takes us outside the scope of the present review. Depression in childhood has been less studied. One study (Caplan and Douglas, 1969) linked loss of a parent with depressive disorder in children, but as the association was confined to children who had been placed in a foster home (it was not present in those losing a parent but remaining with the other parent), it is unlikely that bond disruption was the mechanism involved.

The evidence, then, from human studies suggests that although bond disruption is a potent source of short-term distress, it is not a particularly important factor in the development of serious long-term disturbance of any type. This conclusion seems at first sight to run counter to the findings from studies with subhuman primates, which show that even relatively short periods of separation from the mother are associated with measurable behavioural change in some (but not all) animals, certainly as long as six months, and probably two years later (Hinde and Spencer-Booth, 1971b; Spencer-Booth and Hinde, 1971b). In terms of the proportion of lifespan this is equivalent to several years in humans.

This may be only an apparent difference in that the monkey studies were largely concerned with behavioural differences within the normal range and mostly in relation to responses to strange situations, rather than pathological outcomes. Even in humans, unhappy separations may sometimes lead to clinging behaviour lasting many months or even a year or so. These experiences may also render the child more likely to be distressed by separations when older. However, many children show *no* such long-term effects and even in those that do the effects are generally relatively minor.

To what extent there are real differences between man and monkey in the response to separation is not yet clear. The diminished activity and play found in monkeys five months after separation appears a greater effect than that usually seen in children after a comparable period of time, but comparative data are lacking. If it should turn out that there are differences, there are several possible explanations of why they might exist. In the first place, there are important neuropsychological differences between man and monkey (Drewe, Ettlinger, Milner and Passingham, 1970) and it is known that there are inter-species differences (perhaps between monkey and chimpanzee – Mason, Davenport and Menzel, 1968) in the response to various traumata. One mediating factor in this connection may be the presence of language. Although some extremely rudimentary features of language may be present in chimpanzees (Gardner and Gardner, 1969; Premack, 1971), language has not been demonstrated in monkeys. It may be that the opportunity to explain to children the nature of a separation experience makes it a less stressful experience than it would be without this possibility. Another possible factor is the nature of the care during separation. Unlike humans, other adult monkeys do not usually adequately take over the care of abandoned infants.* Although it is possible to ensure that all material needs are met during separation as before, nevertheless the infant's social experiences are quite different.

Whatever differences there may be between man and monkey, the available evidence from human studies suggests that mother–child separation in itself is not an important cause of *serious* long-term disorder. However, as we have already discussed with respect to short-term effects, separation experiences should not necessarily be equated with bond disruption. It may be that separation does not usually have long-term effects just because children can maintain bonds in a person's absence with the consequence that separation does not necessarily involve bond disruption.

## Disruption of bonds or deprivation of stimulation?
### Cognitive effects

The question of bond disruption or stimulus deprivation arises most clearly with respect to the effects of long-term

*Although there is a shortage of good data on the point it seems that there are considerable inter-species differences in the behaviour of females towards young other than their own (Spencer-Booth, 1970). In many primates adult females do care for other young but, at least in the short term, such care generally falls well short of that provided by the natural mother.

institutional care. Numerous studies have shown that children reared in institutions are frequently retarded in language, general cognitive skills and scholastic attainment (Haywood, 1967; Tizard, 1969). An institutional upbringing frequently involves both bond disruption and stimulus deprivation, so that in order to determine the psychological mechanisms involved it is necessary to seek situations where one occurs without the other.

First, we may consider what happens when there is bond disruption without stimulus deprivation. This probably occurs when a child loses a parent through death or divorce but remains at home with the rest of his family. Douglas's National Survey showed that parental death following an acute illness had no effect on intellectual development (Douglas, Ross and Simpson, 1968), Vernon (1969) found no association between 'broken homes' and intelligence, and the Isle of Wight study found no relationship between a 'broken home' and either intellectual retardation or reading retardation (Rutter, Tizard and Whitmore, 1970). Bond disruption, as such, is therefore not associated with mental subnormality or educational retardation. The fact that Bowlby and his colleagues (1956) found that children who had spent several years of their childhood in a T B sanatorium were of normal intelligence is also in keeping with this conclusion, although in this case it could just mean that the separation had not involved bond disruption.

If that conclusion is correct, institutions with a good level of cognitive 'stimulation' and adequate child care should *not* lead to intellectual impairment. That seems to be the case with respect to children reared in good-quality residential nurseries where there is plenty of staff–child interaction and stimulation but where relationships tend to be rather impersonal and where many adults look after each child (Tizard and Tizard, 1971). Such a setting would seem to involve little perceptual privation but might be likely to impede bond formation. The Tizards found that children in residential nurseries were more clinging and more fearful of strangers than children reared with their own families, but there was no intellectual or language retardation at three years (Tizard, 1971) and only very slight retardation at two years (Tizard and Joseph, 1970). It seems that it is not whether you are brought up at home or in an institution which matters for cognitive growth, but rather the type of care you receive.

Again, if that is so, it follows that if the quality of care is improved in institutions, intellectual and language development should improve even though the children remain separated from their parents. There is good evidence in support of this proposition. In one of the very early studies, Skeels and Dye (1939) reported a marked rise in cognitive level in a small group of children transferred from a very poor orphanage to a rather better subnormality hospital. McKinney and Keele (1963) found that increased physical attention led to more purposeful behaviour and verbal expression in severely retarded boys in a long-stay institution. Kirk (1958) showed that retarded children in an institution made significant gains in I Q (compared with contrast subjects) when given a special nursery-school programme. In the better controlled Brooklands experiment, Tizard and Lyle also found that the provision of better care for mentally subnormal children in hospital led to a significant gain in verbal development (Lyle, 1960; Tizard, 1964). Over an eighteen-month period the experimental group showed a ten-month gain on the verbal section of the Minnesota Pre-School Scale, compared with only four months for the matched control group. The exposure of children to environments differing in the range of environmental experience and amount of stimulation they provide can have an appreciable effect on mental growth (Stein and Susser, 1970).

The importance of stimulus deprivation rather than bond disruption is also shown by other findings. Douglas, Ross and Simpson (1968) found that children whose parent died after a chronic illness showed some intellectual impairment whereas those whose parent died after an acute illness did not. Presumably some aspect of child care was adversely affected by chronic parental illness, but the parental loss as such did not influence cognitive development. Secondly, many studies (Douglas, 1964; Douglas, Ross and Simpson,

1968; Nisbet, 1953a, 1953b) have shown that children in large families have a poor verbal intellectual development compared with children in small families. The effect seems to be environmental rather than genetic (Rutter and Mittler, 1972) and whereas the exact mechanism is not known, it clearly cannot involve bond disruption. Rather some aspect of parent–child interaction (probably involving communication), appears influential.

The same applies to children reared in homes which supply inadequate intellectual stimulation. Early studies of English gypsy and canal-boat children (Gaw, 1925; Gordon, 1923) and of children from isolated communities in the Kentucky (Asher, 1935) and Tennessee mountains (Wheeler, 1942) all showed that verbal abilities were seriously retarded and were more so in older children than in youngsters, suggesting progressive impairment due to deprivation of some aspect of experience. Visuo-spatial abilities were much less impaired. Again bond disruption could not be involved.

The evidence all points to the conclusion that bond disruption *per se* has a negligible influence on intellectual development whereas lack of experience or stimulation has important deleterious effects on cognitive growth. The extensive animal evidence showing the importance of experience in the development of intelligence was discussed in chapter 3. Because the effects on cognition appear to be due to a *lack* of 'stimulation' rather than a *loss* of 'stimulation', privation is a more accurate term than deprivation.

## Emotional and behavioural effects

The conclusion is different for the emotional and behavioural consequences of deprivation. Unlike the finding with regard to cognition, 'broken homes' *are* strongly associated with emotional and behavioural disturbance, particularly of an antisocial nature (Rutter, 1971a). Children not admitted to an institution but separated from a parent through parental divorce or separation have a much increased risk of delinquency. This is a circumstance involving bond disruption but probably not involving any alteration in the amount of stimulation. Accordingly, deprivation of stimulation can be ruled out as the effective mechanism. Whether bond disruption or rather distortion of relationships (either of which might be operative) is the relevant factor is considered below.

Very little is known about the emotional consequences of situations involving a lack of stimulation but no separation or bond disruption. There are well-established differences in the intellectual level of children from different social classes (Hess, 1970; Rutter, Tizard and Whitmore, 1970). These differences are probably partly genetic and partly environmental. In so far as they are environmental in origin, they presumably reflect differences in the type and quality of experience provided for the children. If stimulation differences were associated with emotional as well as cognitive effects, there should presumably be equally marked social-class differences in rates of psychiatric disturbance in childhood. However, this is not the case (Rutter, 1971a; Rutter, Tizard and Whitmore, 1970; Shepherd, Oppenheim and Mitchell, 1971).

In summary, bond disruption or some factor accompanying it is known to be associated with emotional and behavioural disturbance. The very limited available evidence suggests that pure perceptual restriction or poverty of stimulation has only limited long-term emotional consequences but considerable long-term effects on cognition.

### 'Sensory privation' or 'social privation'?

The conclusion that privation of stimulation has a deleterious effect on cognitive growth leads to the further question of what sort of 'stimulation' is important, and in particular, is it 'social stimulation' or 'sensory stimulation' which has the predominant effect? These are difficult to differentiate because in ordinary circumstances sensory stimuli are dispensed by people, with the consequence that if one is lacking so is the other.

Nevertheless, the distinction is a fundamental one which is of major importance in determining the direction of efforts to remedy the ill-effects of privation. The implications are most readily appreciated by contrasting the views of Casler (1961, 1968) and of Ainsworth (1962) with regard to the effects of institutional care. Casler has argued that what is crucial is the degree of stimulation and the range of experiences provided for the child. It is irrelevant whether or not these happen to be supplied by people, although in practice they usually are. Hence his claim that 'the human organism does not need mother love' (Casler, 1968). On this basis presumably it should be possible to furnish the child with all that he needs by the utilization of robots which can speak (computers which can do just this, admittedly at a very primitive level, have already been developed), playthings and a rich and varied environment. In sharp contrast, Ainsworth (1962) has concluded that 'the deprivation offered by the institution chiefly stems from insufficiency of intimate interpersonal interaction'. She regarded perceptual stimulation as a merely incidental factor (at least over the age of six months), which had importance only in so far as this was provided by the mother. Accordingly, 'efforts to enrich the institutional environment by providing nursery-school experience seem to be less effective in stemming retardation of development than efforts to facilitate the attachment of the child to a substitute mother.' On the basis of Ainsworth's view, presumably, speaking robots, playthings and a rich and varied environment would be of negligible value in counteracting the intellectual impairment which occurs in many children reared in old-style institutions.

By polarizing views in this way it is possible that the argument has been taken a little further than Casler or Ainsworth intended by what they wrote. Even so, there is a very real and substantial difference in the way they view the effects of institutional care, which can be summarized in the distinction between 'sensory stimulation' and 'social stimulation' as the crucial elements.

The animal work showing the far-reaching effects of early sensory restriction in leading to intellectual impairment has already been discussed. Animals reared in enclosed cages with opaque sides were much inferior on problem solving to animals reared in a free environment. Because this difference involves both sensory and social restriction (the free environment allowed contact with other animals) it is necessary to look for experiments which differentiated between the two. As noted previously, rats reared in cages which limited vision were retarded compared with those reared in cages which allowed the sight of a varied environment, although in both cases there was no contact with other rats. Similarly, rats reared in a free environment showed a superior performance if there was ample provision of apparatus and playthings than if the room was barren, in spite of the fact that in both cases there was free contact with other rats. The conclusion must be that, in rats, changes in 'sensory' stimulation can influence 'intellectual' development even if there are no changes in social contact. It is not possible to say from the results to what extent 'social' stimulation is also beneficial. The fact that animals reared in a free environment were usually superior to caged animals regardless of apparatus provided might indicate the benefits of social contact or might merely mean that a free environment gave more sensory stimulation and a wider range of experiences.

There can be no directly comparable experiments with children and it cannot necessarily be assumed that what is important for rats is also important for humans. Yet what limited evidence there is suggests that 'sensory stimulation' also plays an important part in man's intellectual development. The benefits of pre-school compensatory education (Starr, 1971) point to this conclusion, as do the studies of the short-term effects of sensory privation and stimulation (see chapter 3). The fact that children reared in institutions which do not provide them with a regular mother-surrogate may have a normal level of intelligence is even stronger supporting evidence. The only direct comparison was undertaken by Brossard and Décarie (1971). They examined the effects on developmental quotient of extra perceptual stimulation (mobiles and tape-recorded sounds) and extra social stimulation (talking and playing with the baby) in two- to three-month-old physically normal infants in a large institution for babies born out of wedlock. The developmental progress of both groups was superior to that of a matched control group of unstimulated children in the same institution. But, up to the age of five months (the limit of the study), perceptual and social stimulation had the *same* beneficial effect. It seems clear then that in humans as well as in lower animals the range of activities and experiences in infancy affects intellectual development.

Much less is known about the relative importance of sensory and social stimulation with regard to *emotional* development. Certainly isolation in infancy has been shown to lead to later emotional disturbance in a wide range of species. Unfortunately, for present purposes, the environmental restriction in these studies involved both sensory and social privation and there are very few investigations which have separated the two. Mason (1968) has some preliminary findings which indicate that deprived monkeys are less fearful and more active if reared with moving dummies than if reared with stationary devices. Similarly, Sidowski (1970) found that physical restraint affected the social and play behaviour of isolated infant monkeys. However, not only are the findings tentative and in need of replication, but also they are concerned with medium- and short-term social disturbances rather than long-term cognitive impairment.

So far in this section 'sensory stimulation' has been discussed as if it referred to a specific set of experiences, but of course it does not. The stimulation may involve different sensory modalities and it may be self-induced or the result of passive exposure. The animal studies described in chapter 4 made it clear that these differences matter. Different forms of stimulation are likely to have quite different effects on development. It is not that one form is more important than another, but rather that 'intelligence' involves many different skills each of which requires slightly differing early life experiences for optimal development.

A lack of visual, kinaesthetic or other perceptual experiences can and does impair intellectual growth in humans. Nevertheless, within English and white American cultures it has been found that environmental privation in childhood leads to a greater impairment of *verbal* intelligence than it does of visuo-spatial abilities (Haywood, 1967; Tizard, 1964, 1969).* This suggests that one aspect of the importance of different types of stimulation may be gauged by examining environmental influences on the development of language and verbal intelligence. In considering human studies in this connection it is relevant that the intellectual effects of privation are similar for children reared in their own homes and for those brought up in institutions (Jones, 1954). This implies that the type of stimulation thought to be needed must apply both to institutions and to private homes.

Intellectual privation, apparently increasing with age, has been noted in canal-boat and gypsy children in England and in children from relatively isolated mountain communities in the USA (see page 87). Little is known of the way of life of these children but what evidence there is suggests that it is most unlikely that they suffered from lack of contact with people, in view of their close family life. In this respect, social privation appears an improbable explanation. Similarly, it seems dubious whether the canal-boat and mountain children suffered from a deficiency of sensory stimulation. On the other hand, the *quality* of the social contact (especially with respect to conversation) and the range and quality of sensory stimulation probably were restricted.

A similar impairment of verbal intelligence is found in children reared in large families (Douglas, 1964; Douglas, Ross and Simpson, 1968; Nisbet, 1953a, 1953b), and the evidence suggests that the mechanism is environmental rather than genetic in origin (Rutter and Mittler, 1972). Again, it appears highly unlikely that the children experience diminished social or sensory stimulation as measured in quantitative terms. Rather, it has been suggested that, because their contacts are more with other children than with adults, their language environment is less rich and less com-

*This may not be true of other cultures. For example, Jamaican children from an impoverished environment show a greater deficit on certain non-verbal tests (Vernon, 1969). Whether this is due to a lack of important life experiences is not known. It could be due, for example, to malnutrition, which is also often a feature of their early life.

plex. However, it may be the *clarity* of the language environment, rather than its complexity, which is the key variable. Deutsch (1964) suggested that children's verbal intellectual development is impaired in homes where there is a predominance of meaningless noise over meaningful communication. In a study of tape-recordings of family conversations in the home, Friedlander (1971) found that the presence of children tends to lead to a tumultuous clamour in which several people speak at once on different topics. Perhaps, this kind of linguistic chaos makes language acquisition more difficult in large families.

Much the same conclusions stem from an examination of environmental influences on verbal development (Rutter and Mittler, 1972). Babies vocalize more if they are spoken to each time they make a noise. The presence of a non-speaking adult has little effect on vocalization; a tape-recorded voice markedly increases babble, but a somewhat greater effect is seen with a speaking person who is actually present in the room (Todd and Palmer, 1968; Weisberg, 1963). In other words, the main effect is produced by non-social verbal stimulation rather than by non-verbal social stimulation. On the other hand it is probably necessary for the verbal stimulation to be *meaningful* to the child. Mere repetition of words is not enough (Casler, 1965).

The same applies to effects on language development in older pre-school children (Brown, Cazden and Bellugi-Klima, 1969; Cazden, 1966). The provision of extra play sessions with toys has little effect unless there is also conversation with adults. But the special provision of sessions when adults deliberately engage the children in conversation has a significantly beneficial effect on language development.

Putting the evidence together, it may be concluded that the absolute restriction of sensory stimulation undoubtedly can impair development, including intellectual development. All forms of perceptual restriction may impede cognitive growth; different forms of restriction affect different intellectual skills. However, humans differ from animals in the additional, and crucial, importance of language with regard to intellectual development. Probably the single most crucial

factor for the development of verbal intelligence is the
quality of the child's language environment; how much he
is talked to but more than that the richness of the conversational interchange he experiences. Because this must be
meaningful to the child and because it is important that
what the adult says develops and responds to the child's
utterances, in all ordinary circumstances it is necessary for
the verbal stimulation to be provided by people. However,
several studies indicate that it is the conversation that matters; the mere presence of an interested adult is not enough
in itself. Particularly in this connection, but probably in
all forms of stimulation, the evidence suggests that it is
the distinctiveness and meaningfulness of the stimuli which
are more important than the absolute level of stimulation.

## Emotional privation or nutritional privation?

The alternatives of emotional privation or nutritional privation largely arise with respect to the syndrome of 'deprivation dwarfism', a condition characterized by extremely short
stature and (often) voracious appetite and marked delay
in skeletal and sexual maturation, found in children who
have experienced extreme and long-standing emotional and
psychological deprivation (Patton and Gardner, 1963). Typi-
cally the children come from grossly disturbed families
where they have been subjected to rejection, isolation and,
in some cases, physical abuse; usually there is rapid weight
gain following admission to hospital. Similar effects have
been observed in children reared in poor-quality institutions
(Fried and Mayer, 1948; Widdowson, 1951). The syndrome
has become increasingly widely recognized in recent years
and it has frequently been concluded that emotional deprivation leads to dwarfism even when nutritional intake remains
adequate (Silver and Finkelstein, 1967).

The evidence for this view is circumstantial. Parents often
report that the children eat large quantities (Silver and
Finkelstein, 1967) and the improvement following removal
from home suggests that the home circumstances have
caused the dwarfing. Fried and Mayer (1948), in an early
study, noted an association between growth rate and emo-

tional adjustment in institutional children. They observed that the provision of an adequate diet did not improve growth until the emotional disorders had been corrected. However, there was no caloric control and no measurement of caloric intake. A study of orphanage children by Widdowson (1951) has been particularly influential. It was found that dietary supplements did not lead to weight gain in children in an orphanage with a harsh and unsympathetic supervisor. A difference in supervisor led to weight gain where the change in diet had not. Nutritional factors were carefully controlled so far as the food provided was concerned, but one may doubt whether food *intake* ran parallel. In the 'bad' orphanage it was said that when the supervisor had finished harassing the children 'the soup would be cold, all the children would be in a state of considerable agitation and several might be in tears'. Perhaps when they were so upset they left their food on the plate.

Several different mechanisms could operate to produce dwarfism. These include endocrine dysfunction, anorexia, distortion of diet, malabsorption and inadequate food intake.

In abnormal emotional states hypothalamic function may be depressed or cortisol secretion may increase (Powell, Brasel, Raiti and Blizzard, 1967), either of which could lead to impaired physical growth through hormonal mechanisms (Acheson, 1960). Powell, Brasel and Blizzard (1967) investigated thirteen children with short stature, polydipsia, polyphagia and who stole food. After hospital admission the behavioural abnormalities remitted and the children gained weight. The children came from very disturbed families and the growth retardation was attributed to emotional deprivation. Endocrine studies showed deficiencies of A C T H and growth hormone in many of the children and the authors suggested that psychic disturbance had led to the hypothalamic dysfunction and so hypopituitarism. The significance of these endocrine findings remains uncertain in that other investigators have found normal steroid output (Silver and Finkelstein, 1967) and normal growth-hormone level (Apley, Davies, Davis and Silk, 1971) in children with deprivation dwarfism. It is possible that endocrine abnormalities are present in only some cases, but even when present it is uncertain whether they are the result of emotional deprivation or inadequate nutrition. That severe prolonged malnutrition (from any cause) can lead to a similar endocrine picture has been found in several studies (Powell *et al.*, 1967) so the endocrine dysfunction could be no more than a side-effect of malnutrition.

It is well recognized that affective disturbance can depress appetite and this could constitute the main effect of deprivation on growth, with anorexia leading to impaired food intake. This could scarely be the mechanism in the dwarfed children with voracious appetites, but some studies have reported that a number of 'deprivation dwarfs' have a low caloric intake and anorexia (Apley *et al.*, 1971; Talbot, Sobel, Burke, Lindemann and Kaufman, 1947). In these cases this could be the operative factor, as increasing growth seems to accompany rising food consumption.

In other cases there is also a qualitative deficiency of diet resulting from extreme food fads (Apley *et al.*, 1971). In this connection it is notable that feeding difficulties going back to infancy have often been reported (Silver and Finkelstein, 1967). These fads are only present in some children and it seems unlikely that the dietary distortion could be sufficient to account for growth failure, but it might constitute a contributory factor.

Another possibility is that changes in intestinal mobility, secretion and absorption might prevent proper assimilation of ingested food. Certainly, emotional factors can influence intestinal function as shown by experimental studies of individuals with a fistula (Beaumont, 1833; Engel, Reichsman and Segal, 1956). The presence of bulky offensive stools in some cases (Powell, Brasel and Blizzard, 1967) is in keeping with the concept of malabsorption, but where present this defect has not prevented rapid weight gain on hospital admission. This mechanism provides a feasible explanation but abnormalities of intestinal function have yet to be demonstrated in dwarfed children and clinical findings suggest that, even if found, malabsorption is unlikely to be more than of minor importance. Furthermore, it should be noted that early malnutrition may well be able itself to lead to later poor food utilization (Chow, Blackwell, Blackwell, Hou, Anilane and Sherwin, 1968).

Finally it could be that the deprived children are under-fed in spite of parental reports to the contrary. A retro-spective dietary history obtained from parents who may feel themselves subject to criticism is unlikely to be very accu-rate. The hypothesis of inadequate food intake has been tested in several experimental studies with results that sup-port the view that this accounts for 'deprivation dwarfism'.

Normal weight gain was found in chimpanzees subjected to severe social isolation both in infancy (Davenport, Men-zel and Rogers, 1961) and when older (Davenport, Menzel and Rogers, 1966). Similarly, Kerr, Chamove and Harlow (1969) showed that when infant rhesus monkeys were reared under conditions of total isolation but with normal oppor-tunities for dietary intake, they developed gross behavioural abnormalities but their growth rates were entirely normal. In a study of three of these adult monkeys who had been subject to total social isolation in infancy, polyphagia and polydipsia were found (Miller, Caul and Mirsky, 1971), but this was apparently associated with no increased weight gain, so that some metabolic alteration may have occurred, even though there was no dwarfism.

Similarly, in deprived human infants growth retardation has not been found when the infants were adequately fed, as shown in a well-controlled study by Whitten and his colleagues (1969). Thirteen maternally deprived infants with height and weight below the third percentile were investi-gated. The inadequate mothering at home was simulated in hospital by solitary confinement for two weeks in a window-less room,* but the infants were offered a generous diet. In spite of the continuing emotional and sensory deprivation, eleven of the thirteen infants showed accelerated weight gain. The two others failed to eat properly although offered

*This rather drastic treatment raises questions of how far it is justifiable to provide a restricted environment to human infants even for a brief period.

food. This finding suggested that in most cases adequate calories were enough to reverse growth failure even when other types of deprivation persisted.

Following the period of understimulation the infants were given a high level of mothering and sensory stimulation, but the diet remained as before. This caused no change in rate of weight gain. The infants who gained during the period of understimulation continued to gain at the same rate and the two who did not gain in those circumstances still did not gain.

Following this study, three other infants were investigated. They were not admitted to hospital nor were the parents told of the suspected diagnosis of maternal deprivation. Instead, under the guise of investigation of caloric intake, feeding was carried out by mothers in the presence of an observer, no attempt being made to alter maternal handling or social circumstances. All infants gained weight at a markedly accelerated rate and the mothers subsequently admitted that the infants ate more food during the experimental period than previously although the diets were duplicates of what the mothers *claimed* they fed the infants. Other evidence also suggested that the mothers' dietary histories were often grossly inaccurate.

The evidence from this study points strongly to the conclusion that nutritional privation is the crucial factor in dwarfism. Nevertheless the findings cannot be conclusive in that short-term weight gain was studied rather than long-term height gain and the infants were younger than most cases of 'deprivation dwarfism'. The Talbot study suggests that anorexia is important in some cases and the Miller investigation of isolated monkeys indicated that metabolic alterations may sometimes follow social isolation. In individual children a variety of mechanisms may operate (Mac-Carthy and Booth, 1970), but the balance of evidence suggests that, over all, impaired food intake is the most important factor. The impaired food intake may be due to either the child being given insufficient food or to his eating too little because of poor appetite. Emotional effects on metabolism or intestinal function remain theoretical possibilities, but there is no evidence that such mechanisms in fact operate to cause dwarfism, whereas there is good evidence that nutritional privation does occur.

## Social privation or nutritional privation?

The alternatives of social privation or nutritional privation have to be considered with regard to the intellectual retardation found in children living in extremely poor circumstances. There is abundant evidence that mild mental retardation is extremely common among children brought up in city slums and rural poverty in the affluent countries of the world as well as in children living in poverty and social disadvantage in the emerging nations (Kushlik, 1968; Wortis, 1970). The hazards faced by children in these situations are multiple. Their mothers are likely to be in poor health, prenatal care may be substandard and the children are likely to be delivered in unsatisfactory circumstances with increased risks of damage during pregnancy and the birth process. During their growing years the children are more liable to illness than their counterparts living in better conditions, more liable to malnutrition, more likely to live in disorganized overcrowded homes providing inadequate stimulation and educational opportunities, and are probably educated in poorly staffed, overcrowded, ill-endowed schools subject to high staff and child turnover. Each of these circumstances could lead to intellectual and educational handicap and the question arises which is the most important in this respect.

Intelligence develops and is not a 'given' capacity. Its development is a social process strictly dependent upon the quality and organization of the human environment in which it evolves (Eisenberg, 1969). That is not to deny that genetic factors play a major part in the development of intelligence. Indeed they do (see pages 150 to 151), but as geneticists have repeatedly emphasized. the aspects of behaviour that are polygenically inherited are not specific traits but patterns of growth and ways of responding to the environment (Dobzhansky, 1967).

Until recently most emphasis has been placed on the

importance of social experience in intellectual development (Haywood, 1967). The evidence that experience and social stimulation are required for the development of intelligence has already been considered and there can be no doubt that social and linguistic privation in itself can and does lead to retardation of intelligence, particularly verbal intelligence.

However, it has become clear that this may not be the whole story. Firstly, it is well established that reproductive complications increase as one moves from more favoured to less favoured socio-economic groups (Birch and Gussow, 1970; Illsley and Kincaid, 1963), and the associations between perinatal damage, cerebral palsy and severe mental retardation have long been known (Illingworth, 1958; McDonald, 1967). More recently, Pasamanick and his colleagues (Pasamanick and Knobloch, 1961) have suggested that prematurity and perinatal complications may lead to lesser mental handicaps even when there is no overt neurological disorder – that there is a 'continuum of reproductive casualty'. The evidence on this point is difficult to interpret and to some extent contradictory (Douglas, 1960; Drillien, 1964; Harper and Wiener, 1965; McDonald, 1964). It is evident that some of the I Q differences associated with prematurity are accountable for in terms of social handicap, but it seems likely that even after the effects of social privation have been ironed out, some intellectual disadvantage may remain as a consequence of low birth weight (Birch and Gussow, 1970). In good social conditions the disadvantage is negligible or non-existent, but there seems to be an interaction effect so that the effects of low birth weight are greatest in deprived social circumstances. The biological handicap acts by lowering the organism's adaptability and increasing its vulnerability to environmental hazard. Even so, the effects of reproductive complications appear relatively small once the group with overt neurological disorder or severe mental retardation have been excluded.

The second possibility is that post-natal malnutrition leads to intellectual retardation. The evidence on this possibility has been reviewed by Birch and Gussow (1970), Cravioto,

DeLicardie and Birch (1966), Stein and Kassab (1970) and in a series of papers in Scrimshaw and Gordon (1968). Nutritional privation in animals has resulted in a reduction in brain weight, histological and biochemical changes in the central nervous system, and behavioural deficits. These effects are probably most marked during the period of maximum brain growth (Dobbing, 1968). Thus, there can be no doubt that malnutrition during early development can damage the brain, but how marked an effect this has on intellectual development in the human is very difficult to assess. There are studies showing that children malnourished in infancy are often intellectually retarded when older. The difficulties in interpretation lie in the fact that under-nourished infants almost always come from homes with gross social handicaps as well and it has not been possible to partition accurately the effects of social deprivation and malnutrition. This is particularly so as it is likely that only a small proportion of malnourished children come under medical care. This may account for Garrow and Pike's (1967) finding that Jamaican children admitted with Kwashiorkor in infancy were no shorter than their sibs at six to eight years of age.

In summary it seems that prematurity and pre-natal damage, post-natal malnutrition and social privation can all lead to intellectual retardation, and it is not possible at present to determine the relative influence of each factor. In any case the relative importance of each will be influenced by the particular social circumstances operating. In Britain it seems likely that social privation is the most influential factor, but the balance may be quite different in India or South America. It should also be added that the effects of each may well be different. Social privation (at least in an English or white American culture) probably has its main effect on language development and verbal intelligence whereas it is likely that both pre-natal damage and post-natal malnutrition cause a more global retardation of cognitive development.

## Failure to form bonds or disruption of bonds?

Surprisingly little attention has been paid to this issue yet it is of great theoretical interest and practical importance. For example, it has extensive implications for the organization of institutional care for young children. If bond disruption is the damaging factor then it may be that institutional life should be so organized that none of the caretakers have sufficient intensive contact with the children for bonds to develop. If bonds are not formed then the children are less likely to suffer when the caretaker moves elsewhere leaving the child behind. On the other hand, if failure to form bonds is more deleterious, every effort should be made to ensure that the caretakers do have an intensive and stable interaction with individual children to encourage the development of attachments. If persisting bonds are developed with several caretakers, damage is less likely when one caretaker has to leave.

Unfortunately, there is very little evidence on this crucial issue. It should also be said that it is not necessarily a question of one alternative being worse than the other. Rather it may be that failure to form bonds and bond disruption have *different* effects. What little evidence is available supports this view.

To investigate the problem it is necessary to search for situations where the children will have had little or no opportunity to form stable bonds in early childhood. On the slender and incomplete findings available (see chapter 2) it may be postulated that bond formation is least likely to occur in a non-stimulating environment, where there is only low intensity of personal interaction, where infants tend to be left when they cry, where care is provided at routine times rather than in response to the infant's demands and where there are multiple caretakers none of whom have regular interaction with the child over a period of many months or longer. Such an environment is provided by the old-style large institution. Attachments normally develop during the first eighteen months of life, so that an institutional upbringing during the first two or three years of life is probably the single situation most likely to be associated with impaired bond formation.* Accordingly, failure to form bonds and bond disruption may be compared by contrasting children who enter institutions early in life and children who enter only after bonds have been formed.

Pringle and her colleagues investigated possible reasons for differences between stable and maladjusted children in long-term institutional care. They found that the stable children had almost always remained with their mothers until well after the first year and so had had the opportunity of forming bonds prior to admission. This suggests that failure to form bonds was most likely to lead to 'maladjustment'. The stable children had also more often experienced a dependable and lasting relationship with a parent or parent-substitute after going into care. In contrast, the maladjusted children had not had the same opportunity to establish or maintain stable bonds and their outstanding characteristic was an inability to make relationships with adults or children (Pringle and Bossio, 1960). Apparently, regular visiting by parents was often sufficient to maintain relationships while the children were in institutions (Pringle and Clifford, 1962).

In his study of working mothers, Moore (1963) found that the only group to suffer were the children who went from 'pillar to post' in a succession of unsatisfactory and unstable child-minding arrangements. In most cases these children had also had periods in institutions or residential nurseries. Their behaviour in early childhood was characteristically clinging, dependent and attention-seeking. In a more recent study, the Tizards (1971) found similarly that these were also the features which most clearly differentiated children in residential nurseries from those reared in their own homes.

---

* But institutional care certainly cannot be the only cause of an 'affectionless character'. Lewis (1954), for example, in her study of 500 deprived children admitted into care found that only five of the nineteen children with this syndrome had suffered prolonged separation from their families.

Further evidence is provided by Wolkind's (1974) study of children in care. Psychiatric disturbance in these children took several forms, but the characteristics of indiscriminate friendliness and lack of social inhibition were especially a feature of children admitted before the age of two years. This suggests that failure to form bonds may lead not only to greater emotional disturbance, as suggested by the studies mentioned above, but also it may lead to a particular type of disturbance.

The special features of a failure to form bonds may also be examined by studying children reared in an institution from infancy and then comparing those placed in homes before three years when bonds may develop more readily and those not placed until after three years when bond formation may not occur for the first time so easily. This comparison was made by Goldfarb (1955), who found that although both groups showed emotional problems, those who remained in the institution until after age three years were especially characterized by an inability to keep rules, a lack of guilt, a craving for affection and an inability to make lasting relationships. They were also of lower intelligence and had poorer speech. The study is open to a number of criticisms in terms of the measures used and an uncertainty regarding the factors which determined whether the children stayed in the institution or were placed in foster homes. Nevertheless, for whatever reason, there were differences in the type of disturbance between the two groups; differences which may have been due to a failure to form bonds and differences which are strikingly similar to Bowlby's (1946) concept of 'affectionless character'.

In his study of forty-four thieves, Bowlby (1946) linked this inability to form relationships with separation experiences in early childhood. However, an examination of his case histories suggests that an affectionless character is associated not so much with a prolonged separation as with multiple changes of mother-figure or home in infancy or early childhood. This had occurred in seven out of fourteen affectionless characters, but only three of the other thirty thieves. It could well be that frequent changes of mother-figures during the period when attachments are normally formed could also impair bond formation. Two of the other affectionless characters had spent nine months in hospital unvisited during their second year of life, when attachments would normally be consolidated.

It may be hypothesized on these findings that a failure to form bonds in early childhood is particularly associated with the later development of an 'affectionless character'. Can a disruption of bonds have the same effect? The studies already discussed imply that this outcome is only rarely a consequence of bond disruption. Follow-up studies of children admitted to institutions *after* the age when attachments develop confirm that affectionless psychopathy is *not* characteristic of children who have developed bonds and then had them broken or stressed by a prolonged separation. For example, this was not a feature of the children admitted to a T B sanatorium in Bowlby's study (Bowlby *et al.*, 1956), nor of children evacuated from London and placed in residential nurseries in Maas' study (1963).

No firm conclusions are yet possible from the patchy findings of these diverse studies. Nevertheless, the evidence does suggest that the effects of bond disruption and a failure to form bonds are different. It appears possible that a failure to form bonds in early childhood is particularly liable to lead to an initial phase of clinging, dependent behaviour, followed by attention-seeking, uninhibited, indiscriminate friendliness and finally a personality characterized by lack of guilt, an inability to keep rules and an inability to form lasting relationships. In contrast, this type of personality does *not* often follow bond disruption.

It may be thought that the clinging, dependent behaviour seen in young children is out of keeping with the failure to form relationships observed in later childhood. However, this is in keeping with cross-sectional age differences in the behaviour of institutional children (Dennis, 1960). There are no longitudinal studies in humans showing this progression, but this course of development is just what was found in Harlow's studies of monkeys reared in complete social isolation. As infants they clung to their mechanical mother-surrogates, sucked parts of their own body and were fearful in new situations. Later, they remained fearful, but also showed a striking deficiency in all forms of sexual, mothering and relationship behaviour (Harlow and Griffin, 1965; Harlow and Harlow, 1969, 1970).

It seems clear that experiences involving bond disruption do *not* normally lead to an 'affectionless character', but there are grounds for suggesting that a failure to form bonds in early childhood may have this outcome. This implies that there may be a sensitive period for the development of attachment behaviour after which bond formation becomes increasingly less likely. If such a period exists (and it has yet to be demonstrated) it begins about five or six months of age and it must last up to at least age two or three years in view of the usually good outcome of children placed in adoptive or foster homes at this age after early institutional care. The matter warrants further investigation.

### Failure to form bonds or failure to form bonds with mother?

As a sub-issue on the question of the effects of failure of bond formation it may be asked whether the bonds have to be with the mother or whether any bonds serve the same purpose. In one of his earlier papers Harlow (1963) claimed that the mother–child affectional system differed qualitatively from other affectional systems, and observed that the clinging of monkeys reared only with peers differed from the attachment formed to the mother monkey. Clearly, there will be differences in the relationship as a function of the type of interaction – caretaking with the mother or play with peers. However, the question is whether the bonds with peers or other adults serve the same function in psychological development as do the bonds with mother. The Harlow studies with rhesus monkeys suggest that in spite of differences at the outset, the long-term effects are remarkably similar (Harlow and Harlow, 1970). Few negative long-term effects have been found for monkeys reared with multiple-age mates but without a mother.

On the other hand, Bowlby (1969) still maintains that playmate relationships are quite different from attachments and he equates attachment with the mother-figure. Indeed mother is defined as 'the person who mothers the child and to whom he becomes attached'. However, Bowlby argues that social interaction is the most important part of mother-care and that feeding is not an essential part of mothering. If the essence of 'mothering' is no more than social interaction between the child and some adult it could well be suggested that the term has come to have such a wide application that it has ceased to have much meaning. Nevertheless, what evidence there is supports Bowlby's view that social inter-action constitutes the basis of attachment behaviour (see chapter 2) and it is difficult to see what merit there is in tying the concept of attachment to motherhood if it is not neces-sarily tied to a female, not a function of feeding and only indirectly related to caretaking activities.

The factors leading to attachment listed above are ones which make it unlikely that in ordinary circumstances a child of the same age could provide what is needed for the development of a strong stable attachment. On the other hand, any adult or older child in close interaction with the infant could do so, whether or not he or she was a parent or caretaker.

Empirical findings on the benefits of bond formation with someone other than the mother are not available and this is an issue meriting much more study than it has received. How-ever, there is Freud and Dann's (1951) classical study of six pre-school children who lost their parents as a result of Nazi persecution and who remained together as a group through-out a series of changes of concentration camps and thence to an English nursery. In these very abnormal circumstances the children developed unusually strong ties with each other and these seemed to have had a protective influence. While the children showed various emotional problems they did not show the gross disturbances which might be expected as a result of the total loss of mothering experiences and gross rejection that they had suffered.

There is no adequate evidence upon which to base any conclusions, but it may be suggested that for the development of social and emotional relationships in later childhood and adult life it is bond formation which matters and that it is of less consequence to whom the attachment is formed. In addition to this, caretaking and 'mothering' experiences are needed as are also play activities, but they serve a different role. Bonding, caretaking and play are three separate functions which may or may not be performed by the same person. It is hypothesized that so long as all three are available, it is of no matter, with regard to the prevention of 'affectionless psychopathy', who provides them, and in particular it does not matter if the mother does so.

That is not to say that it makes no difference in terms of individual psychological development with whom the young child forms bonds. A child, for example, who fails to develop a bond with his father or any other male figure in early childhood may not be able to make a really close relationship with him later. Although we still know little about the factors influencing psychosexual development, it is evident that early family relationships and attitudes are important (Rutter, 1971b). It may well be that youngsters who have developed bonds with adults of only one sex are at a disadvantage later with respect to heterosexual relationships and to the development of sex-appropriate attitudes and behaviour (Biller, 1971). It is probable that for optimal development bonds need to be formed with people of *both* sexes, and from what has been said about attachment behaviour it is very likely that early attachments will influence the kind of close relationships which are possible later.

### Privation or deprivation?

As already discussed, the cognitive effects of inadequate stimulation are explicable in terms of privation (lack) rather than deprivation (loss). Similarly, the development of 'affectionless psychopathy' is probably due to a privation, rather than deprivation, of opportunity for bond formation. Deprivation has only seemed crucial with respect to long-term effects in the case of enuresis and stressful events in early childhood. However, surprisingly little attention has been paid in the literature to the distinction between not having some necessary experience as against having it but then losing it. The experience of loss appears important in the case of short-term effects of 'maternal deprivation'. The limited available evidence suggests that it is much less important for long-term consequences, but the issue requires further study.

As an extension of the concept of deprivation, there is the question of whether the most favoured children suffer more from loss than those already relatively deprived and so with less to lose. Gibson (1969) found that loss of a mother was more strongly associated with delinquency in families without social handicap, in keeping with the view that children with most to lose suffer more from loss. On the other hand, the reverse was true for fathers. In our studies (Rutter, 1971a), separation experiences were *only* associated with disturbance in children from *un*happy homes. Other investigations, too, have shown that the short-term effects of hospital admission tend to be worse for children with a poor relationship with their parents (see chapter 3). The evidence is most unsatisfactory, but on the whole it appears that children with the most favourable home environments are *least* affected by deprivation, and that those who have least to lose are most affected when they lose even that little. However, it is evident that the issue has been very little investigated and it remains quite possible that there is a form of long-term distress associated with deprivation or loss which differs from the results stemming from privation.

## Disruption of bonds or distortion of relationships?

In an earlier section of this book the strong association between 'broken homes' and delinquency was noted. This association has commonly been held to demonstrate the seriously deleterious long-term effects of disruption of affectional bonds (Bowlby, 1968). The evidence on this point has been considered in detail elsewhere (Rutter, 1971a), but it may be briefly summarized here.

The main question is whether the harm comes from disruption of bonds or distortion of relationships. This may be considered by comparing homes broken by death (where relationships are likely to have been fairly normal prior to the break and where the bond is irrevocably disrupted) and homes broken by divorce or separation (where the break is likely to have been preceded by discord and quarrelling, or at least by a lack of warmth and affection, and yet where the break-up of the home may not necessarily disrupt the bonds). This comparison has been made in several independent studies (Brown, 1961; Douglas, Ross, Hammond and Mulligan, 1966; Gibson, 1969; Glueck and Glueck, 1950; Gregory, 1965). In each case the delinquency rate has been about double (compared to that for boys in intact homes) for boys whose parents had divorced or separated, whereas the delinquency rate has been only slightly (and non-significantly) raised for those who had lost a parent by death.

This suggests that it may be the discord and disharmony preceding the break (rather than the break itself) which led to the children developing antisocial behaviour. If that suggestion is correct parental discord should be associated with antisocial disorder in children even when the home is unbroken. There is good evidence from several studies (Craig and Glick, 1965; McCord and McCord, 1959; Tait and Hodges, 1962), including our own (Rutter, 1971a), that this is the case. In children from unbroken homes there was a strong association between parental marital disharmony and antisocial disorder in the sons. The McCords (1959) also showed that broken homes resulted in significantly less juvenile delinquency than did unbroken but quarrelsome and neglecting homes.

Delinquency is thus associated with breaks which follow parental discord, or discord without a break, but *not* with a break-up of the home as such. In fact, delinquency is *less* associated with parental death, with its necessary disruption of bonds, than it is with parental divorce, where bonds may still be maintained by intermittent contact after the break-up of the marriage. It may be concluded that it is distortion of relationships rather than bond disruption as such which causes the damage.

The same conclusion applies to temporary separations. In our own studies we examined the issue with respect to separations of at least one month's duration (Rutter, 1971a). There was no association between separation from one parent only and deviant behaviour in the children. There was an association between separation from *both* parents and anti-social disorder in the boys, but this applied only in homes where there was a very poor marriage relationship between the parents. Again this suggested that the association might not be due to the fact of separation from parents but rather to the discord and disturbance which surrounded the separation. To investigate this possibility separations were divided into those due to some event *not* associated with family discord (the child's admission to hospital for some physical illness, or a prolonged holiday) and those in which the separation was the result of family disorder or disharmony (usually break-up following a quarrel). Only when the separation was a consequence of family deviance was there an association with antisocial disorder (and in this case the association was strong). Transient separations as such are unrelated to the development of antisocial behaviour; they only appear to be so on occasions because separation often occurs as a result of family disturbance.

The issue was examined in a different way by Wardle (1961) who studied children attending a child-guidance clinic. He found that conduct disorder was not only associated with the child's coming from a broken home, but also with one *parent* coming from a broken home. The finding suggested that it was not the direct experience of bond disruption which mattered but rather the difficulties in interpersonal relations with which bond disruption was associated.

Little is known about the specific nature of disturbed relationships which tend to cause antisocial disorder in the children, but our studies provided some findings on this issue (Rutter, 1971a). Both active discord and lack of affection were associated with the development of antisocial disorder, but the combination of the two was particularly harmful. The longer the family discord lasted the greater the effect on the child, but the effects were not necessarily permanent. If the child later lived in a harmonious home the risk of antisocial disorder dropped. Whereas any type of prolonged family discord was associated with an increased risk of antisocial disorder, a good relationship with one parent went some way towards mitigating the harmful effect of a quarrelsome unhappy home. In short, the findings emphasized the importance of good relationships in personality development, but did not suggest that any one specific type of defect in relationship was of predominant importance.

Altogether the results strongly suggest that it is the *quality* of relationships which matter rather than the presence or absence of separations. It could still be argued that bond formation was nevertheless the crucial factor (a) if separations do not imply bond disruption and (b) if distorted relationships seriously impair bond formation. As already discussed, it is certainly unjustified to assume that separation is synonymous with bond disruption. In some circumstances children can maintain bonds through quite prolonged separations. On the other hand there is no evidence that distorted relationships lead to inadequate bonding. As Bowlby (1951, p. 69) observed: 'The attachment of children to parents who by all ordinary standards are very bad is a never-ceasing source of wonder to those who seek to help them.'

That is not to say that parental behaviour is irrelevant to the formation of attachments: on the contrary it plays a most important role. Among the factors thought to be important on the basis of systematic observations of infants are frequent and sustained physical contact, mother's ability to soothe her baby when distressed, her sensitivity to her baby's signals and the promptness with which she responds to his crying (Ainsworth and Bell, 1969; Ainsworth and Wittig, 1969; Schaffer and Emerson, 1964). These factors might well be influenced by parental pathology or parental discord. Yet it should be noted that, at least with younger children, maternal rebuffs and rejection seem to *increase*, not decrease, attachment behaviour (Bowlby, 1969). This observation is in keeping with animal studies. Scott (1963) found that puppies showed greater attachment (to the experimenter) when punished than when not. Similar results were obtained by Cairns (1966a, 1966b) with lambs. Harlow (Harlow, 1961; Rosenblum and Harlow, 1963) examined infant monkeys' attachment to a surrogate cloth 'mother' and found that a strong aversive stimulus from the surrogate (a blast of compressed air) only served to increase clinging behaviour. In the same way infant monkeys who were severely maltreated by their mothers nevertheless developed strong attachments to them (Harlow and Griffin, 1965; Seay, Alexander and Harlow, 1964).

It must be said that there is a lack of evidence on what happens in the long term to bonding in the presence of family discord and disharmony. Doubtless this depends among other things on the child's stage of development when rejection takes place. For example, it has been tentatively suggested that rejection very early in life may deter attachment, rejection at the period of most intense attachment behaviour may enhance it and rejection later when attachment is waning may encourage its dissolution (Rosenblum, 1971b). Whether this is so is not yet known. However, it certainly cannot be assumed that family deviance will necessarily lead to impaired bonding – indeed the animal evidence suggests that in some circumstances it might even lead to increased (although possibly less secure) bonding.

Part of the difficulty in successfully differentiating the effects of disruption of bonds and distortion of relationships is the fact that whereas the latter can be defined the former cannot, or at least has not yet been satisfactorily defined (Bowlby, 1969). That attachment behaviour occurs and is a crucial part of development is not in dispute. That bonds develop and are important is also not a matter for argument. The difficulty arises in differentiating approach (or attachment) behaviour from the existence of a persisting bond. This difficulty is multiplied many times when the existence of a bond has to be measured in the absence of the attachment figure, as is necessary to differentiate the effects of bond disruption from mere separation. The concept of bonds has proved useful in focusing attention on the minutiae of parent–child interaction, but it is important to remember that it is a concept (in the same way as 'drive' or 'instinct') and unless further specified does not provide an explanation. So far there is good evidence that disturbed relationships in the home are associated with the development of antisocial disorder in the children. As far as can be judged, this association cannot be explained in terms of bond disruption, but until a satisfactory operational definition can be provided for bond disruption it is not possible to take the matter any further.

## Distortion of relationships or distortion of relationships with mother?

As the issue of deprivation has been discussed in the literature almost entirely in terms of *maternal* deprivation, it is necessary to ask if the harm to the child comes from distorted relationships in general, or specifically from a distorted relationship with mother. In our own study of family relationships it did not make much difference which parent the child got on well with so long as he got on well with one parent (Rutter, 1971a). Conversely, disturbed relationships with *either* parent led to an increased risk of antisocial disorder. Furthermore, disturbed relationships *between* the parents also put the child at risk. The Gluecks (1950, 1962) also found that affection and discipline from both mother and father were important factors in the genesis (or prevention) of delinquency.

Nevertheless, it would be wrong to assume that the mother and father had identical roles in the children's upbringing. In an earlier study it was found that boys were more likely to show psychiatric disorder if the father had died or if the father was mentally ill (Rutter, 1966). The apparent particular importance of the same-sexed parent also emerged in a study by Gregory (1965), which showed that delinquency rates were higher in boys if the father was absent from the home but in girls the rate was higher if the mother was missing. Thus, there are several studies which have shown the special role of the same-sexed parent. However, other studies (Gibson, 1969; Rutter, 1971a) have not found this and the matter remains unresolved at the moment. One suggestion is that the same-sexed parent is particularly important only at certain ages – perhaps in adolescence.

What is abundantly clear, however, is that it is not just the relationship with the mother that matters. It is true that mother generally has more contact with very young children and her influence on them often predominates (Wolff and

Acton, 1968). On the other hand the father–child relationship is also important and sometimes it may even be the most influential (Bronfenbrenner, 1961; Peterson, Becker, Hellmer, Shoemaker and Quay, 1959; Robins, 1966). Both parents influence their children's development and which parent is more important varies with the child's age, sex, temperament and environmental circumstances. Furthermore, it is not always meaningful to regard the influence of each parent as separate and independent. The mental health of one parent may influence that of the other (Kreitman, Collins, Nelson and Troop, 1970) and may also influence the marriage relationship (Barry, 1970). The family consists of individuals and pairs of individuals, but it is also a social group of its own and needs to be considered as such (Handel, 1968).

## Distortion of relationships or deviant model?

Before concluding finally that it is the distortion of relationships as such which leads to antisocial behaviour in the children, three other possibilities have to be considered. First, there is a large body of experimental data which show how readily children imitate other people's behaviour and how a model of aggressive or deviant behaviour may influence the children to behave similarly (Bandura, 1969). These studies have been largely concerned with children's *immediate* response to an aggressive model, and the children's behaviour measured has mostly consisted of assertive or mildly aggressive behaviour within the range of normality. Nevertheless, it is quite possible that similar mechanisms might operate with more severe and more prolonged behavioural disturbances. Thus, it could be suggested that children in discordant families become antisocial, not because of any disturbance of relationships, but because they are following a deviant parental model of behaviour.

In keeping with this hypothesis is the fact that many of the parents in the most disturbed and unhappy families showed marked abnormalities of personality outside the family situation. Also in keeping with the hypothesis is our finding (Rutter, 1971a) that children are more likely to become antisocial when there is active discord in the home as well as a lack of warmth. On the other hand, there is a good deal of contrary evidence. Our own studies showed that parental personality disorder was *not* associated with antisocial disorder in the child unless there was also parental discord (Rutter, 1971a). Conversely, the adverse effect on the child of a very poor parental marriage was markedly ameliorated if the child had a good relationship with one parent. This is just what would be predicted if distorted relationships were what mattered. Contrariwise, given a quarrelsome home, if the child was only influenced by means of a parental model it should not make any difference if he happened to have a good relationship with one parent. West (1969) in his prospective study of city children produced similar findings. The characteristics of the family proved to be an important predictor of his later disturbed conduct and delinquency. However, once these family characteristics had been taken into account, the presence of a criminal parent did *not* add to the risk of delinquency.

In summary, the evidence is circumstantial but it points to the conclusion that distorted relationships are most important in the genesis of antisocial disorder, but that the presence of a deviant model may well be a contributory factor. Perhaps the best test would be what happens to children in a home which is without affection for the children but also without discord, deviant behaviour or criminality. The relationship hypothesis would predict delinquency in the children whereas the model hypothesis would not. Unfortunately, there are no satisfactory data on what happens to children in this situation. A follow-up study of children admitted in infancy to a well-run, harmonious institution, but one which did not provide close or affectionate relationships with the children, might provide the answer.

### Distortion of relationships or ineffective discipline?

There is evidence from both retrospective and prospective studies that the parents of delinquent boys differ from other parents in their approach to the discipline and supervision of their children (Craig and Glick, 1965; Glueck and Glueck, 1962; Sprott, Jephcott and Carter, 1955; West, 1969). It is possible that it is the child-rearing practices which matter in the genesis of delinquency and that the family discord is important only in so far as it is associated with erratic and deviant methods of bringing up children. This possibility could be tested only by some form of multivariate analysis in which the association of discipline with delinquency was examined after ironing out the effects of family discord, and vice versa. This has so far not been carried out in any of the published studies. It is hard to judge how likely it is that ineffective discipline could explain the findings. On the one hand there is little association in the normal range between methods of child rearing and child behaviour (Becker, 1964). On the other hand, associations at the extremes of a distribution often differ from those in the middle. The issue requires further study.

## Nature or nurture?

One of the chief objections raised against the view that deprivation (in any of its forms) leads to adverse effects in children is that the association might well be explicable in genetic terms (Wootton, 1959, 1962). This objection could not apply to some of the varieties of deprivation discussed in this book, but it could apply to the association between distortion of relationships and the development of antisocial behaviour.

Before discussing the evidence on this point, it is necessary to make clear what is at issue. In the first place the question is not whether antisocial behaviour is due to heredity or environment. This is a nonsensical question as it must result from an interaction between the two. Secondly, the question is not whether *differences* between antisocial and other children are largely genetically or environmentally determined. This is a meaningful question, although it is always necessary to specify the environmental circumstances to which the answer applies.* Rather, the question is very much more specific: that is, to what extent is the association between

* Where environmental circumstances experienced by individuals are extremely different, the influence of genetic factors in accounting for individual differences will necessarily be less than when environmental circumstances are closely similar.

disturbed family relationships and antisocial behaviour genetically determined? It should be appreciated that it is quite
possible for this association to operate entirely through environmental influences and yet antisocial behaviour still have
a strong genetic element (by virtue of other mechanisms).

The whole association could be accounted for in terms of
heredity if a gene led to both delinquent behaviour and to
personality difficulties giving rise to marital disharmony. In
our own studies we found that within the group of families
with a satisfactory marriage there was *no* association between
parental personality disorder and antisocial disturbance in
the children. This finding makes a genetic explanation less
plausible, but a more direct test is offered by studies of
adopted or foster children. When children are reared by their
biological parents there is an association between parental
criminality or alcoholism and deviant behaviour in the children (Jonsson, 1967; Nylander, 1960; Otterström, 1946;
Robins, 1966). This does not appear to be the case to the
same extent when the children are brought up away from
their biological parents. Thus, in a recent Swedish study
Bohman (1970) examined associations between deviant behaviour in adopted children and criminality or alcohol abuse
in the true fathers (who of course had no contact with the
children). No association was found. Similar results have
come from less well-controlled studies. For example, Theis
(1924) found little association between 'unsatisfactory' heredity in the biological parents and the social adjustment of
their children who had been placed away from home. In a
study of foster children, Roe and Burks (1945), too, found
little difference between the adult outcome of those whose
true parents were alcoholic and those whose biological
parents were 'normal'. However, the offspring of alcoholic
parents did have more serious difficulties of an antisocial type
during adolescence.

There have been few twin studies of delinquents, but those
that have been undertaken suggest that genetic factors play
a relatively small part in the pathogenesis of delinquency and
antisocial behaviour (Rosanoff, Handy and Plesset, 1941;
Shields, 1954, 1968). The concordance rates are high in both

monozygotic and dizygotic pairs and only slightly higher in the former.

The evidence is not very satisfactory, but it seems to show that the association between disturbed family relationships and antisocial behaviour in the children is environmentally determined to a considerable extent. However, studies do not differentiate between transient antisocial disturbance in childhood and the more severe delinquent disorders which frequently persist into adult life (Robins, 1970). It may well be that the genetic component differs in these two cases.

It should be added that the findings do not suggest that genetic factors play no part in delinquency. They probably are important with respect to the differences in temperamental features which render children more or less susceptible to psychological stress (see pages 33 and 75).

## Privation or stigma?

This book has been solely concerned with the effects of objective deprivation. It only remains to note that deprivation has a subjective side – the individual's view of his position relative to that of others whom he perceives as being better or less well off than himself (Eckland and Kent, 1968). By means of stigma, people may be socialized to disabling roles in life. It has been suggested that the effects of stigma may account for many of the consequences of socio-cultural deprivation, particularly when the deprivation is associated with membership of a minority or socially depressed racial group. Investigation of this issue is of the greatest social importance, but in the area of child development it is so far distinguished more by its promise than its achievements (Jessor and Richardson, 1968). There is some reason to suppose that an individual's immediate response in the test situation may be influenced by motivational factors associated with stigma (Deutsch, Katz and Jensen, 1968; Watson, 1970), but findings that similar effects may influence more long-term cognitive and educational progress (Rosenthal and Jacobson, 1968) have not been confirmed on replication (Claiborn, 1969). Even less is known about the emotional and behavioural effects of stigma. It could be that some of the consequences of 'maternal deprivation' discussed in this chapter are attributable in part to the influence of stigma on social interaction, but this speculation remains a matter for further research.

## Conclusions

In view of the many areas of research into 'deprivation' which lack sound data, it would be quite inappropriate to draw any firm conclusions at this stage. Interim conclusions of a tentative kind have been mentioned throughout the chapter, but the main findings can perhaps be drawn together by considering what mechanisms *might* underlie the main long-term consequences of 'maternal deprivation'.

A nutritional deficiency is probably the main factor responsible for the syndrome of 'deprivation dwarfism'. In parts of the world where malnutrition is rife it probably also plays a part in the genesis of mental retardation, but in Britain this is likely to be an uncommon occurrence.

A deficiency in 'stimulation' and necessary life experiences is likely to be largely responsible for those cases of intellectual retardation due to 'deprivation'. Perceptual privation is important in causing certain types of developmental and intellectual retardation, but humans differ from lower animals in the special role of language in intellectual development. Linguistic privation is probably most important in the poor vocalization of institutional infants and in the impairment of verbal intelligence seen in older children. In each case, although a certain minimum is required, the absolute amount of stimulation seems less important than the distinctiveness and meaningfulness of the stimulation to the child.

Distorted intra-familial relationships involving both lack of affection and hostility or discord are associated with the development of later antisocial behaviour and delinquency. Although the presence of a deviant parental model and inefficient discipline may be contributing factors, the lack of a stable, persistent, harmonious relationship with a parent appears to be the crucial variable.

Less is known about the syndrome of 'affectionless psychopathy', but the little evidence available suggests that the most tenable hypothesis is that a failure to develop attachments (or bonds) in early childhood is the main factor. A bond to one or other parent, usually the mother, is the strongest attachment formed by most normal young children. However, the evidence suggests that what is needed is a bond. Whether this is to the mother seems irrelevant in this connection and indeed it is doubtful whether it even has to be to an adult. Nevertheless, *which* person it is with whom bonds form is important for other reasons. Although the necessary facts are lacking it is probable that bonds with both men *and* women are advantageous for optimal psychosexual development.

Stress during the first six years (often but probably not necessarily involving parent–child separation) is a factor in the genesis of enuresis. However, some aspect of an institutional upbringing also appears important in that enuresis is common among children in a wide range of institutions. Which aspect of institutional care is pertinent in this connection is not known.

Loss of an attachment figure, although a major factor in the causation of short-term effects, seems of only minor importance with respect to long-term consequences, in spite of many previous claims to the contrary. Such a loss may play a part in enuresis, as one of several stress factors. Also, it may have a more specific connection with depression in adults. However, in this case the association is more with parental loss during adolescence than with loss in early childhood. Loss may be a minor contributory factor in other types of outcome, but so far as can be judged from the evidence it is not the main influence.

Indeed, the evidence strongly suggests that most of the long-term consequences are due to privation or lack of some kind, rather than to any type of loss. Accordingly the 'deprivation' half of the concept is somewhat misleading. The 'maternal' half of the concept is also inaccurate in that, with but few exceptions, the deleterious influences concern the care of the child or relationships with people rather than any specific defect of the mother.

# 6. Conclusions

It may be appropriate to end this reconsideration of 'maternal deprivation' by comparing the present state of knowledge with that extant at the time of Bowlby's review of the field in 1951. At that time there had been some fifteen years of research into the adverse effects of early deprivation of maternal care, but he was the first person to draw the strands together into one coherent argument. His report to the World Health Organization rightly became a most influential document, which stimulated a wealth of research and led to a reconsideration of the care provided for children being reared in institutions. Bowlby's exposure (by bringing together the results of a diverse range of reports) of 'the prevalence of deplorable patterns of institutional upbringing and of the crass indifference of certain hospitals to childish sensitivities' was likened in importance to Elizabeth Fry's exposure of the insanitary conditions in prisons in the nineteenth century (Wootton, 1962). His indictment of residential care of children led to a remarkable change in outlook that was followed by a widespread improvement in the institutional care of children.

On the other hand, his claim that maternal deprivation might have grave and far-reaching effects on a child's personality and intellect was met with considerable criticism and theoretical dispute. Several influential reviews pointed to the serious methodological deficiencies in many of the studies he cited. It was suggested that some of the supposed *sequelae* of deprivation might be merely artefacts consequent upon the biases existing in how children are chosen to be admitted to institutions, or might be due to hereditary conditions, or might represent the consequences of biological damage resulting from malnutrition, birth complications and the like. These criticisms were correct, but have not been discussed in this book as they have been amply documented by previous writers and because better controlled studies have replaced some of the weaker investigations upon which the 1951 report had to rely. Those faults in research design in the earlier investigations led, in some quarters, to a serious lack of appreciation of the importance of genetic and physical factors in children's development. It is necessary to redress the balance in this respect, as done in Berger and Passingham's (1972) review of 'deprivation'. Nevertheless, a parallel but opposite reliance on an outdated and incorrect deterministic view of development as a mere unfolding of hereditarily determined characteristics also requires redressing. It is fortunate that Bowlby's 1951 WHO report was immediately preceded by Hebb's (1949) classic, *The Organization of Behavior*, in which he outlined his ideas on the importance of experience in the development of intelligence. In the field of the study of animal behaviour this had as revolutionary an impact as Bowlby's book did on the world of child care. As a consequence, there is now a large body of animal evidence on the effects of early life experiences. These, together with a smaller group of well-controlled human studies, have amply demonstrated that early life experiences may have serious and lasting effects on development. This conclusion of Bowlby's which was regarded as very controversial twenty years ago is now generally accepted as true.

We may now take for granted

the extensive evidence that many children admitted to hospital or to a residential nursery show an immediate reaction of acute distress; that many infants show developmental retardation following admission to a poor-quality institution and may exhibit intellectual impairment if they remain there for a long time; that there is an association between delinquency and broken homes; that affectionless psychopathy sometimes follows multiple separation experiences and institutional care in early childhood; and that dwarfism is particularly seen in children from rejecting and affectionless homes (Rutter, 1972b).

Because this is widely accepted it is now possible to focus

on the very important questions of *why* and *how* children are adversely affected by those experiences included under the term 'maternal deprivation', rather than spend time on *whether* they are affected. The diversity of experiences covered by 'maternal deprivation' was noted by Bowlby in his 1951 report and has been re-emphasized in numerous subsequent reviews. Nevertheless, the very existence of a single term, 'maternal deprivation', has had the most unfortunate consequence of implying one specific syndrome of unitary causation. This is apparent, for example, in Ainsworth's excellent and thoughtful reappraisal of the topic in 1962. Her whole review is explicitly based on the fact that 'maternal deprivation' covers a wide range of different experiences, but the unitary concept creeps back in her summary of findings (Ainsworth, 1962, p. 153), where the term 'deprivation' is repeatedly used as if it referred to a single stress. Manifestly it is not a single stress.

Twenty, and even ten, years ago there was a paucity of evidence upon which to base any analysis of the different mechanisms involved. Today things have moved forward somewhat and it has been possible to put forward some suggestions concerning possible psychological mechanisms. It has been hypothesized that the syndrome of acute distress is probably due in part to a disruption of the bonding process (not necessarily with the mother); developmental retardation and intellectual impairment are both a consequence of privation of perceptual and linguistic experience; dwarfism is usually due to nutritional privation; enuresis is sometimes a result of stressful experiences in the first five years; delinquency follows family discord; and psychopathy may be the end-product of a failure to develop bonds or attachments in the first three years of life. None of these suggestions has yet got firm and unequivocal empirical support and it is important to remember that they remain hypotheses which require rigorous testing. What is important is that it is now clear that the different elements in a child's early life experiences play quite different parts in the development process, so that the end-results of an insufficiency or distortion of each are equally dissimilar.

Throughout this book, reference has been made to age differences in children's responses to various forms of privation and deprivation. It has been apparent that these differ according to the type of life experience being considered. This reflects the important fact that children's needs differ according to their stage of development. No statement can be made about environmental influences without some specification of the age of the child being discussed. This has been implicit in the whole of this account of 'maternal deprivation', but because of the lack of data on many aspects of age differences the effects have been discussed primarily in terms of different psychological mechanisms rather than in terms of developmental level. Nevertheless, in seeking to confirm or refute the hypotheses advanced it will be crucial to consider the effects in terms of how various experiences impinge on the developmental process.

Another problem in the use of the concept of 'maternal deprivation' stems from the actual words used. The term is misleading in that it appears that in most cases the deleterious influences are *not* specifically tied to the mother and are *not* due to deprivation (Rutter, 1972b). Reference to *The Shorter Oxford English Dictionary* shows that deprivation means 'dispossession' or 'loss'. While loss is probably an important factor in one of the syndromes associated with 'maternal deprivation', a review of the evidence suggests that in most cases the damage comes from 'lack' or 'distortion' of care rather than any form of 'loss'. Bowlby's claim in 1951 that 'mother-love in infancy and childhood is as important for mental health as are vitamins and proteins for physical health' was probably correct, but unfortunately it led some people (mistakenly) to place an almost mystical importance on the mother and to regard love as the only important element in child rearing. This is a nonsense and it has always been a *mis*-interpretation of what was said in the 1951 report. Nevertheless, this view has come to be widespread among those involved in child care.

Bowlby's own work in the last twenty years has gone a long way towards the specification of what are the crucial elements in 'mother-love'. His emphasis on the importance of attachment behaviour and on a young child's need to form lasting bonds with other people (Bowlby, 1969) has received increasing experimental support. This aspect of the mother–child relationship appears particularly important in connection with children's distress following certain kinds of separation experiences and with the (rather rare) syndrome of 'affectionless psychopathy'.

Nevertheless, some details of Bowlby's views on bonding have been questioned in this book. He has sometimes seemed to suggest that these two syndromes arise in a similar way, but the current evidence points to different mechanisms. Distress probably arises in part through *disruption* of bonds, whereas affectionless psychopathy probably arises because firm bonds *fail to develop*.

The whole notion of bonding also gives rise to some difficult questions. It is now clear that separation need not involve bond disruption and the two should not be regarded as synonymous. This assumption in the past led to a misleading emphasis on the supposedly deleterious effects of separation as such. This now appears incorrect and is one of the points on which the 1951 report needs major modification. Separation may or may not be harmful according to its effects on bonds and on attachment behaviour. It is the relationship itself which needs to be studied. But that raises another issue: if bonds can be maintained during a separation, then obviously bonds cannot be equated with attachment behaviour. But in that case how should one measure the strength of a bond (or even its presence) when the person with whom bonds have developed is absent? Further elucidation of the bonding process requires resolution of that difficulty.

A further point of departure from Bowlby's views concerns the supposedly special importance of the mother. He has argued that the child is innately monotropic and that the bond with the mother (or mother-surrogate) is different in kind from the bonds developed with others. The evidence on that point is unsatisfactory but what there is seems not to support that view. Two issues are involved. The first is whether or not the main bond differs from all others. It is suggested here that it does not. The chief bond is especially important because of its greater strength, but most children develop bonds with several people and it appears likely that these bonds are basically similar. The second concerns the assumption that the 'mother' or 'mother-surrogate' is the person to whom the child is necessarily most attached. Of course in most families the mother has most to do with the young child and as a consequence she is usually the person with whom the strongest bond is formed. But it should be appreciated that the chief bond need not be with a biological parent, it need not be with the chief caretaker and it need not be with a female.

Furthermore, it seems to be incorrect to regard the person with whom there is the main bond as necessarily and generally the most important person in the child's life. That person will be most important for some things but not for others. For some aspects of development the same-sexed parent seems to have a special role, for some the person who plays and talks most with the child and for others the person who feeds the child. The father, the mother, brother and sisters, friends, school-teachers and others all have an impact on development, but their influences and importance differ for different aspects of development. A less exclusive focus on the mother is required. Children also have fathers!

The studies into the development of antisocial behaviour in children show the importance of family relationships. Discord, tension and lack of affection in the home all appear to increase the likelihood of the children showing disorders of conduct. The exact mechanisms involved remain unclear, but it seems that father–mother and parent–child relationships are both influential, and that this effect is not necessarily associated with defects in attachment behaviour. Distorted relationships rather than weak bonds seem to be responsible. This effect, unlike some of the others, is not one particularly associated with influences in early childhood and it serves to emphasize the importance of life experiences in middle childhood for some aspects of development.

Adult disorders have not been considered in this book, but later childhood and adolescence may be especially important periods for the genesis of depression, one of the psychiatric conditions in adult life associated with 'maternal deprivation'. Depression is probably particularly associated with being orphaned during early adolescence (Hill, 1972). It is likely that the mechanisms involved are multiple, but this may constitute another example of the effects of disruption of bonds. In keeping with this view (Bowlby, 1968; Bowlby and Parkes, 1970) is the fact that depression and suicide are associated with recent bereavement (Bunch, 1972; Parkes, 1964, 1965), with divorce or separation (Barraclough and Nelson, 1971), and with moving to a new neighbourhood (Sainsbury, 1971). Whether these associations reflect the same or different mechanisms should be further investigated.

Quite apart from 'love' and harmonious family relationships other features of the environment greatly influence children's development. This is most clearly evident with regard to intellectual development where experience with different forms of perception and of perceptuo-motor activity has been shown to influence later skills in perceptual discrimination and problem solving, which constitute important elements in the group of abilities called 'intelligence'. Animal studies show that although there are general effects, to a considerable extent effects are specific. The more limited human evidence is in keeping with this suggestion. Thus, visual experience is particularly important in the development of visual discrimination skills, experience of movement in the development of coordination, and so forth. However, human development differs from that in other animals in one key respect – the role of language. Verbal skills are an important part of 'intelligence' in man and those aspects of the environment which influence language are thereby especially important. It is in this connection that the amount, type and clarity of conversation experienced by the child are most influential. The appreciation today of the importance of these perceptual and linguistic experiences in development departs from Ainsworth's conclusions in 1962 and differs from Bowlby's emphasis in 1951.

Feeding was at one time given a disproportionate role in child development by theorists. Hunger was seen as the source of 'drive' and activity and the relief of hunger was seen as the chief reason why children became attached to their parents – the theory of 'cupboard love'. These views have been shown to be largely mistaken (Bowlby, 1969), but there is a danger now of overlooking the importance of nutrition in other ways. The evidence suggests that privation of food may be an important cause of dwarfism in children from rejecting and neglectful homes, and chronic malnutrition may also sometimes lead to mental retardation.

Perhaps the most important recent development in 'maternal deprivation' research has been the emphasis on individual differences in children's responses to 'deprivation'. That some children are damaged and some escape damage has long been observed, but the differences in vulnerability have been regarded as largely inexplicable (Ainsworth, 1962). At last, some reasons are emerging for research. In the field of animal research, Hinde's studies of separation experiences in rhesus monkeys are most important in this respect. He has clearly shown that the mother–infant relationship *prior* to separation influences the infant's response to separation. This relationship is a reciprocal one and is influenced both by variables in the mother and by variables in the child. The importance of child variables as determinants of mother–child interaction in humans has been emphasized by Bell (1968, 1971), and Graham and George's (1972) work examining differences in children's responses to parental illness has made an important beginning to the study of temperamental differences in children's reactions to stressful experiences. Much remains to be done, but what has been achieved so far shows that this is a fruitful field for study.

Curiously, one of the omissions until recently in this connection has been the study of sex differences. That boys and girls differ in their behaviour has long been known, but only in the last few years has attention been focused on sex differences in early mother–child interaction (Moss, 1967) and in responses to stress (Rutter, 1970b). It is now evident that boys and girls do differ in these respects although exactly how they do remains ill-understood – another area requiring further research.

In a recent review of the effects of 'psychosocial deprivation' on human development in infancy (a topic closely related to 'maternal deprivation'), Bettye Caldwell (1970) suggested that three of the tasks requiring massive research efforts were: improved techniques of assessing the psychosocial environment, better measures of those aspects of human behaviour which react to changes of environment, and an exploration of the relationship between constitutional factors and the susceptibility to the influence of deprivation. Exactly the same applies to parent–child interaction and the effects of distortion, privation or deprivation of any kind of parental care.

The concept of 'maternal deprivation' has undoubtedly been useful in focusing attention on the sometimes grave consequences of deficient or disturbed care in early life. However, it is now evident that the experiences included under the term 'maternal deprivation' are too heterogeneous and the effects too varied for it to continue to have any usefulness. It has served its purpose and should now be abandoned. That 'bad' care of children in early life can have 'bad' effects, both short-term and long-term, can be accepted as proven. What is now needed is a more precise delineation of the different aspects of 'badness', together with an analysis of their separate effects and of the reasons why children differ in their responses. The chief purpose of this book has been to discuss some of the possible psychological mechanisms which might be investigated in this connection.

# Postscript: New Developments in 'Maternal Deprivation' 1972-80

## 7. Concepts of Deprivation Reviewed

### Introduction

The first edition of *Maternal Deprivation Reassessed* ended with the conclusion that Bowlby's claim – first put forward in 1951 – that early life experiences may have serious effects on intellectual and on psychosocial development, was no longer controversial. On the other hand, the same evidence which provided support for this claim also indicated that the term 'maternal deprivation' covered a most heterogeneous range of experiences and of outcomes due to quite disparate mechanisms. Research findings were used to discuss some of these possible mechanisms.

In many respects the suggestions which were made as a result of the review of research were no more than restatements of ideas already apparent in Bowlby's (1951) WHO report or Ainsworth's (1962) reappraisal of the topic a decade later. But there were a few crucial differences (see also Rutter, 1974), some of which proved more controversial than expected.

Firstly, it was argued that the original emphasis on the supposedly deleterious effects of separation *as such* were incorrect (Rutter, 1971a, 1979a). Antisocial disorders were linked with broken homes *not* because of the separation involved but rather because of the discord and disharmony which led to the break. Affectionless psychopathy was due *not* to the breaking of relationships but rather to the initial failure to form bonds. Intellectual retardation was due to a lack of appropriate experiences and *not* to separations.

Secondly, there was disagreement with Bowlby's views on the supposedly special importance of the mother. In particular, it was suggested that the evidence did not support the notion that the child's main bond with the mother differed in kind and in quality from all his other bonds.

Thirdly, the review indicated that 'the most important recent development in "maternal deprivation" research has been the emphasis on individual differences in children's responses to "deprivation".' All investigations had shown that many children are *not* damaged by deprivation, and it was argued that exploration of the reasons for their apparent invulnerability should prove a particularly fruitful field for study.

The findings from research undertaken during the eight years since 1972 allow a better judgement on the extent to which these initial formulations have proved valid. That evidence is briefly surveyed here. However, many of the issues which were current in 1972 are no longer those which excite most interest today. New concepts and new ideas have come to the forefront and in this postscript most attention is paid to the research findings which underlie these new approaches. These recent investigations have their roots in the work of the pioneers who introduced the notion of 'maternal deprivation' over a quarter of a century ago (cf. Bowlby, 1951; Goldfarb, 1955; Spitz, 1946), but the picture now looks very different from the way it appeared then.

### Syndromes

It is appropriate to begin this update with a consideration of the four principal syndromes thought to result from 'maternal deprivation', and of the mechanisms proposed in 1972 for their causation.

### Acute distress syndrome

Firstly, there is the acute distress reaction shown by many young children admitted to hospitals or residential nurseries. About a third of children are admitted to hospital at least once and about 1 in 20 have repeated admissions (Douglas, 1975; Quinton and Rutter, 1976). As discussed in earlier chapters, this is a quite frequent cause of distress among pre-school children. However, in considering the mechanisms involved it is important to differentiate two phases: (a) the distress during admission; and (b) the disturbance on returning home *after* the admission (see Rutter, 1979a).

So far as the distress during admission is concerned, there is little to add to the earlier account. The evidence indicates that some kind of interference with attachment behaviour constitutes one element in the syndrome. Thus, the Robertsons (1971) found that young children separated from their parents but cared for in a family (rather than institutional) setting did *not* show the same acute distress reaction exhibited by children admitted to hospitals or residential nurseries. This indicates that separation *per se* cannot be the explanation. Of course, the children fostered in a family setting showed *some* response to their separation from their parents, but the point is that they did not exhibit the marked distress seen in children admitted to hospital. The strong inference is that separation, although a crucial precipitant, is not the essential causal agent in the distress syndrome. Moreover, insofar as separation plays a part it is separation from the family which is important and not just separation from the mother. Separation protest tends to be greater in strange circumstances than in a familiar situation (Ross *et al.*, 1975; Littenberg *et al.*, 1971), and tends to be reduced if the child has the opportunity to form new attachments (Robertson and Robertson, 1971). In short, the immediate disturbance during hospital or residential nursery admission seems to be a function of (a) separation from all people to whom the child is attached; (b) a lack of opportunity to form new attachments (because caretakers keep changing); and (c) a strange environment. Alteration of any of these (as by having some of the family present for as much of the time as possible, by altered patterns of care, and by trying to keep to the child's familiar routines as much as possible) should all help in reducing the likelihood of emotional disturbance.

However, in addition to these mechanisms, children admitted to hospital may become upset both because their parents are anxious and worried, and also because medical and surgical procedures are strange and frightening to the child. Several studies have now shown that preparing children and their parents for admission by letting them know what to expect, by showing them how to cope and by providing emotional support may significantly reduce anxiety in the parents and emotional disturbance in the children (Ferguson, 1979; Wolfer and Visintainer, 1979).

The factors involved with disturbance following reunion are probably somewhat different. Of course, *sequelae* afterwards are more likely in children upset at the time (and to that extent the mechanisms are similar) but in addition other processes come into operation. Curiously, there has been little direct study of this in humans, but the findings from monkeys' studies are striking and probably relevant (Hinde and McGinnis, 1977). The most important observation is that the infant's disturbance *after* the separation is strongly connected with the quality of the mother–infant relationship. When the relationship *before* separation was tense and difficult, the infants were more likely to be disturbed *afterwards*. Moreover, when the circumstances during or after the separation aggravated the mother–infant relationship, this too increased the likelihood that the infant would be disturbed. In short, it appeared that the main mechanism leading to disordered psychological function in the infant was tension and difficulty in the mother–infant relationship.

Circumstantial evidence suggests that the same may apply in humans. Thus, what evidence there is suggests that disturbance is more likely if the child comes from a deprived or disturbed family or if the previous parent–child relationship was poor (Stacey *et al.*, 1970; Douglas, 1975; Quinton and Rutter, 1976; Vernon *et al.*, 1965). It has long been observed that children may be hostile and difficult, as well as clinging, after returning home from hospital, and it appears that the parental response to this behaviour may be crucial. If the animal evidence is anything to go by it would seem that an increase in 'mothering' at this time may facilitate a return to normality.

## Conduct disorders

The second syndrome to consider is that of conduct disorders or antisocial problems. Earlier work (Rutter, 1971a) had shown that conduct disorders were strongly associated with family discord and disharmony even when there had been *no* break or separation. Furthermore, whereas parental divorce was strongly linked with delinquency, parental death was not. Thus, it appeared that the key variable involved disturbed interpersonal relationships rather than separation.

Further research during recent years has consistently confirmed these findings. For example, several recent general population epidemiological studies (Rutter, Cox, Tupling, Berger and Yule, 1975a; West and Farrington, 1973, 1977) have all shown important links between marital discord and disorders of conduct in the children. Moreover, Power and his colleagues (1974) found that among boys who had already made a court appearance for delinquency, those from intact homes with severe and persistent family problems were more likely to become recidivist than those from broken homes (or from intact homes without serious problems). Lambert, Essen and Head (1977), using longitudinal data, showed that most of the behavioural disturbance found in children removed from their homes into the care of the local authority *preceded* the removal. The separation may have added to the stresses but it was not the prime cause of the children's problems. Hetherington, Cox and Cox (1979) found that during the transition period of family disequilibrium and reorganization following divorce, children's problems may be exacerbated. However, improvement then tends to follow, and two years after divorce the children showed significantly less disturbance than those remaining in intact homes with continuing marital conflict.

It seems quite clear that family discord and disharmony are indeed the most important damaging factors. Of course that still leaves open the question of why and how disturbed interpersonal relationships lead to conduct disorders. Also, it should be emphasized that family discord is only one of many causal influences for delinquency (Rutter and Madge, 1976; West and Farrington, 1973, 1977).

It should be added, too, that the research since 1972 has also indicated that it would be unwarranted to infer that divorce necessarily either brings marital conflict to an end or produces an easy solution to the children's problems (Hetherington, Cox and Cox, 1979; Levitin, 1979; Wallerstein and Kelly, 1980). Divorce may well be an appropriate step when it is not possible to resolve serious chronic marital difficulties by any other means, but it constitutes an extended process requiring a variety of adaptations and adjustments. As a consequence, the transition period following divorce is often a stressful one for both parents and children, with behavioural disturbance getting worse before it gets better.

## Intellectual retardation

Intellectual retardation is the third syndrome to be discussed. The earlier review of the evidence suggested that perceptual and linguistic experiences played the main environmental role in the development of intelligence and that personal mothering (although important for other aspects of development) was largely irrelevant for cognitive growth.

The role of mothering and of interpersonal relationships can be assessed by examining the intellectual development of children reared in environments which are deviant in these respects. Barbara Tizard's important studies of children reared in institutions from infancy and followed to age eight years have shown them to be of normal intelligence (Tizard and Joseph, 1970; Tizard and Rees, 1974). Their mean WISC full scale IQ was 99 compared with 110 in the general population family-reared control group (Tizard and Hodges, 1978). This was so despite the fact that they had experienced some fifty to eighty parent-surrogates with quite appalling discontinuities in parent–child relationships. This had ill-effects on their psychosocial development, but it did *not* appreciably retard their intellectual growth.

Dixon's findings (1980) on larger samples are closely comparable. She too has studied children reared in institutions from the first year of life. At five to eight years they showed various social problems but they were of normal intelligence. Their mean W I S C full scale I Q was 108 compared with 106 in a comparable group of fostered children and 116 in a general population control group.

It is evident that roughly normal levels of functioning on standard I Q tests are usually attained by children reared in environments which lack personal mothering but which nevertheless provide experiences which are adequate in other respects. There is the clear implication that continuities in family relationships do not have the central role in intellectual development that they do in social development (see below). To an important extent, intellectual growth and social growth have their main influences from rather different sources.*

The evidence for the view that perceptual and linguistic experiences do influence intellectual development comes from both natural and contrived experiments. For example, Dennis (1973) showed that a shift from a poor institutional environment in the Lebanon to an adoptive home was associated with a marked gain in I Q. Heber and Garber (1974; Garber and Heber, 1977; Heber, 1971 and 1978; Heber, Garber, Harrington, Hoffman and Falender, 1972) have demonstrated marked intellectual gains compared with controls in socially disadvantaged black children given a very intensive educational intervention programme (see also Bronfenbrenner, 1974). It is also relevant that

* Even so, it would be absurd to regard intellectual development as something which is independent of personal relationships or isolated from the emotional and social life of the child. The same studies of institutional children show them to have poor task involvement in the classroom (see below) and this is very likely to affect their learning and some aspects of their cognitive growth, even if it does not have much impact on their overall I Q scores. Similarly, Matas *et al.* (1978) showed continuities between measures of attachment and of problem-solving style but not between attachment and Bayley scores at two years.

Scarr and Weinberg (1976) found that black children reared by white parents have a mean I Q some fifteen points above black children reared in their own homes.

Caldwell and her colleagues (Bradley and Caldwell, 1976; Elardo, Bradley and Caldwell, 1975) have shown that systematic measures of home stimulation are related to children's I Q scores at three; Clarke-Stewart (1973) found that maternal attention was correlated with changes in children's developmental quotient; and McCall, Appelbaum and Hogarty (1973) have concluded that parental behaviour related to I Q in later childhood. Furthermore, Tizard, Cooperman, Joseph and Tizard (1972) have shown significant (but low) correlations between institutional children's experiences and their language comprehension.

It would be wrong to exaggerate the strength of any of these findings. All the relationships are quite modest and many are statistically insignificant (Fisch, Bilek, Deinard and Chang, 1976). Some reflect the effect of the child on the parents rather than the other way round (Bradley et al., 1979), and replications often give rise to inconsistent findings (Clarke-Stewart et al., 1979). Nevertheless, there is evidence that learning experiences in and outside the home influence cognitive development. We do not yet know precisely what mechanisms are involved. However, it is clear that the sheer amount of stimulation is irrelevant (some of the most disadvantaging environments are full of noise – with shouting and the blare of the radio at full blast). Rather, the quality and meaningfulness of active experience (especially conversational interchange) seem crucial.

## Affectionless psychopathy

The fourth syndrome, so-called affectionless psychopathy, has been the subject of very little direct research in the last eight years and hence there is nothing to add to the 1972 review in terms of findings on the syndrome itself. On the other hand, there have been important advances in knowledge on the development of social relationships and on the abnormalities of bonding thought to underlie the syndrome. These warrant some detailed discussion.

## Development of social relationships

Bowlby (1969, 1973, 1980) has put forward a theory of attachment in which early bonding to the mother is seen as the essential precursor of later social relationships. There is now abundant evidence that infants usually develop an attachment to a specific person some time about six to twelve months of age. Also, something is known regarding the factors most likely to foster the development of attachments (see Ainsworth, 1973, and Rutter, 1980a). A baby's tendency to seek attachments is increased by anxiety and fear, and also by illness and fatigue (Bowlby, 1969; Maccoby and Masters, 1970). Attachments are probably particularly likely to develop to the person who brings comfort at such times. However, the *way* a parent responds to the infant is also important. Attachments are most likely to develop to people who *actively* interact with the baby and who are responsive to the baby's cues (see Ainsworth, 1973). Moreover these same parental qualities seem to predispose to secure rather than anxious attachments (Blehar, Lieberman and Ainsworth, 1977). As Ainsworth suggested, sensitive responsiveness seems to be the one quality in any interaction most likely to foster secure personal bonding.

These rather general conclusions would be accepted by most workers, but five areas of controversy and uncertainty remain; the concept of 'sensitive responsiveness', Bowlby's (1969) notion of monotropy, the distinctions to be made within the overall group of attachment behaviours, early bonding and later social relationships, and the process by which attachments develop.

### *'Sensitive responsiveness'*

The concept of 'sensitive responsiveness' reflects the general shift of view from parenting as doing things *to* the baby to parenting as a process of reciprocal interaction – an active dialogue between parent and child (see Lewis and Rosenblum, 1974). For example, Brazelton and his colleagues (Brazelton, Tronick, Adamson, Als and Weise, 1975) have examined the rhythms and patterns involved in face-to-

face interaction in the neonatal period; Condon and Sander (1974) and Stern (Stern, Jaffe, Beebe and Bennett, 1975)
have done the same with early communication; and Dunn
(1975) has investigated the longitudinal development of
styles of mothering in the first years of life. Brown and
Bateman (1978) showed that mothers responded differently
to premature than to full-term babies. The premature infants were less active and responsive and it seemed that as
a consequence the mothers became more active and more
likely to initiate interactions. Clarke-Stewart's findings (1973,
1978), from her cross-lagged correlational analysis of longitudinal data, suggested not only a two-way interaction, in
which parents both influenced and were influenced by their
children, but also a reciprocal relationship which changed
in balance and characteristics as the children grew older.

Everyone is agreed that parenting involves reciprocity
and sensitivity to the baby's cues and signals, but study
of this sequential process had proved extremely difficult.
Ainsworth and her colleagues (1974) found that rapid responses to the baby's crying were effective in reducing the
amount of crying both immediately and later in the first
year of life (Bell and Ainsworth, 1972). On the other hand,
there are problems in the interpretation of her results
(Gewirtz and Boyd, 1977) and the findings from other studies
have been quite different (Etzel and Gewirtz, 1967; Sander,
1969; Sander, Stechler, Burns and Julia, 1970) in showing
that rapid responses may *increase* babies' crying and in
showing weak correlations between measures of responsiveness in the neonatal period and in later infancy (Dunn,
1975). Babies' cries are of several quite different kinds
(Wasz-Höckert, Lind, Vuorenkoski, Partanen and Valanne,
1968; Wolff, 1969), and it may be that it is the parent's
ability to discriminate between these and to respond appropriately which is important.

Clearly, we have some way to go yet before we have
either adequate concepts or adequate measures of what is
meant by sensitive responsiveness. However, it is likely that
it involves not only the discrimination between different
cues provided by the baby, but in addition the giving of

appropriate differentiating responses, the ability to get pleasure from the baby's reciprocity and the initiation of interactions.

## Monotropy

All studies have shown that most children develop multiple attachments. However, there is continuing controversy on whether these attachments all have the same meaning. Bowlby (1969) has suggested that there is an innate bias for a child to attach himself especially to *one* figure and that this main attachment differs in kind from those to other subsidiary figures. However, this statement involves two rather different propositions, one of which is supported by the evidence and one of which is not. The first proposition is that the several attachments are not of equal strength and are not freely interchangeable. This is well supported by the findings from several studies which show that there is a persisting hierarchy among attachments, with some continuing to be stronger than others (Ainsworth, 1967; Schaffer and Emerson, 1964). Even in institutions, children tend to have their 'favourite' adult to whom they will go in preference to others (Stevens, 1975).

The second proposition is that the first or main attachment differs *in kind* from all other subsidiary ones. Most research findings suggest that this is not the case. The proposition may be tested in two different ways. Firstly, it may be determined whether the function or effects of all attachments are similar in *quality* even though they differ in *intensity*. The evidence indicates that they are. Attachment may be shown by protest or distress if the attached person leaves the child, by reduction of anxiety and increase of exploration. in a strange situation when the attached person is present, and by following or the seeking of closeness (see below). Each of these qualities have been shown for attachments to sibs (Heinicke and Westheimer, 1965), to peers (Kissel, 1965; Schwarz, 1972), to fathers (Cohen and Campos, 1974; Lamb, 1977a and b; Spelke, Zelazo, Kagan and Kotelchuck, 1973), to adult caretakers in a nursery (Arsenian, 1943) and to inanimate objects

(Harlow and Zimmermann, 1959; Mason and Berkson, 1975; Passman, 1977; Passman and Weisberg, 1975) as well as to mothers (Ainsworth, 1967; Ainsworth and Wittig, 1969; Corter, 1973; Cox and Campbell, 1968; Maccoby and Feldman, 1972; Morgan and Ricciuti, 1969; Stayton *et al.*, 1973; Tracy, Lamb and Ainsworth, 1976). It is also crucial that these attachment responses to other persons occur even in children who have developed bonds with their mothers. However, the responses do not occur with strangers.

Secondly, the proposition may be tested by determining if the difference in intensity of attachment between the person at the top of the hierarchy and the person second in the hierarchy is greater than that between the second and third persons. Stevens (1975) found that in most cases it was not (although in some it was). It may be concluded that multiple attachments tend to have rather *similar* functions in spite of a persisting hierarchy among them which differs markedly in intensity. Of course, it is not suggested that all relationships are similar in quality and function. The evidence that this is *not* the case is more fully discussed below. However, Bowlby's argument is that the child's relationship with mother differs from other relationships specifically with respect to its *attachment* qualities, and the evidence indicates that this is not so.

### Attachment behaviours

In early writings on attachment there tended to be an implicit assumption that it was a unitary concept. However, it is now clear that this is not so (Coates, Anderson and Hartup, 1972; Rosenthal, 1973; Stayton and Ainsworth, 1973). Attachment is not a personality trait but rather a construct (Sroufe and Waters, 1977) which involves several different features. Probably at least two distinctions need to be made. Firstly, there is the difference between attachment behaviour and persisting bonds. Infants show a general tendency to seek attachments to other people (Robertson and Robertson, 1971). However, the concept of bonding implies selective attachment (Cohen, 1974) which *persists* over time even during a period of *no contact* with the person with whom bonds exist. The importance of this distinction was shown in the Harlow experiments with rhesus monkeys. Infants reared in social isolation clung to inanimate models (so-called 'cloth mothers') and rushed back to them when threatened or frightened, as by a blast of air in their face (Harlow, 1958; Harlow and Zimmermann, 1959). The behaviour clearly indicates attachment. However, follow-up studies have indicated that these early attachments to inanimate objects did *not* lead on to normal social relationships in adult life, as peer or parent attachments usually do (Harlow and Harlow, 1969; Ruppenthal, Arling, Harlow, Sackett and Suomi, 1976). The difference between *human* attachment behaviour and bonding is shown by Tizard and Rees' (1974) findings regarding institutional children. Four-year-old children reared in institutions showed *more* clinging and following behaviour than family-reared children, but also they were *less* likely to show selective bonding or deep relationships. The findings may mean that the processes involved are different or, more likely, that the nature of the attached object's *response* to the infant will influence the *quality* of the relationship formed and hence its function in relation to later development.

The second distinction is between secure and insecure bonding (Stayton and Ainsworth, 1973). One of the characteristics of bonding is that it enables children to feel secure in strange situations. The apparent 'purpose' of bonding is to give the child security of relationships in order to stop clinging and following, and in that sense to become detached. Thus, Stayton and Ainsworth (1973) found that the children of sensitive responsive mothers showed more positive greeting on reunion and more following behaviour (suggesting stronger attachments) than the children of insensitive unresponsive mothers, but they showed *less* crying on separation which suggested that they had a more 'secure' attachment. Children who are securely attached to one parent are likely also to be securely attached to the other but there is sufficient variability in a child's relationships with his two parents to suggest that to an appreciable extent the quality of security is specific to the relationship (Lamb,

1978). It is also relevant that Hinde and Spencer-Booth (1970) showed that infant rhesus monkeys who exhibited most distress after separation were those who had experienced most rejection from their mothers and for whom there was the most tension in the infant–mother relationship.

One further question is whether the concept of attachment encompasses all positive social interactions in young children. The evidence suggests that it does *not*. In particular, the effects of anxiety sharply differentiate attachment from other forms of social interaction; whereas social play is *inhibited* by anxiety, attachment is *intensified*. Thus, Lamb (1977b) found that when a child was with his parents the entrance of a stranger inhibited playful interactions but intensified attachment behaviour. Children may prefer to play with peers (Eckerman, Whatley and Katz, 1975) or a stranger (Ross and Goldman, 1977) but will nevertheless prefer to go to a parent for comfort. The same applies to rhesus monkeys (Patterson, Bonvillian, Reynolds and Maccoby, 1975). Similarly in an unfamiliar situation infants are much more likely to follow their mother than a stranger when both leave the room out of different doors (Corter, 1973). Following and the seeking of proximity are characteristic of attachment and both tend to increase at times of stress. It should be noted that this differential reaction to anxiety is *not* a consequence of parents being more skilled at providing comfort at times of stress. Harlow and his colleagues showed that infant monkeys clung tightly even to cloth models which repeatedly punished them with a blast of compressed air (Rosenblum and Harlow, 1963) or to deprived mothers who severely abused them (Seay, Alexander and Harlow, 1964). Anxiety seems to increase attachment *regardless* of the response of the attachment object. Systematic data are lacking for humans but the same seems to apply (Bowlby, 1969).

Play and attachment clearly overlap greatly but they exhibit rather different qualities (Hartup, 1979, 1980). The ways children play together (Heathers, 1955) and the ways they interact with a stranger (Ross and Goldman, 1977) are rather different from their style of interaction with parents. Clinging, or hugging one another, is rarely seen in peer play except in the unusual circumstances of rearing in the absence of parents (Freud and Dann, 1951). The same applies to monkey interactions with peers (Harlow, 1969; Harlow and Harlow, 1972). If there are no parents, peer relationships may serve as a fair substitute in providing attachments, but in these circumstances fully adequate social development may be more difficult to achieve (Goldberger, 1972; Ruppenthal et al., 1976).

Lamb's studies (Lamb and Stevenson, 1978) also indicate that father–child interactions differ in some respects from mother–child interactions. Fathers tend to spend less time in caretaking but are more likely to engage in physically stimulating and unpredictable play which is often preferred by infants. Somewhat comparable findings have been reported for rhesus monkeys (Suomi, 1977).

Taken together, the findings suggest that any one relationship may involve both attachment and playful interactions. On the whole the former is most characteristic of parent–child relationships and the latter is most characteristic of peer relationships – but there is overlap. Clearly, it is useful conceptually to separate the two types of interactions. However, it remains uncertain how far they are linked and, in particular, how far early bonding is necessary for the optimal development of later playful interaction (see chapter 9).

Further research is necessary to sort out the various dimensions of social interaction. However, it may be that attachment behaviours are most readily differentiated from play by the amount of close physical contact in attachment and by its tendency to increase (rather than decrease) at times of fear. Within the overall concept of attachment, specific bonding is probably best differentiated from general attachment behaviour by the presence of selectivity in relationships which persist over time and place. The strength of bonding may be best determined by the degree of reduction of distress in a frightened situation when the bonded person is present. The security of bonding, on the other hand, may perhaps be assessed by the relative lack of distress following separation, or by the extent of moving away from the bonded person in a strange situation (obviously this measurement would have to control for strength of bonding).

## Process of bonding

The fourth area of controversy concerns the process by which attachments and bonds develop (Cairns, 1977; Corter, 1974; Gewirtz, 1972a; Rajeki, Lamb and Obmascher, 1978; Rutter, 1980a). The topic has attracted the attention and interest of many theorists and there is a wide variety of quite disparate explanations of attachment behaviour (see Rajeki, Lamb and Obmascher, 1978, for a good summary and appraisal). Some, although historically important, no longer warrant serious attention in view of the mass of findings inconsistent with the theory. Thus, Lorenz's (1937) original view of imprinting has had to be greatly modified in the light of research data; Freud's (1946) notion that object relations develop on the basis of feeding, and Dollard and Miller's (1950) view of attachment as the result of secondary reinforcement are both inconsistent with the findings showing the irrelevance of feeding and physical caretaking; Schneirla's (1965) epigenetic model lacks empirical support; and Scott's (1971) concept that attachment develops as a response to separation is out of keeping with research findings.

Bowlby (1969) and Ainsworth (1973) have both suggested that infants are born with a biological propensity to behave in ways which promote proximity and contact with their mother-figure. According to their view, attachment then develops as a consequence of parental responsiveness to these innate behaviours during a sensitive period in the first years of life. In this way attachment is seen as a specific phenomenon which differs qualitatively from dependency.

Gewirtz (1961 and 1972a and b), in contrast, argues that both develop as a result of differential reinforcement, the difference being simply that positive stimulus control is restricted to a particular person (rather than to a class of objects) in the case of attachment. Cairns (1966a and b), on the other hand, proposes a contiguity conditioning process which does not rely on any rewarding properties of the attached-object. In his view, attachment occurs because a proximate relationship with a salient object predisposes to conditioning. Hoffman and Ratner (1973) suggest a somewhat different form of conditioning model, and Solomon and Corbit (1974), Sears (1972) and Salzen (1978) posit a more central role for the child's emotional state.

Theorists are agreed on several crucial issues. Firstly, the process of bonding obviously involves a *reciprocal* interaction between infant and parent in which *both* play an active role (see e.g. Bowlby, 1969; Cairns, 1977; Gewirtz and Boyd, 1976). Secondly, maturational as well as environmental factors are important in determining *when* bonding occurs (see Cairns, 1972 and 1977; Schaffer, 1971). Thus, the development of selective attachment necessarily presupposes that the child can differentiate between people and has a repertoire of social signals and responses. However, while this is a necessary condition it is not a sufficient one as bonding does not occur until some weeks or months later and may be even further delayed if the environment lacks adequate social opportunities. Thirdly, selective bonds clearly develop as a result of some form of social learning. Moreover, differential reinforcement manifestly plays an important role in determining the patterning and quality of social interactions (Hinde and Stevenson-Hinde, 1976).

Dispute mainly centres on the question of how far bonding is a process which is qualitatively distinct from other forms of social learning, and on the nature and importance of possible innate propensities. Five key observations demand explanation and together these pose problems for all of the theories. Firstly, there is the secure base effect – the fact that the presence of an attachment object makes it more likely that the infant will move *away* and explore (Cox and Campbell, 1968; Morgan and Ricciuti, 1969; Rheingold and Eckerman, 1973). Ainsworth and Bowlby's ethological model accounts best for the phenomenon but it is not at all clear from their theory why inanimate objects should serve this purpose. The various learning theories can only account for the behaviour by making several assumptions that do not arise directly from the theories.

Secondly, there is the consistent observation that attachment still develops in the face of maltreatment and severe punishment (Harlow and Harlow, 1971; Kovach and Hess, 1963; Seay, Alexander and Harlow, 1964). Ethological theory correctly predicts that stress should enhance attachment behaviour, but the emphasis of Bowlby (1969) and Lamb (1978) on the importance of an 'appropriate' parental response does not seem to fit easily with the findings. Cairn's contiguity conditioning theory is in keeping, but it is difficult to see how Gewirtz's reinforcement model could satisfactorily account for the observations.

Thirdly, there is the observation that attachments develop to inanimate objects (Harlow and Zimmermann, 1959; Mason and Berkson, 1975; Passman, 1977; Passman and Weisberg, 1975; Boniface and Graham, 1979). In this instance, the monkey data and human observations seem to be somewhat in conflict. Socially isolated monkeys readily develop attachments to cloth surrogates but it has been found that institutional children (who show impaired human attachments) do not. Indeed it seems that institutional children are *less* likely than family-reared children to be attached to blankets and cuddly toys. On the Bowlby–Ainsworth theory it is easy to see how strongly attached children might 'generalize' their attachments to inanimate objects. On the other hand, if there is a strong biological propensity to seek attachments (as they suggest) it is not at all clear why institutional children do not use cuddly blankets when they lack adequate human bonds. Of course, it might be suggested that the inanimate objects gain their bonding properties through association with the mother (in learning theory terms) or because of their symbolic link with the mother (in psychodynamic terms). This might explain the occurrence in normal children and its lack in institutional children, but it does not account for the animal observations, or for the fact that many normal children do *not* become attached to inanimate objects, or for the observation that autistic children (who lack attachments to their parents) show attachments to (usually non-soft) inanimate objects (Marchant, Howlin, Yule and Rutter, 1974). It may be that the mechanisms involved in these various cases are different but, so far, the observations are not well explained by any of the theories.

Fourthly, it is necessary to account for the finding that anxiety *inhibits* play but *intensifies* attachment. This is exactly what the Bowlby–Ainsworth theory predicts. The phenomenon in normal individuals is also readily explicable in social learning terms in view of the very different responses elicited by infants in the two situations. On the other hand, it is less obvious in reinforcement terms why the attachment effect should apply to inanimate objects.

Fifthly, there are the observations which suggest that not all forms of attachment are equivalent. In particular, it is necessary to explain why the monkey attachments to cloth surrogates do not lead on to normal social relationships in the way that parent and (to a lesser extent) peer attachments usually do. The distinction between secure and insecure attachment has also to be accounted for. In both instances the nature of the attached-object's response to the infant seems crucial. Social learning provides an adequate explanation as part of most of the main theories but the findings are out of keeping with a mechanistic imprinting view.

It may be concluded that none of the theories fully accounts for all the phenomena, and theoretical closure is not yet possible. The widespread occurrence of attachment in many animal species certainly suggests some kind of biological propensity, as the ethological theory suggests. Also, as suggested by almost all theories, social learning plays a major role in the process of bonding and in determining the characteristics of the parent–child relationship. However, several crucial questions have still to receive satisfactory answers.

### Early bonding and later social relationships

The last issue of controversy concerning the development of social relationships concerns the *sequelae* of early bonding. It has usually been thought that early selective bonds in some way provide the basis for later social development (Bowlby, 1969; Rutter 1978a; Sroufe, 1979), but there has been an extreme paucity of evidence on whether or not this is actually the case. There is good evidence that social bonds continue to play an important role throughout the whole of life (see Bowlby, 1980). Moreover, in many respects these adult ties seem to share many of the properties of infantile attachments. Thus, the onset of depression in adulthood is often preceded by acute life stresses which involve the loss of an important relationship by death, moving away or rebuff (Paykel *et al.*, 1969 and 1980; Brown and Harris, 1978). Also, a close confiding relationship seems to be protective when severe stresses are encountered (Eaton, 1978; Nuckolls *et al.*, 1972; Brown and Harris, 1978; Paykel *et al.*, 1980). However, what remains uncertain is whether infantile attachments are a necessary precursor of these adult relationships and whether there is developmental continuity between the two. The research findings relevant to that issue are discussed in chapter 9.

### Nature and nurture

One further point in relation to the first edition needs to be discussed in order to correct a common misconception. In the introduction it was stated that:

Quite apart from the effects of different types of 'maternal deprivation', there is good evidence that hereditary factors and organic damage or dysfunction of the brain play an important part in the genesis of emotional and behavioural disorders.

In spite of this unambiguous statement, the focus on environmental influences in the remainder of the text was sometimes interpreted as implying that genetic and other biological influences on development must be rather *un*important. It should be made clear that that assumption is not only logically unjustified but also wrong. To the contrary, there is a body of increasingly strong evidence that genetic factors are very important in development (Shields, 1973, 1977 and 1980) and that brain injury is followed by definite cognitive and psychiatric *sequelae* (Rutter, 1980d).

Intelligence may be taken as an example to illustrate the nature of the genetic evidence and its implications for the effects of 'maternal deprivation'. The findings from twin studies are well known and, in spite of the need to reject Burt's results in view of the evidence of their falsification (see Hearnshaw, 1979), the twin findings remain suggestive of genetic influences. However the genetic argument rests on very much stronger grounds than those. Perhaps the two most convincing pieces of evidence stem from adoption studies and from the findings on the offspring of twins. The adoptive studies show that adopted children's I Q scores correlate more strongly with the characteristics of their biological parents (with whom they have had no contact since early infancy) than with the characteristics of their adoptive parents who reared them; and that within adoptive families that have both biological and adopted children the parent–child correlations are substantially stronger for the biological offspring than for the adopted offspring (Scarr and Weinberg, 1978; Willerman, 1979). The findings point strongly to a genetic effect. However, even more striking evidence is provided by the recent study by Rose and his colleagues (1979) on the offspring of identical twins. They point out that, genetically speaking, the offspring of identical twin mothers comprise a maternal half-sibship who relate to their twin aunt as closely as they do to their own mother. As a result, it is possible to compare the twin aunt–niece or –nephew relationships which have this special genetic feature with the spouse aunt–niece or –nephew relationships which do not. The important point in this comparison is that environmentally the two are directly comparable. The results show the genetically predicted significant correlation, comparable to that between parent and child, in the former comparison, but a zero correlation in the latter. We are forced to conclude that, undoubtedly, there is a strong genetic influence with respect to intelligence (although there is legitimate argument on the precise level of heritability).

Does this mean, then, that there is little room for environmental influences on intellectual development? Certainly not! Firstly, as summarized in an earlier report (Rutter and Madge, 1976), there is substantial direct evidence of non-genetic influences. This applies to the adoptive groups which form the basis of the genetic studies as well as to the general population (Scarr and Weinberg, 1976; Schiff *et al.*, 1978). Secondly, even when there is a very high heritability, environmental factors may still exert a major influence. For example, it may be calculated that if I Q has an eighty-three per cent heritability (an estimate which is rather higher than generally accepted), it would still be expected on *environmental grounds alone* that the most advantaged million people in Britain would have a mean I Q some twenty-four points above the least advantaged million (Rutter and Madge, 1976). That is quite a sizeable effect by any standard. Thirdly, environmental influences may have a massive effect in raising the overall *level* of intelligence without there being any substantial effect on *individual differences*, which may still be due largely to genetic factors (Rutter and Madge, 1976). For example, this actually occurs in the case of children born to socially deprived mothers when the children are adopted in infancy into professional or otherwise advantaged homes (Skodak and Skeels, 1949; Schiff *et al.*, 1978).

On the basis, then, of this and other similar evidence (Rutter and Madge, 1976) we may conclude with some confidence both that there are very substantial genetic influences on intellectual development *and* also that there are most important environmental effects. This volume focuses on some of the issues which arise with respect to these environmental effects but it should not be assumed that this means that genetic factors are not also important.

Intelligence has been used as an example here but comparable arguments could be applied to psychosocial development. The unresolved question of whether environmental influences exert a greater or lesser effect on social behaviour than on intelligence is irrelevant to present considerations. The point is that both genetic and experimental factors are important. It should be added that, as well as genetic factors, physical disease and especially organic brain damage also exert important effects on intelligence and on psycho-social development (Rutter and Madge, 1976; Rutter, 1980d).

## Conclusions

This chapter has been mainly concerned with the review of new evidence relevant to the concepts of 'maternal deprivation' and to the hypotheses about mechanisms advanced in the first edition. It may be concluded that most of the suggestions put forward then have proved valid although, inevitably, with the growth of knowledge, the emphases on some points need some modification. However, during the last eight years attention has come to be focused on a variety of new topics which were touched on only rather lightly in the 1972 text. These are discussed in more detail in the remaining three chapters.

# 8. Social/Emotional Consequences of Day Care

In chapter 4 (page 64) it was concluded that 'the available evidence gives no reason to suppose that the use of day nurseries has any long-term psychological or physical ill-effects'. However, the evidence available in 1972 was quite limited and, in particular, there had been few studies on either the youngest children or on the social/emotional (rather than cognitive) *sequelae*. As a result of further research during the last eight years (see Rutter, 1981) we are now in a better position to review the issues. Before turning to the empirical findings, however, it may be useful to summarize the main reasons why people have worried that day care *might* have important adverse effects on social/emotional development.

The concerns over day care stem from the fear that if the child has prolonged daily separations from his parents, and if caretaking is divided among a large number of different adults, then either the bonding process may be impaired or the attachments formed will be in some way less secure or less effective in bringing comfort and security. These fears seemed to have been borne out by the evidence (discussed in more detail in chapter 9) that an institutional upbringing which involves multiple changing caretakers *has* been shown to lead to important social deficits and problems in interpersonal relationships (Tizard and Hodges, 1978; Dixon, 1980; Wolkind, 1974). Of course, there is a world of difference between institutional care without any parental involvement and day care in which the mother remains a key figure who continues to actively participate in looking after the child. For these reasons, little weight can be attached to the results of *residential* group care as a basis for assessing the probable *sequelae* of group *day* care.

Nevertheless, some links have seemed to be evident in the observations that children who experience 'pillar to post' day-care arrangements which lack both stability and continuity do appear to suffer an increased risk of emotional and social difficulties (Moore, 1963 and 1975). Unfortunately, the strength of this argument is much weakened by the fact that the day-care arrangements which lack continuity also tend to be of poor quality in many other respects. Nevertheless, although the findings are contradictory and inconclusive (see below), a few empirical studies have appeared to demonstrate that group day care does lead to insecurity and anxiety or aggression in some children. Writers who argue that day care for very young children is often damaging tend to dismiss the research findings which show that day-care children are not more often maladjusted than other children by pointing out that most of the evidence applies to children *over* the age of three years, whereas developmental considerations arising out of attachment theory suggest that it is those under three years who are most at risk (Robertson and Robertson, 1977). Moreover, the range of psychological outcome variables in most investigations has been so narrow and so limited that it would be misleading to conclude that their negative findings rule out the presence of damage. These various strands of argument, then, provide a reasonable basis both for assuming that social experiences during the first three years might well have an important influence on psychosocial development and also that there are aspects of group day care which might constitute adverse circumstances for the optimal social development of very young children. But, it is not enough to conclude on *a priori* grounds that day nurseries and child-minding centres *might* be harmful to toddlers; we need to go on to ask whether the empirical evidence suggests that group day care does in fact have the disadvantageous features that the critics allege and furthermore, if it does, whether these features often or sometimes have the ill-effects that they are supposed to have.

These matters are most conveniently examined by discussing first the overall findings on the different aspects of the psychosocial *sequelae* of day care and then secondly by proceeding to consider both the possible mechanisms involved and the possible modifying variables.

## Attachment

Initially, the concern was that group day care might in some way either prevent the development of primary selective attachments or cause the bonds to be made with the day-care staff rather than with the child's own parents (and hence possibly damage family cohesion), or result in anxious insecure attachments. The first two of these concerns have been consistently negated by the empirical findings. Not only do day-care children develop emotional bonds in much the same way and at much the same time as children reared at home, but also the main bonds are usually with the parents rather than with the child-care staff (Caldwell *et al.*, 1970; Farran and Ramey, 1977; Kagan *et al.*, 1978; Rubenstein and Howes, 1979; Ricciuti, 1974; Fox, 1977; Cummings, 1980; Reed and Leiderman, 1981). There can be reasonable confidence in this finding in that the results are so consistent across a variety of different ways of assessing attachment. Thus, children generally show more distress when separated from their mothers than from their day centre caretakers, they are more likely to go to mothers for comfort when upset, and they seem more responsive to reunion with their mothers. Furthermore, as shown by Kagan *et al.* (1978), the developmental course of separation anxiety seems very similar for day-care and home-reared children. These findings apply not only to children who experience day care for the first time at age two or three years (when it might be assumed that parent–child bonds are already well established), but also to children who attend day-care centres from the first twelve months of life when primary attachments are still forming. For example, Fox's (1977) kibbutzim children were born on the kibbutz and reared by metaplot in a group situation from four days onwards; Cummings's (1980) children first attended day-care centres at a mean age of 10·5 months; and in Kagan *et al.*'s (1978) study the children were enrolled at the centre between 3·5 and 5·5 months of age. The only serious caveats regarding the conclusion that day-care children ordinarily develop their primary bonds with parents rather than with day-centre staff is that most of the research has been undertaken with stable non-deprived families and with centres which almost certainly are of well-above-average quality.

The further question of whether day care might lead to anxious insecure attachments was raised by Blehar's (1974) finding that, compared with home-reared children, day-care children cried more, showed more oral behaviour and showed more avoidance of the stranger during Ainsworth's experimental strange person situation procedure; further-more they exhibited more avoidant and resistant behaviour upon reunion with the mother. It should be noted that the children in this study had entered day care only at two or three years of age and had been reared at home during the period when selective attachments are usually first formed.

Blehar's (1974) study has several methodological limi-tations (see Kagan *et al.*, 1978; Belsky and Steinberg, 1978) including the fact that the day-care group included more first-born children who in other studies have been found to be more liable to show adverse responses to separation (Fox, 1977). However, more importantly, other research has tended to produce rather different findings. Thus, Moskowitz *et al.* (1977) used a basically similar research design with children entering day care at about age three years. Few differences were found between the day-care and home-care children but such differences as there were suggested that, contrary to Blehar's findings, the day-care children were less upset by the strange person situation. Cornelius and Denney (1975) also found that children entering day care at about age three years were no more anxious and insecure than home-reared children (although it did seem that day care altered sex differences in the response to separation). Portnoy and Simmons (1978) looked at the responses of children who started day care at about one year of age and also at those starting at age three years; neither showed differences from the home-care children.

It is clear that most studies have failed to confirm Ble-har's findings and it is necessary to consider why her results were different. Various explanations may be suggested. Thus, it could be that Blehar's findings were an artefact of limitations in the design of the study. Alternatively, it might be that her results reflected transient short-term effects (she obained measures some four to five months after the children started at the day centre, whereas other investigators have tended to make their assessments rather later than that). Some support for this suggestion is provided by Blanchard and Main's (1979) finding (based on cross-sectional data) with younger (one- to two-year-old) children that both parental avoidance on reunion and social-emotional maladjustment *diminished* the longer a child was in day care.

However, it is also possible that the differences between the day-care and home-care children reflected patterns of parent–child interaction which *ante-dated* the day-care experience and which were not due to the experience at all. It is relevant, in this connection, that none of the studies discussed thus far had any measures of the children's behaviour before starting day care. The one exception is the investigation by Roopnarine and Lamb (1979) which used the same Ainsworth 'strange situation' procedure. Their findings suggested that the day-care children were *more* anxious and insecure than the home-care children when assessed during the week *preceding* their enrolment in day care but that they became *less* distressed and more friendly while in day care; so that three months later there were no day-care–home-care group differences. The pre-admission findings are curious and it is unclear whether they represent differences in the prior characteristics of families and children using day centres, or the children's anticipatory anxiety about a new experience. It should be noted that this study, like most others, suffers from un-certainties about the comparability of groups (this uncer-tainty is increased by the information that forty per cent of eligible families declined to participate – a possibly im-portant source of bias as shown by Cox *et al.*, 1977). Nevertheless, it is clear that the balance of the evidence from the research taken as a whole is that, at least with three-year-olds, insecure and anxious attachments are certainly not the *usual* result of day care.

Other researchers have examined the same issues with children entering day care during the infancy or toddler age-period. It is important to consider these separately, as the effects of day care at a time when selective attachments are first developing could well be different from the effects at a later age when parent–child bonds are well established. Cummings (1980) studied thirty children, all of whom had begun group care before two years of age (mean of 10·5 months) and who had experienced day care for at least two months (mean of 10·4 months). Fourteen children from the day centre waiting lists constituted the home-care comparison group (the use of waiting-list children has the major advantage of going a long way towards ensuring reasonable comparability prior to day care). Eight trials using the Cohen and Campos (1974) stranger procedure were planned. Although the day-care and home-care children did not differ in their behaviour during the first trial, far more day-care children became upset during subsequent trials; only nine of the thirty completed all conditions, compared with thirteen of the fourteen home-care children. On the other hand, although more of the day-care children became distressed in the strange situation of the laboratory, few showed distress in the familiar setting of the day-care centre.

Cochran (1977) studied 120 children aged twelve to eighteen months comparing those reared in their own home, those in a family setting being looked after by a 'day mother' together with one or two other children, and those in a group day centre with a 1:4 caretaker-to-child staff ratio. The first two groups were obtained from the day centre waiting lists, so providing reasonable control for family characteristics. Observations were made in a semi-structured separation situation in the child's own home (rather than the more commonly used laboratory setting). No differences between the groups were found in the children's responses to separation (however, few details are given and it seems that the measures may not have been either very detailed or very subtle). Doyle (1975) studied twenty-four five- to thirty-month day-care children with a matched home-care control group using the Ainsworth 'strange situation' procedure in the laboratory and a modification of the same procedure in the child's own home. Not unexpectedly the laboratory setting produced more clinging behaviour in both groups. While no overall significant differences between the home-reared and day-care infants were evident in either setting, there was a significant group by sex/by location interaction in which day-care boys showed less contact with the stranger in the lab than home-care boys whereas the reverse applied to girls.

It is obvious that too few data are available for firm conclusions to be drawn. The Cochran, Doyle, and Brookhart and Hock findings are generally reassuring about the infrequency of adverse effects on the quality of attachment, as are the Cummings observations in the day centre. On the other hand, the day-centre children in the Cummings (1980) study were much more likely to become insecure and anxious in the stressful circumstances of repeated separation procedures under unusual conditions in the laboratory. This was not the case in the Brookhart and Hock (1976) study, but it may be relevant that the experimental procedures were not identical. Although Blanchard and Main (1979) found that the pattern of parent reunion was generally similar in a day-care centre and in a laboratory, Brookhart and Hock (1976) found the latter to be more stressful. It seems likely that curious procedures involving mother, caretakers and strangers not only going in and out of rooms every minute for reasons quite obscure to the child but also not initiating interactions in the way they might usually do, could well bring latent anxieties to the surface. The findings are not consistent and it is not evident why the Brookhart and Hock (1976) and Cummings (1980) results disagree. However, questions must remain about the effects of day care on the security of toddlers' attachments. The evidence is inconclusive, but it seems that although most young children do not become overtly insecure and anxious as a result of day care, nevertheless it is possible that more subtle ill-effects occur in some children. The matter warrants further study.

## Social-emotional adjustment and behaviour

Up to this point, research findings have been considered solely in relation to attachment, which constitutes just one specific aspect of psychosocial development. It is necessary now to examine other indices of outcome, once more differentiating findings according to the age of the child. Schwarz et al. (1973) studied affect, tension and social interaction on the first day and fifth week after 3½-year-old children started attending a new day-care centre. Children who had experienced day care from before twenty-two months of age (the mean age of starting was 9·5 months) were compared with those attending a day centre for the first time (although several of these had experienced other forms of substitute care). Few statistically significant differences were found but the early day-care children tended to show more positive affect, less tension and more social interaction – especially immediately after starting at the new centre. The findings are particularly difficult to interpret because the early day-care group not only differed in having experienced day care from infancy but also in their starting at the new centre as part of a pre-existing group of children who already knew one another well. The same children were rated by their day-centre teachers four months after starting at the centre (Schwarz et al., 1974). The children who experienced day care from infancy were rated as significantly less cooperative with adults, more physically and verbally aggressive with peers and adults, and more active; there was also a tendency ($p < 0.1$ for them to be less tolerant of frustration. Putting the results of the two studies together, we may tentatively conclude that early day care had probably resulted in some differences in style of social interactions (although this did not amount to maladjustment and the differences could be a consequence of characteristics of the families rather than of the day care as such), but that the presence of familiar peers had made starting at a new centre a less strange, and probably less stressful, experience.

Macrae and Herbert-Jackson (1976) compared two-year-olds at a day centre according to whether they had experienced day care for less than six months or more than thirteen months. More prolonged day-care experience was associated with better peer relationships, but non-significant tendencies towards a lower level of frustration tolerance, a higher level of activity, and more aggression – on ratings made by caregivers. The authors comment on the differences from the Schwarz study but the similarities appear rather greater. Nevertheless, detailed comparisons are not warranted in that the age groups in the two studies were different.

Other studies, too, have tended to show both that most (but not all) infants and toddlers adapt fairly rapidly to a day-care setting and also that early day-care experiences lead to slight differences in social behaviour, although there is no particular tendency for any increase (or decrease) in maladjustment or psychosocial disorder as such. However, many of the changes in social interaction which take place during the pre-school years seem to be largely a function of maturation and of peer-group experiences rather than specifically home care or day care. For example, in one of the most detailed and systematic studies undertaken, with all the advantages of a longitudinal design, Kagan et al. (1978) showed systematic growth functions across age for interactions with other children. Apprehension in the presence of an unfamiliar child tended to peak at about twenty months, with a gradual lessening of social inhibition thereafter associated with a concomitant increase in reciprocal play during the subsequent months. However, in group-reared children the apprehension tended to diminish more quickly (in a comparison of kibbutz and family-reared Israeli children) or to wax and wane at an earlier age (as in the study of day-care and home-reared children in the USA). American children who had experienced day care from infancy played more than home-reared children in an unfamiliar day-care centre, suggesting that they may have been less apprehensive. The finding is not unexpected as, of course, the situation would be a less novel one for them. While day care did not seem to substantially alter children's basic social behaviour, the mothers of day-care children regarded them as more patient and less shy with adults, compared with home-care children.

It also seems that day-care experiences may alter patterns of parent–child interaction at home. Vandell (1979) compared six play-group and six home-care families with sixteen-month-old boys, using observations in a semistructured laboratory setting furnished as a living room. Measures were taken before the beginning of the play group and three and six months later. The changes over time indicated that the play-group experience was associated with an increase in proximity-seeking and in object-related social acts (i.e. showing, offering or demonstrating objects) together with a decrease in the extent to which the toddlers terminated parent–child interactions. It is uncertain whether the changes reflect an increase in insecurity or a rise in social skills.

McCutcheon and Calhoun (1976) observed five- to thirty-month-old infants one week and again one month after entering a day-care programme. During that first month at the centre, crying decreased in frequency (from 9·5 per cent to 4·3 per cent of observations) and interactions with other children increased. Finkelstein *et al.* (1978) observed two groups of day-centre children, infants in the seven- to fourteen-month age range and toddlers in the fifteen- to thirty-one-month age range. The toddlers showed more peer interactions and greater social responsiveness. The implication that peers are likely to play a greater role in the socialization of older pre-school children is also borne out by other research (Rubenstein and Howes, 1979). Raph *et al.* (1968) found that social interactions increased with age, irrespective of nursery school experience. Negative interactions with other children *decreased* and negative interactions with teachers *increased* between three and five years; this tendency was marginally greater in those with the greatest prior nursery group experience.

The only study of the long-term effects of day care is that by Moore (1975). As part of a longitudinal study of London children, he compared those who had experienced full-time home care by the mother ('exclusive mothering') and those who had had some form of substitute day care ('diffused mothering'), usually beginning just before age three years. Interview and questionnaire measures were taken at six to eight years and fifteen years. For boys, the findings from the mothers' inventory indicated that exclusive mothering tended to result in 'sensitive fastidious conformity' to adult- rather than peer-group standards, self-control, timidity and academic interests. In contrast, diffused mothering tended to result in 'fearless aggressive non-conformity' to parental requirements with outgoing, active, social interests which showed a peer-group orientation. The group differences for girls were fewer, smaller, and less consistent. However, the exclusive and diffused mothering groups (especially for boys) also differed in terms of maternal personality measures, so that the differences in the children might well reflect family features as much as the experience or non-experience of day care. It should be added that there was substantial overlap between the groups and also that the findings generally reflected personality variations within the normal range rather than maladjustment. However, there was a tendency for the exclusively mothered boys to have more fears at age four to five years; the observation that this difference only emerged after day care began implies that day care in the older pre-school child may actually somewhat *diminish* fearfulness. On the other hand, day care which began before age two years was associated with an *increase* in fearfulness. Because early day care tended to involve unstable changing patterns of child care, it remains uncertain whether the findings reflect the age of the child when group day care commenced or rather the consequences of frequent changes of substitute care and generally unstable family circumstances.

Thus, the results suggest that group day care may well incline children to be somewhat more assertive and peer-oriented but that it does not usually result in any increase or decrease in psychosocial disorder as such. However, Moore's (1975) findings emphasize that the consequences may well depend on the quality, consistency and overall pattern of substitute care provided.* So far the research findings have been discussed simply in terms of whether children had or had not experienced group day care. While most studies have been reported in this way, the implicit assumption that 'day care' encompasses a homogeneous set of experiences is obviously untenable. The other implicit assumption, that the parents who utilize day care are similar to those who do not, is equally questionable. Accordingly, we need to turn now to those investigations which provide data on either point.

## Characteristics of day care

Not only does day care take several different forms, but it also differs from home care on a variety of dimensions, including multiplicity of caretakers, continuity in caretaking, upbringing as part of a same-age peer group, and the experience of new environments. Of course, too, it might also vary in the characteristics of adult–child interaction.

### Caregiver–child interactions

That possibility has been examined in several different studies of rather different types of day care. Rubenstein *et al.* (1977) observed the interactions with thirty-eight mother-reared and seventeen substitute-reared black infants aged five to six months. Fifteen of the latter group had been looked after by relatives and twelve by non-related baby-sitters, some of whom provided care in their own and some in the infants' homes. It was found that the mothers provided a more stimulating and responsive environment than did the substitute

* Bryant, Harris and Newton (1980) reported that a quarter of the children cared for by childminders were rather detached and inactive, and nearly half were quiet at the minders' but lively at home. As no control group was employed it is not known if this is a higher rate of inactivity than in children not in day care. However, the children's socio-emotional disturbance at the minders' was *very strongly* associated with serious family difficulties and only moderately associated with characteristics of the mother–child relationship. This suggests that the socio-emotional problems stemmed in large part from disturbances *outside* day care in the child's own family, but that such vulnerable children are also more likely to be adversely affected by cold, unaffectionate minding.

caretakers – as shown by more positive affect, more playful interactions and a greater variety of experiences. However, the substitute caretakers who had had the infants for a longer period of time were more like the mothers, suggesting that some of the differences were a function of the short duration of the caretaker–infant relationship.

Rubenstein and Howes (1979) also compared caretaker–infant interaction with eighteen-month-old Caucasian children attending day-care centres and comparable children being reared at home. In many respects the interactions in the two settings were very similar but there were some differences. For example, adults in the day-care centres patted the children more frequently and held them longer; were more likely physically to intervene to help infants with objects and were more likely to enter into a game with the infant and toy. On the other hand, mothers were more verbally directive and were more restrictive of infant exploration and play. Positive affective exchanges between infant and caretaker (such as reciprocal smiling, hugging and mutual play) were more frequent in day care; and more negative affect was expressed at home by both infants and caretakers – as shown by more crying and more reprimanding. Obviously, peer interactions were more frequent in the day centres just because in many instances there were no peers in the home. However, a comparison of the eight home-reared infants who had a peer with whom they played regularly and twelve day-care infants matched for ordinal position, showed that peer interactions were generally similar in the two settings. It appeared, too, that the presence of peers influenced caretaker–infant interaction; maternal reprimands were reduced in the home-reared sample when peers came to visit (Rubenstein and Howes, 1976).

Cochran (1977) also compared interactions with twelve- to eighteen-month-old children in day centres and in the infants' own homes; in addition he also studied day care in which the infant was with a substitute caretaker in her own home with just one or two other children. Like Rubenstein and Howes (1979) he found that interactions were similar in many respects but mothers were more controlling (as shown by a higher frequency of 'do's' and 'dont's'), with the family home caretakers more like mothers than day-centre caretakers. Verbal interactions were also more frequent in both types of family home than in the day centres.

From these findings it appears that the social context is likely to influence caretaker–child interaction. Family homes must function as living quarters for parents as well as children while day centres are designed exclusively for child care. As a consequence, mothers may need to exercise more control than do centre caretakers simply because there are more objects about that are not suitable for infant play. It may also be that the isolated setting of the home makes more demands on the mother; the infant's needs compete with the need to undertake household chores and to have social contact with other adults (Rubenstein and Howes, 1979). The presence of another child with whom the infant may play may also reduce the intensity of pressure on the caretaker. The amount and quality of adult–child interaction in day centres is also likely to be influenced by the staff–child ratio. Centre staff have the advantage over mothers of not having many other competing activities so that they are able to devote all their time to child care. On the other hand, this advantage may be reversed if the centre caretaker has many children to look after, so that there is inadequate opportunity for individual play and interaction with any one child.

This issue was examined systematically by Stallings and Porter (1980) in a study of 303 family day-care homes (i.e. substitute care in private homes rather than in day centres). In general it was found that caregivers provided a positive and supportive environment for the children, with positive affect much more frequent than negative. The caregivers spent about half their time interacting with the children and the other half in different activities. Caregivers in officially sponsored or regulated homes tended to be more actively involved with the children and talked with them more; such homes also tended to provide a safer physical environment. In homes with several infants and toddlers, individual children received less caretaker attention and it appeared that toddlers were likely to fare best in homes with only a few children. The findings suggested that children become a little more unruly when there are several toddlers together and the caregiver spends more time controlling their behaviour and less time engaged in developmental activities. In short, it seems that the presence of another similar-aged child is an advantage for toddlers but that homes with several toddlers all together may place undue strains on caretakers with subsequent disadvantages for the children.

The family day care provided in the homes studied by Stallings and Porter (1980) was of a generally satisfactory standard but this is not universally so. In Mayall and Petrie's (1977) study of British childminders the quality of care proved to be very variable. In some cases it was fine but in others it was not. Many children looked after by childminders spent a low-level under-stimulated day in cramped surroundings; some lacked love and attention, and some experienced frequent unsettling changes of minder.*

## Polymatric versus monomatric upbringing

Day care also differs from home care in terms of the number of adults who look after the child. A traditional home upbringing is usually described as monomatric, as if there was only one adult who provided parenting for the child. Of course, this is misleading. There may be only one mother but fathers often take an active role in looking after and playing with the children (Lamb, 1976), and in addition grandparents, older brothers and sisters and other relatives or neighbours may also play a role. Nevertheless, it certainly is the case that day care usually involves a greater dispersion of child care among a larger number of adults than is usually the case with infants reared solely at home. Patterns of polymatric infant care take many forms: ranging from the Israeli kibbutzim (Fox, 1977) where the caretaking is provided in a setting designed specifically for the purpose; to

* The Oxford studies of childminding (Bryant, Harris and Newton, 1980) and of group day care (Garland and White, 1980) also showed variations in quality and characteristics of care which had possible implications for the development of the children (Bruner, 1980).

the more informal, less structured arrangements of shared care in the East African Highlands (Leiderman and Leiderman, 1974); to the rather varied arrangements associated with day care in Western societies. While it seems evident that the development of attachments* follows much the same course when there are several stable caretakers rather than just one (Fox, 1977; Reed and Leiderman, 1981), nevertheless questions remain on the consequences of having *many* different caretakers and especially of having a roster of changing caretakers. It has been shown that the latter situation is associated with anomalous psychosocial development if it constitutes the *only* care arrangement, as it does in residential care (Tizard and Hodges, 1978; Dixon, 1980). However, the circumstances of day care are different in that stability is provided in the form of the child's own parents who share the care with the day-centre staff. The issue, then is: what are the effects of consistency or inconsistency of individualized caretaking in the day centre, when there is consistency in parenting at home? The matter has been little studied so far but there are a few relevant investigations.

Cummings (1980) compared attachment behaviours in twelve- to twenty-eight-month-old infants in relation to 'stable' caretakers (i.e. those who had worked at the centre a long time) and 'unstable' caretakers (i.e. those who had been there only a brief time). In the day-care environment the infants showed a preference for 'stable' caretakers, but the trend was less marked and short of statistical significance in the more strange and stressful laboratory situation. The findings were not particularly clearcut, but they suggested that children formed a sort of intermediate attachment to caretakers, greater than that to strangers but substantially less than that to mothers – with the attachment to 'stable' caretakers greater than that to 'unstable' caretakers. While the findings show that attachments to caretakers tend to be greater when the children have known them some time, they

---

* As already discussed, 'attachment' is not a unitary concept and it may well be misleading either to rely on just one measure or to pool all together as if they all meant the same thing, as in many studies up to now.

do not deal with the crucial comparison between day care in which there is consistency in individualized caregiving and day care in which there is not.

That comparison was made, however, by Wilcox *et al.* (1980) in a study in which twelve- to twenty-four-month-old infants were assigned in a quasi-random fashion to two otherwise identical nurseries: in one there were five caregivers and twenty infants with care so arranged that each caregiver was assigned to four specific infants; in the other nursery there was multiple caretaking so that the five adults shared responsibility for all twenty children. Most of the infants came from socially disadvantaged black families. Observations were made of social contacts at the day centre and of separations from and reunions with the mother. No differences in mother-attachment (as judged from the child's observed behaviour during separations from and reunions with the mother) were found between the infants in the individual and in the multiple caregiver assignment settings. However, there was a rather limited range of outcome variables and, perhaps more importantly, it was found that in the supposedly individually assigned caregiver setting, nearly half of the child's adult contacts were with someone other than the assigned caregiver – a proportion no different from that in the multiple assignment setting. It appears that in a group day-care setting with as many as twenty children in one room, practicalities mean that very little individualized caregiving is possible. As a result, this investigation failed to provide an adequate test of individualized versus multiple caregiving.

Mention has already been made of Moore's (1963 and 1975) study which showed that unstable, frequently changing day-care arrangements seemed to lead to insecurity and emotional upset. However, not only is it uncertain how far the ill-effects stemmed from the pattern of day care itself (rather than the family difficulties which led to it), but it is also unclear how far the insecurity was a result of multiplicity of caregivers and how far a consequence of the repeated major changes in caregiving arrangements.

It is all too obvious that we have insufficient data for any firm conclusions on this important issue. Nevertheless, it may be useful to look at the described characteristics of the day centres concerned in the reports suggesting possibly adverse effects of day care. In the Blehar (1974) study, the staff–child ratio was 1 : 6 to 1 : 8; from the statement that 'two caregivers were assigned to each group' it may be inferred that the children were probably in groups of twelve to sixteen; nothing is said about individualized assignment of caregivers. In the Schwarz *et al.* (1974) study, the staff–pupil ratio was similar (1 : 7) and there was no individualized assignment. In the Cummings (1980) study, the staffing ratio was better (1 : 4), but again there was no individualized assignment and the group size was fifteen to twenty. The Moore (1975) report involved a variety of day centres and settings but the adverse effects were found in children with an early experience of care with changing caregivers and settings. Of course, all of these characteristics also applied to centres where studies have *not* shown adverse effects, and neither the numbers nor the nature of the data allow systematic comparisons. However, certain tentative suggestions may be made. Firstly, it seems highly likely that the effects of multiple non-individualized caregiving in an institution which lacks any primary caregiver will be quite different from the effects of multiple caregiving which is supplemental to an ordinary upbringing by the child's parent in his own home – the former is often damaging whereas the latter may not be. Secondly, however, truly individualized caregiving during day care is more likely than multiple caregiving to foster attachments which will bring the child comfort and security at times of stress. We do not know how important this difference is in practice and it may well vary according to the quality and security of the child's relationships at home. Thirdly, both because it will involve adaptation to new environments and because it may involve loss of attachment-figures, it seems likely that multiple changes of day-care arrangements will prove unsettling for many children.

One further issue in this connection is whether there are advantages in polymatric child-rearing just because it allows the child to develop multiple attachments and hence a greater range of sources of security and a less precarious reliance on a single relationship. Once again, the crucial data are lacking. However, it may be that the key question is how far the pattern of care *actually* leads to multiple attachments of any strength and utility. In this connection, the kibbutzim findings (Fox, 1977) and the East African findings (Leiderman and Leiderman, 1974; Reed and Leiderman, 1981) both suggest that these forms of polymatric care *do* lead to multiple functional attachments, although the attachments to the substitute caretakers are generally less strong than those to the mothers. On the other hand, Cummings's (1980) data suggest that group day care with multiple shared caregiving leads to such weak attachments (forty per cent of the children failed to approach the caregiver in any of the test conditions), that the attachments are of little use to the child.

## Employed and unemployed mothers

A further issue concerns the differences between employed and unemployed mothers. Actually, this involves several rather different questions including the differences between families that use and families that do not use day care; the effect of having a job outside the home on the mother's self-esteem, satisfaction and mental health; the effects of the use of day care on parent–child interaction; and the consequences for the child of having two working parents.

The issues were well reviewed by Hoffman (1974) who has recently updated her appraisal of maternal employment (Hoffman, 1979). The main findings may be summarized as follows. Firstly, there are differences between families using and not using day care. These involve social and ethnic features, (as illustrated in the study by Winett *et al.*, 1977) and they involve marital circumstances (for example, Cohen, 1978, found that employed mothers were more likely to be without a cohabiting husband). In addition, however, working mothers may differ in their attitudes in ways which could influence their infant's response to day care. Thus, Hock (1978) found that, as well as being more career-oriented, working mothers perceived less infant distress at separation, were less anxious about separation and were generally less apprehensive about other caregivers. Of course, these findings could mean both that the mothers' lack of anxiety may make it easier for their children to adapt positively to day care, and also that the mothers may be less perceptive of insecurities when and if they arise. Thus, Cohen (1978) found a tendency for employed mothers to show less 'reciprocal positive attentiveness' than non-employed mothers.

Secondly, a variety of studies have shown that when the mother has a job outside the home fathers tend to take a more active role in family life (although this is likely to be influenced by the father's attitude to his wife's return to work; Lamb, 1979), children tend to take on more household responsibilities and it is more likely that someone outside the home will be involved in child care (Hoffman, 1974; Winett *et al.*, 1977; Gold and Andres, 1978a and b). Not surprisingly, the fact that there tends to be less differentiation between the parents in both work and parenting roles has meant a similar tendency for the children to have a less differentiated or otherwise modified perception of sex roles (Marantz and Mansfield, 1977; Vogel *et al.*, 1970; Gold and Andres, 1978a and b). On the other hand, the evidence is consistent in showing that this is not associated with any increase in rates of psychosocial disorder (Hoffman, 1974; Rutter, 1979d).

Thirdly, it has been found that the experience of having a paid job outside the home may have beneficial effects on the mother's sense of well-being. Most studies have found that, compared with housewives, employed women have a greater sense of self-esteem and personal satisfaction in their role (Gold and Andres, 1978a and b; Radloff, 1975; Newberry *et al.*, 1979). The findings with respect to mental health are more contradictory, with some finding no differences between employed and non-employed women, but others finding that employment serves as a factor protecting working-class women from depression (Brown and Harris, 1978; Roy, 1978). Many (but by no means all) full-time housewives are dissatisfied with their situation (Gavron, 1966; Oakley, 1974), and Yarrow *et al.* (1962) found that child-rearing posed most difficulties for women who wanted to work but who remained at home out of a sense of duty. Clearly, what remaining at home or having a job does for the mother's mental state is likely to make a big difference to the children (Hoffman, 1974). It may well be more important to have a satisfied, happy mother than to have a mother at home all day (Rutter, 1979d). Whether maternal employment is or is not a good thing for the family is likely to depend very much on whether the mother wants to work. Presumably, too, it matters whether the job proves to be a satisfying one and not so tiring as to lead to role strain or conflict. Many mothers of young children prefer part-time work; stress and fatigue may result if full-time work is the only available alternative.

Fourthly, there are scattered, rather contradictory findings that employed women may differ from housewives in their styles of interaction with their children either as a result of pre-existing differences or as a result of their having been away from their child all day (Winett et al., 1977; Belsky and Steinberg, 1978; Cohen, 1978; Vandell, 1979). It is not self-evident that day care will necessarily reduce the amount of exclusive, intensive parent–child interaction. It could mean that on return from work parents are more likely to arrange uninterrupted time to play and talk with their children – or it could mean that the involvement in a job outside the home reduces interest in the children. The data to decide between these and other alternatives are not yet available, but there is a need to consider both maternal employment and day care in terms of its impact on the broader ecological systems within which children develop (Belsky and Steinberg, 1978).

## Modifying factors in children's responses to day care

Finally, it is important to consider possible modifying factors which may influence how children respond to day care. The few research findings available to date suggest that the relevant variables may include the child's age, sex, ordinal position, temperament, prior experiences and relationship with his own parents.

It is well established that children's responses to hospital admission are much influenced by their age at the time (see chapter 3) and it seems that developmental maturity similarly influences responses to other separation experiences (Robertson and Robertson, 1971). On these grounds and on what is known about the course of the development of selective attachments (Kagan *et al.*, 1978; Rutter, 1980a; Reed and Leiderman, 1981) it would be expected that reactions to day care would also vary according to the age at which commenced. Actually, there are surprisingly few direct examinations of age differences. However, it is known that children's responses to peers change with increasing age (Kagan *et al.*, 1978), and that peer interactions and reciprocal social behaviours are more frequent among toddlers than among infants (Finkelstein *et al.*, 1978), and still more common among three- to five-year-olds than among toddlers (Stallings and Porter, 1980). The importance of peers in influencing young children's play, interaction with adults, and response to separation has been suggested by Rubenstein and Howes' (1976 and 1979) findings and it may be that older pre-school children are better able to take advantage of the peer group opportunities; although even toddlers do so to some extent. Findings on age trends in separation-protest would suggest that day care might be more stressful for infants under the age of $2\frac{1}{2}$ or three years than for older pre-school children, but empirical evidence to indicate whether or not this is in fact the case is lacking. (Moore's 1975 results are consistent with the suggestion, but there are too many confounding variables to have confidence in the finding; moreover, other studies suggest the converse (Blehar, 1974) or no differences (Portnoy and Simmons, 1978), so the matter must remain open.)

Several studies have shown that the effects of day care are more marked, more consistent and somewhat different in the case of boys compared with girls (Cornelius and Denney, 1975; Brookhart and Hock, 1976; Portnoy and Simmons, 1978; Moskowitz *et al.*, 1977; Moore, 1975). The sex differences in these various studies are not identical, so no coherent set of conclusions is yet possible. Cornelius and Denney (1975) found that day-care boys were more independent and interacted more with the strange male adult; Brookhart and Hock (1976) found that with respect to contact-maintaining behaviours boys and girls responded in the opposite fashion to day care; Moskowitz *et al.* (1977) found that day-care boys functioned more independently in the mother's presence but were responsive to her return from a separation (note that all these results refer to a group by sex interaction effect); Portnoy and Simmons (1978) found that boys cried more and showed more resistance and avoidance of the strange than did girls; Moore (1975) found that the personality differences which followed day care were more marked and more consistent in boys. While the sex difference findings remain rather inconclusive so far, it is highly probable that ultimately they will prove to be valid and meaningful in view of the evidence of sex differences in children's responses to other forms of stress (see chapter 10).

Fox (1977) found that first-born children were more anxious than later-born children during an experimental separation procedure. The matter has been little investigated otherwise but there is a substantial body of evidence indicating that parents tend to interact differently with their first-born than with their later-born children (see below). Thus, it would seem plausible that ordinal position might influence responses to day care – the matter warrants study.

Although there is a growing body of evidence indicating the importance of temperamental differences in relation to various aspects of psychosocial development and of responses to stress (see Ruter, 1977c; Dunn, 1980), little is known regarding its importance with respect to day care. However, it may be relevant that Kagan *et al.* (1978) found quite marked differences between Chinese and Caucasian babies in their responses to separation. Once more, the variable requires investigation.

It would be expected that children's prior experiences of happy and of unhappy separations as well as of interaction with peers might well influence their responses to day care. There are suggestive findings that this may be the case for children's responses to hospital admission (Stacey *et al.*, 1970) and there is some indication that this also applies to day care

(Schwarz *et al.*, 1973) but the data so far provide no more than tentative leads.

Lastly, it is necessary to consider family characteristics and the nature of the child's relationships with his own parents. The whole notion of 'insecure' attachments (Stayton and Ainsworth, 1973) implies that the quality of bonding will influence the child's response to separation-experiences and hence one might infer that children with 'insecure' attachments (whether as a result of their own temperament or the quality of their upbringing) might be more vulnerable to the adverse effects of day care. Circumstantial support is provided by the animal data (Hinde and Spencer-Booth, 1970) which showed that the infant monkeys who showed most distress after separation were those whose relationship with their mothers had shown most tension *before* the separation. Also, it appears that human infants from discordant or otherwise troubled homes are more likely to show disorder following repeated hospital admissions (Quinton and Rutter, 1976). However, both situations are rather remote from that of day care and it would be unwise to do more than conclude that the findings suggest that it would be most worthwhile to examine the issue further.

## Conclusions

While it is clear that some of the more alarming stereotypes about day care can be rejected, it is equally obvious that we have some way to go before we are in a position to make well-based policy decisions on what type of care is most suitable for which children in which circumstances. Heinicke *et al.* (1973), Pilling and Pringle (1978), Belsky and Steinberg (1978) and Kagan *et al.* (1978) have all made valuable suggestions on some of the key issues to be considered; others have been introduced here. We know that good quality day care does not disrupt a child's emotional bonds with his parents; moreover, children continue to prefer their parents over alternative caregivers. Furthermore, even day care for very young children does not *usually* result in serious emotional disturbance. On the other hand, there are indications that to some extent day care influences the form of children's social behaviour (in ways which may be either helpful or deleterious). Also there are pointers that the ways in which it does so may be determined by the specific characteristics of the day care (and by its quality – it is important to note that most research has concerned day centres of above-average quality), by the age and other characteristics of the child, and by the characteristics of the family (including the meaning of maternal employment and the meaning of day care for the parents). It would be wrong to conclude that day care is without effects and it would be misleading to assume that it carries no risks (even though these have been greatly exaggerated in the past). What is now needed is research which moves beyond the crude day care versus home care comparison in order to determine which aspects of care, in which circumstances, have which effects.

# 9. Long-Term Effects of Early Life Experiences

## Critical periods

The idea that the infancy years have an over-riding importance in development and the related notion of 'critical or sensitive periods' were discussed in chapter 4. Both continue to be controversial concepts (Oyama, 1979; Clarke and Clarke, 1976) and require more extended discussion in the light of new evidence (see Rutter, 1980e).

The original view of 'critical periods' was closely associated with imprinting in birds and it came to carry implications of developmental fixity, of restriction to a very narrow period of development, of a high degree of specificity, and of permanent and irreversible effects. This type of notion of fixed and absolute 'critical periods' has now been shown to involve so many exceptions and to require so many qualifications (even in the case of imprinting – Bateson, 1966; Hinde, 1970; Sluckin, 1973) that probably it no longer warrants further consideration with respect to human psychosocial development.* At the other extreme, the broader notion of 'sensitive periods' sometimes implies no more than the presence of a phase of heightened responsiveness to certain kinds of stimuli (Oyama, 1979). This idea has obvious validity, and controversy centres around the specifics of its application rather than the general idea itself.

Rather than discuss that overall concept any further, attention needs to be focused on the suggestion that infancy and the early years of life have a special over-riding importance

---

*Certain aspects of visual development (see e.g. Wiesel and Hubel, 1965; Daw et al., 1978) may well have a critical period in the original sense, but this provides a rather special exception which probably does not have a parallel in the field of psychosocial development.

in personality development. Alan and Ann Clarke (1976) have documented much of the evidence that runs counter to that suggestion and have proposed instead that the *whole* of development is important, with the infancy period no less so, but equally no more so, than the years of middle and later childhood. Their view has been both vigorously attacked as wrong (Pringle, 1976), and criticized as over-simplistic in focusing on an 'inoculation' view of early experiences rather than the more plausible developmental hypothesis that happenings in infancy have a special importance, *not* because infancy experiences are biologically critical, but rather because early experiences may influence later vulnerability by increasing or decreasing sensitivity to later stresses (Sroufe, 1977). The topic as a whole is a very large one, but most of the theorizing and most of the empirical findings apply to just two aspects of development: cognition and socialization.

In both cases the main arguments in favour of the critical nature of the early years are a) many disorders have their roots in early childhood; b) therapeutic interventions in later childhood have usually been rather unsuccessful in the case of persistent disorders; and c) the correlations (for I Q or personality measures) with adult status rise rapidly during the first half of childhood with much less change in the second half. All three arguments are unsatisfactory (Rutter, 1974). In the first place, critical periods can only be studied when there are major environmental changes. Psychosocial disadvantages tend to be *very persistent* and the continuities in development will necessarily be influenced by continuities in deprivation. In the second place, comparisons between the effects of environmental change at age two after two years of deprivation and environmental change at twelve after twelve years of deprivation are not at all comparable. In no way do these provide an appropriate test of critical periods. In the third place, most therapeutic interventions in later childhood consist of *talking* about adapting to disadvantage – only very rarely do they actually involve complete *changes* of environment. Little is to be gained by considering such arguments. Instead we have to focus on direct investigations of environmental change at different ages.

## The development of language and of intelligence

The first question with respect to intellectual and language development is whether an environment which improves only in middle or later childhood leads to major gains. The evidence is unequivocal that it does. This is most dramatically shown by the achievement of normal intelligence in severely deprived children who have been rescued from their appalling circumstances only at the age of six or seven years (Davis, 1947; Koluchova, 1972 and 1976). Thus, in the Koluchova twins an IQ in the forties at age seven years increased to 100 at age fourteen years; similarly, Dennis (1973) found an increase of some thirty points in Lebanese orphans moved from a poor to a better institution at age six years. Even later improvements were shown by Genie, who was not removed from her appallingly deprived environment until age thirteen years (Curtiss, 1977). When discovered she was incontinent, without language, able to walk only with difficulty, and had a non-verbal mental age of less than five years. Four years later Genie still had many problems but she was talking in phrases and had a non-verbal mental age of eleven years. Less dramatically, Swedish studies have shown that continued schooling in late adolescence also leads to IQ gains (Harnqvist, 1968; Husen, 1951). It is quite clear that major environmental improvements in middle childhood can lead to substantial increases in IQ.

The second question is whether adverse experiences in infancy can lead to *enduring* linguistic or intellectual impairment even when experiences during middle and later childhood are positive and beneficial. Of course, much is likely to depend both on the severity and duration of early deprivation and also on the quality of later experiences. Moreover, as already evident in the answer to the first question, it is clear that even the damage due to very severe early privation is to a considerable extent reversible later in childhood if the environmental change is sufficiently great and if the later experiences are sufficiently good. There is much evidence to indicate that the persistence of ill-effects is heavily dependent on the persistence of the adverse experiences (Clarke and

Clarke, 1976; Kagan *et al.*, 1978). Nevertheless, the question of whether traumata experienced *only* in infancy can have long-term *sequelae* is not an unimportant one. That the adverse effects of early deprivation can be greatly reduced by later beneficial experiences is no longer in doubt, but is the reversibility complete? At first sight it seems surprising that there is so little empirical evidence on this crucial point. However, the main reason for the lack of data is that it is so rare to have severe deprivation in infancy and yet a good environment throughout the rest of childhood.

Studies of late adoption are about the only examples we have of this phenomenon. The findings are consistent in showing that the I Q scores of later-adopted children tend to be slightly lower than those of children adopted in infancy (Goldfarb, 1943a; Dennis, 1973; Tizard and Hodges, 1978). It is difficult to entirely rule out biases due to selective placement but the implication is that later adoption may not entirely remove the impairments consequent upon early privation.

A more stringent test, perhaps, is provided by Winick *et al.*'s (1975) study of Korean orphans adopted into American families at a mean age of eighteen months (but removed from their poor home environment at an unspecified earlier age). At follow-up, during the elementary school years, the children had a mean I Q above 100 and average levels of scholastic achievement, both being well above those expected if the children had returned to their original poor background. The findings suggest a very considerable degree of recovery. However, the children who were originally severely malnourished had a mean I Q at follow-up which was still ten points below that for the well-nourished group (102 *vs* 112), and a level of scholastic attainment which was nearly one standard deviation lower. The implication is that the effects of very early malnutrition had not yet been fully reversed. The findings on the persistence or otherwise of the effects of psychosocial privation are much less clearcut in that no within-group comparisons on this dimension were possible. Moreover, it has to be borne in mind that the adverse experiences in infancy lasted on average only a few months (with a maximum in any individual child of two years), and that a third of the children could not be traced.

It is all too clear that the decisive evidence on the enduring effects of adverse experiences restricted to infancy is still lacking. However, we may tentatively conclude that, although the effects are very greatly modified by later experiences, nevertheless some residual consequences of early adversities may sometimes remain.

The third question is the converse of the second, namely: can *good* experiences which are restricted to the infancy period have a *lasting* beneficial impact even when experiences during middle and later childhood are disadvantageous? The extreme form of the proposition, that is the suggestion that good experiences during the early years can protect children from the ill-effects of later disadvantage, can be firmly ruled out. Numerous investigations have shown that the substantial IQ gains associated with good pre-school compensatory education programmes diminish and then disappear within four or five years, if not sooner (Bronfenbrenner, 1974; Horowitz and Paden, 1973; Rutter and Madge, 1976). Furthermore, as Fogelman and Goldstein (1976) showed, children whose families go down the social scale during the middle years fall in IQ.

However, these findings do not necessarily mean that there are *no* lasting benefits. Indeed, the recent American follow-up of mainly black children from low-income families who attended experimental pre-school programmes suggests that there may be some enduring effects (Darlington *et al.*, 1980). At follow-up, the children were in third to twelfth grade (with a median of seventh grade). Confirming earlier reports, the children from the experimental programmes did not differ from controls in IQ. However, fewer of the experimental children had been assigned to special education classes (fourteen per cent *vs* twenty-nine per cent) and somewhat fewer had had to repeat a school year (twenty-six per cent *vs* thirty-seven per cent).

These findings on aspects of school performance are encouraging (although the possibility of a placement artefact resulting from the school's knowledge that the child had been in an experimental programme can not be ruled out) and stand in contrast to the consistently negative findings regarding lasting effects on I Q scores. The data needed to provide an adequate interpretation of these results are not so far available. However, it should be appreciated that they do not necessarily mean that early experiences had lasting effects which were independent of later experiences. Rather it may be that the pre-school programmes led to changes in the children's approaches to school work which had more enduring benefits just because they altered the teachers' responses to the children.

The fourth question is whether environmental effects on intellectual development are greater in infancy than in later childhood. The already noted finding that later-adopted children tend to have lower I Qs than those of early-adopted children suggest that they may be. Nevertheless, they do not necessarily indicate a real age difference in environmental effects on intellectual growth. Firstly, the durations of deprivation in the two situations are not comparable. By definition, the late-adopted children had been deprived for longer and the lesser gains could be simply a function of that fact. Secondly, the amount and character of parent–child interaction in middle childhood is very different from that in the pre-school years. It may be that the lesser intellectual gains in older late-adopted children was just due to the fact that they had less opportunity for interacting with their parents.

Another approach to the same issue is provided by studies of the effects of schooling. Compensatory educational programmes in the first five years of life have been found to be associated with immediate I Q gains* (Bronfenbrenner, 1974; Horowitz and Paden, 1973). Do similar I Q gains follow schooling during the middle years of childhood? That is a difficult question to answer in industrialized societies because virtually all children attend school and those who do not tend to be handicapped in one way or another. On the other

*As already noted, these tend not to persist if the programmes cease. However, the benefits of more intensive and extensive pre-school interventions may be more lasting, as shown by the Heber and Garber study (Garber and Heber, 1977; Heber, 1978).

hand, there are developing countries where this is not the case and they have provided interesting and relevant findings on this point. Stevenson and his colleagues (1978) investigated the influence of schooling and general environmental conditions on the development of cognitive skills among five- and six-year-old children living in jungle villages and slum settlements in Peru. Attendance at school was related to improvement in all cognitive tasks. In that non-attendance at school seemed to be largely a function of lack of opportunity, the implication is that schooling improved cognitive performance. The conclusion is not entirely certain in that the data were cross-sectional rather than longitudinal, but the circumstantial evidence for a schooling effect on the specific aspects of cognition which were assessed was strong. Sharp, Cole and Lave's (1979) findings for adolescents and adults in rural Yucatan in Mexico point to the same conclusion. The limited results from studies in Western societies are confirmatory. DeGroot (1951) found a drop of some five I Q points for the generation of Dutch youngsters who missed out on their education as a result of the Second World War. Similar effects were found following the closure of some schools in the U S A to avoid integration (Jencks *et al.*, 1972). Moreover, Swedish studies (Husen, 1951; Harnqvist, 1968) have shown that continued schooling during later adolescence is associated with a mean I Q gain of some five to seven points. While the results of these various studies do not allow a quantitative comparison of the effects of schooling in infancy and in later childhood, it is clear that schooling does have beneficial effects on cognitive performance at all times from the pre-school years to adolescence.

The last question we need to consider with respect to the early years and cognitive development is whether there is a sensitive period for language acquisition such that first language acquisition must occur during the first twelve years if it is to proceed normally (Lenneberg, 1967). The notion is primarily based on the finding that the recovery from aphasia-producing brain lesions tends to be better in childhood than in adult life, and on the view that cerebral dominance for language becomes complete only about the time of puberty. Recent research suggests that the age-differences in extent of recovery from aphasia were exaggerated by differences in the types of brain lesions which occur at different age periods (James-Roberts, 1979). Nevertheless, it remains well substantiated that unilateral brain lesions are not only less likely to lead to permanent language impairment if they occur during early childhood, but also that the effects are qualitatively different in being associated with speech delay rather than with aphasic-type abnormalities. Ideas about the timing and nature of the acquisition of cerebral dominance also have had to undergo some modification as a result of new evidence (Segalowitz and Gruber, 1977); and concepts of what is meant by 'plasticity' of brain functioning, too, have developed and changed (Stein *et al.*, 1974).

It is evident that the views of brain functioning which were generally held during the 1960s were not entirely correct. Even so, it is still apparent that there is greater ease of inter-hemispheric transfer or take-up of language functions during early and middle childhood and that this is associated with clinically and developmentally important age-differences in the effects of aphasia-producing lesions on language skills.

There is little direct evidence on how far normal language development can take place if the first language acquisition does not occur until well after the usual age. The problem, of course, is that the cases in which language skills are not first acquired until very late in childhood are necessarily associated with either gross environmental distortions or brain abnormalities or both. Nevertheless, it is known that autistic children may certainly acquire spoken language for the first time after age five years, even though normal language skills are very rarely achieved by such children (Rutter, 1970a). However, children subjected to very extreme psychosocial deprivation not only may acquire language after age five years but also may go on to achieve a normal level of language competence (Davis, 1947; Koluchova, 1972 and 1976). Whether this could still occur after age twelve years is much more doubtful. The study of Genie (Curtiss, 1977), who was not rescued from her appalling circumstances until aged thirteen years, showed that first language acquisition could occur even at that late age. While it is still too early to know whether fully normal language skills will ever be acquired, the follow-up so far suggests that this is unlikely.

Another implication (although not a necessary one) usually drawn from the critical period hypothesis concerning language is that *second* language learning will be similar to first language learning only if it occurs before the age of puberty. This implication has recently been investigated by Snow and Hoefnagel-Hohle (1978) by studying longitudinally the naturalistic acquisition of Dutch by English speakers of different ages. They found that six- to ten-year-olds (closely followed by twelve- to fifteen-year-olds) achieved the greatest fluency in Dutch after one year but that twelve- to fifteen-year-olds and adults showed the most rapid learning in the early months. The three- to five-year-olds were consistently worse throughout, and it was only in this age group that the growing control of Dutch was associated with a breakdown in control of English. Marked individual differences were found in all age groups. The findings are open to more than one interpretation but they are inconsistent with the traditionally expressed view of the critical period hypothesis. Perhaps we may conclude that the first five years are somewhat different in that there are, at least initially, difficulties in consolidating first language acquisition and acquiring a second language at the same time. On the other hand, it seems to be confirmed that fully fluent second language acquisition is more likely to take place in childhood and adolescence than in later life.

Putting together the findings relevant to all five questions it is apparent that the issues are by no means entirely resolved. However, what is quite clear is that children's intellectual development is sensitive to environmental change in both later and earlier childhood. Whether the early years have more effect remains uncertain. To some extent, they may do, but if they do, it is only a relative difference and not a qualitative distinction due to a sharply defined critical period of development in the first five years.

## The development of social relationships

Much the same questions apply to the development of social relationships, and in many cases the answers, too, are similar. Thus, again there is good evidence from studies of late-adopted children that environmental improvements which do not occur until middle or later childhood nevertheless still lead to marked social and behavioural improvement (see Kadushin, 1970; Rathbun, Di Virgilio and Waldfogel, 1958; Rathbun, McLaughlin, Bennett and Garland, 1965; Tizard and Hodges, 1978). We have shown the same in our studies of children from severely disturbed homes who later experience a more harmonious family environment (Rutter, 1971a, 1978b). In addition, there are a host of investigations demonstrating that environmental influences during adolescence (Rutter, 1979c) or even adult life may still exert important effects on people's behaviour and social relationships. No one now supposes that personality is fixed and unalterable by the end of the pre-school years.

Clearly, too, as the other side of the same issue, a good home in the early years does not prevent damage from psychosocial stresses later. This is shown, for example, by the well-demonstrated links between bereavement or other personal losses in adult life and the occurrence of depression (Brown and Harris, 1978). Psychosocial functioning, and indeed psychosocial development, may be influenced by environmental changes at any stage in the child's life.

Also, it is obvious that it is not meaningful to ask whether, in general, environmental effects on behaviour and social relationships are greater in the early years than in later childhood. Much depends on the type of adversity involved and on the kind of psychosocial outcome which is being considered. It makes no sense to discuss the psychosocial effects of different forms of deprivation without specifying the child's age and level of social maturity. Thus, adverse responses to hospital admission are most frequent during the period from about six months to four years (Rutter, 1979a). On the other hand, severe grief reactions following bereavement are less common in earlier childhood and become more frequent during early adolescence (Rutter, 1966).

The ways in which children respond to parental divorce are also influenced by their age at the time (Wallerstein and Kelly, 1980). It is clear that children's susceptibilities and styles of response vary with developmental level, even though adequate data to document the details of this variation are still lacking for many kinds of stress.

These conclusions are non-controversial and generally agreed. But several key questions remain regarding the long-term effects of early life experiences on the development of social relationships. The first question is whether certain experiences *have* to occur during the infancy period or the pre-school years for social development to proceed normally. The most likely candidate for this critical period notion is the initial formation of selective attachments or bonds. It is well demonstrated (see Rutter, 1980a) that in the ordinary course of events these first develop about the age of three to fifteen months (there is considerable individual variation in timing). However, Bowlby (1969) has gone further in suggesting that first bonds *must* develop during the first two years or so if normal social relationships are to be possible later. It is obvious that this hypothesis is one which has most important theoretical and practical implications.

Unfortunately, the evidence to test it remains meagre but the best data are provided by Tizard and Hodges' (1978) study of late-adopted children. The testing of the critical period hypothesis is dependent on the evidence that the children did *not* develop normal selective attachments during the infancy period. This is likely on the grounds of both what is known about their style of rearing and also what was observed regarding their social behaviour. The children were looked after in a residential nursery where they experienced some fifty to eighty different caretakers during the pre-school period – an environment which is likely to impede the development of personal bonds. At two years the children were found to be both more clinging and more diffuse in their attachments than children brought up in ordinary families

(Tizard and Tizard, 1971; Tizard and Rees, 1974). At four years they were still more clinging and less likely to show deep attachments; in addition they had become overly friendly with strangers and attention-seeking. At age eight years less than half of the children who remained in the institution were said to be closely attached to their house-mothers and still they sought affection more than other children (Tizard, 1977; Tizard and Hodges, 1978). At school they were more attention-seeking, restless, disobedient and unpopular. All the evidence suggests that few of these institution-cared children developed normal selective attachments during the infancy period. Hence, we may regard the sample as one that is suitable for testing the critical period hypothesis.

The question then is what happened to the development of social relationships in those institution-reared children who were adopted after the infancy period and therefore who experienced a normal family upbringing which began only after age four years. Two main findings are relevant to this issue. Firstly, even children adopted after the age of four years usually developed deep relationships with their adoptive parents. As this was so for children who had not been closely attached to anyone while they were in the institution, we may conclude that it is possible for first bonds to develop even as late as age four to six years. On that point, either the critical period hypothesis is wrong or the critical period extends to an older age than usually supposed.

On the other hand, secondly, in spite of this later development of parent–child bonds, the late-adopted children showed the same social and attentional problems in school as did those who remained in the institutions. It appears that although attachments can still develop for the first time after infancy, nevertheless fully normal social development may be dependent on early bonding. As the children were only eight years old at the last follow-up, it is still too early to know whether this will turn out to be the case. However, the evidence up to this point is consistent with the possibility of a sensitive period for optimal early socialization, even though there may not be an absolutely critical period for some kind of initial bonding.

For other evidence on this critical period hypothesis we need to turn to studies of sub-human primates. These have convincingly demonstrated that monkeys reared in total social isolation for the first six or twelve months of life (equivalent to several years in human development) failed to develop normal social relationships in adult life and showed severe abnormalities in both sexual and parenting behaviour (Harlow and Harlow, 1969; Ruppenthal *et al.*, 1976). The gross social anomalies of these isolation-reared monkeys persisted into adult life and there was little evidence of spontaneous social recovery. The data seemed to point to a possible critical period for socialization, particularly as social isolation did not have the same effect on older 'juvenile' monkeys (Davenport *et al.*, 1966). Once socialization had become well established in early life, it was less readily disrupted by isolation experiences. However, to test the critical period notion it was necessary to do more to try to remedy the social deficits – the long-term persistence of the social abnormalities could have been a function of the lack of adequate and appropriate social experiences during the years after infancy. This possibility was examined by Novak (1979) by attempting to rehabilitate the isolation-reared monkeys after their removal from isolation at twelve months by a series of procedures including exposure to younger 'therapist' monkeys which took place during the succeeding eight months (Novak and Harlow, 1975) and then by group-rearing with ordinary mother-reared monkeys (Novak, 1979). Testing at age three years showed that the rehabilitated isolation-reared monkeys had acquired a considerable range of appropriate social skills, and on many comparisons they did not differ from controls. On the other hand, some differences still remained. Of course, greater recovery may still take place with further social experience, but so far the general pattern of results is strikingly similar to that found with late-adopted institution-reared children, in showing a very substantial, but not complete later recovery. Final conclusions are not yet justified but the implication is that there may well be a sensitive period in infancy for the development of initial social attachments. With appropriate social conditions, bonds may develop for the first time after that period and a considerable degree of late social recovery is certainly possible. But it remains plausible that fully normal socialization* will be less likely if attachments are not first established in infancy.

However, this argument presupposes that links have been demonstrated between early selective attachments and later social relationships. Even if the results on the late effects of early institution-rearing in humans and of early social isolation experiences on monkeys are confirmed it does not necessarily follow that the relevant mechanism involved selective attachments. For many reasons that constitutes a very reasonable hypothesis but it is hypothesis rather than fact. Actually, we have rather few data on the supposed bonding–socialization links. But in the last few years there have been a handful of studies which have begun to examine the longitudinal course of the development of social relationships during the first few years of life (Waters *et al.*, 1979; Easterbrooks and Lamb, 1979; Matas *et al.*, 1978; Lieberman, 1977). The findings indicate significant correlations between measures of the 'security' of attachments in infancy and measures of various aspects of the quality of peer relationships at age three years. While the data do not indicate whether or not the correlations represent causal connections, the results suggest some kind of continuity between early bonding and later peer relationships.

A further question on psychosocial development is whether *acute* and *transient* stresses in early childhood can have long-lasting effects on psychological development. Douglas's (1975) findings from the National Survey raised this possibility with respect to hospital admission. However, both his study and that of Quinton and Rutter (1976) showed *no* long-term

---

*In this connection, it should be emphasized that most studies have examined long-term outcome in terms of rather gross abnormalities rather than in terms of more subtle changes in social behaviour which fall short of actual disorder.

*sequelae* following single hospital admissions of less than a week. The link with later disorder in both studies applied to *multiple* or recurrent admissions. This might seem to suggest that even quite brief stress events in early life can have long-term effects which extend through middle childhood into adolescence. However, caution is required before making this inference. In the first place, many children are admitted to hospital for social reasons (Wynne and Hull, 1977), and the association might reflect the adverse effects of poor home circumstances rather than anything directly related to hospital admission *per se*. The results suggest that this is indeed part of the explanation, but Quinton and Rutter (1976) found that the association still held even after home circumstances had been taken into account.

The precise mechanisms involved in these long-term effects of acute stresses are rather uncertain. In particular, it is not clear why one admission has no association with disorder years later but yet two admissions substantially increase the psychiatric risk. The finding indicates that it cannot be just the cumulative effect of two separate stresses. Rather, the first admission must in some way sensitize the child so that he is more likely to suffer next time. Also, it should not necessarily be supposed that a brief admission to hospital actually operates as an acute stress. One of the important observations from monkey studies of separation experiences is that the infant monkeys' disturbance after the separation is to a considerable extent a consequence of the fact that separation serves to disturb and increase tensions in the mother–infant relationship (Hinde and McGinnis, 1977). Separation acts as the precipitant but it appears that it is the more enduring problems in the relationship which cause the infants' disordered behaviour. Perhaps this is what happens in the case of hospital admissions with children. Data to test the suggestion are lacking but the notion is given some plausibility by the observation that chronic family adversity seems to render children more likely to be damaged by hospital admission (Quinton and Rutter, 1976). The matter requires investigation. In the meanwhile we may conclude that single isolated stresses in early life only rarely lead to long-term disorder; that multiple acute stresses more often do so; and that long-term damage is most likely when multiple acute stresses arise against a background of chronic adversity.

The next question to be considered is whether stresses in early life might lead to psychosocial disorder many years later, not through any direct effect, but rather through rendering the individual more vulnerable to later stresses. The notion that the experience of a first stress might alter a person's response to a second stress is certainly plausible, but very little evidence is available to test the hypothesis. The observed interactive effect between acute stresses in the hospital admission findings and the further interaction between admissions and chronic family adversities (Quinton and Rutter, 1976) suggest that the first stresses may serve to increase susceptibility to later stresses; but the data were not such as to provide an adequate test of the idea. Brown and Harris (1978) have suggested the same phenomenon as the explanation of the link between parental loss in childhood and depression in adult life. They argue that early parental loss (by separation or death) operates by increasing vulnerability to later losses.

This hypothesis is an important one but there are many issues which require resolution before it can be accepted. In the first place, the statistical links between childhood bereavement and adult depression are both weak and inconsistent (Crook and Eliot, 1980). Bowlby (1980) has discussed this issue at some length and, drawing on detailed clinical accounts of individual cases, has put forward some ideas on why some children become sensitized by early loss and yet others do not. He suggests that the course taken by mourning after the loss in childhood may be important; in this connection the pattern of family relationships both before and after the loss is thought to be influential. So far, empirical evidence to test these suggestions is largely lacking. Secondly, in those cases where there is a link between childhood bereavement and adult depression, there is the further question of whether the association is mediated by the hypothesized mechanism of early loss increasing vulnerability to later losses, or by some quite different process. Brown and Harris (1978) cite the evidence from their own studies in favour of a vulnerability model but, as Bebbington (1980) shows, the argument remains inconclusive in spite of its intuitive plausibility. Thirdly, there is the finding that parental death in childhood seems to be associated with 'psychotic' depression but not with 'neurotic' depression, whereas parental loss through separation shows the reverse pattern of associations. Brown and Harris (1978) have put forward a possible explanation for this finding in terms of the type of mental set likely to be engendered by different types of loss, but their suggestions remain speculative at the moment.

Studies in primates have also investigated the possibility that a stressful separation in infancy may cause an increased predisposition to respond adversely to separation later in life (Mineke and Suomi, 1978). The findings are somewhat equivocal but it appears that this may occur in some instances. However, whether or not the threshold for adverse reactions is lowered seems to depend on the nature of the response to the first stress (the increased vulnerability being more frequent when the reaction to the first stress was severe).

But it should not be thought that infantile stresses only increase vulnerability; they may also decrease it. A quarter of a century ago Levine and his colleagues (1956) showed that rat pups subjected to electric shock showed an enhanced resistance to later stress. Subsequent research has repeatedly confirmed the finding and has shown that it applies to a wide range of aversive experiences in infancy (Hunt, 1979). The explanation seems to lie in changes in the neuro-endocrine system which provide a more adaptive response to later stress (Levine, 1969; Weinberg and Levine, 1977).

Of course, the aversive stimuli given to these rats are a far cry from the social adversities we have been considering in human infants. Nevertheless, there is human evidence that acute stresses in adults can have a 'steeling' effect (Ursin, Baade and Levine, 1978), and in children, too, it seems that some forms of separation experience may *protect* children from the stresses of hospital admission (Stacey *et al.*, 1970), even if others may have the reverse effect (Vernon *et al.*, 1965). Presumably, it matters whether the child emerges successfully from the first stress with improved coping mechanisms, enhanced self-esteem or a more effective physiological response. If he does he may become more stress-resistant. If, on the other hand, he is left distraught, unable to cope, or physiologically impaired by the first stress he may instead become more vulnerable. It is all too apparent that we lack good data; speculation provides an inadequate substitute and further research on this important topic would be most worthwhile.

The finding from rat studies that transient acute stresses in infancy can have long-term physiological consequences leads on to the final question to be considered; namely whether adverse social experiences in the early years can have long-term behavioural effects as a result of altered brain structure or chemistry. The possibility is raised by the well-established observation from investigations in various species of animals that visual privation in infancy is followed by marked changes in the visual cortex (Riesen, 1975) and that environmental impoverishment in infancy results in changes in brain chemistry and histology (Rosenzweig and Bennett, 1977). While the suggestion remains intriguing, the limited evidence available to date suggests that the effects follow a lack of crucial *physical* experiences rather than any kind of social stress or privation (Floeter and Greenough, 1979). The idea that social experiences could alter brain structure* cannot be entirely ruled out but it seems most unlikely that this constitutes the mechanism in most instances.

## Conclusions

We have come a long way from the early views that infantile experiences somehow fixed personality and that thereafter it was too late to remedy the faults of omission or commission in those vital pre-school years. However, it is evident that we have a long way yet to go before we can adequately

---

*Of course, all psychological effects have to operate through some kind of alteration in brain *function*, but this need not necessarily involve changes in *structure*.

appraise the long-term effects of early experiences. It is good that human resilience has proved to be greater than once thought. Continuities between infancy and maturity undoubtedly exist, but the residual effects of early experiences on adult behaviour tend to be quite slight because of both the maturational changes that take place during middle and later childhood and also the effects of beneficial and adverse experiences during all the years after infancy. While it is clear that the long-term effects of early deprivation depend heavily on whether or not the deprivation continues, it would be premature to conclude that infantile experiences are of no importance in their own right. That remains a matter still worthy of further study and one on which there is a surprising paucity of information.

## 10. Influences on Parenting and Resilience in the Presence of Deprivation

### Influences on parenting

One issue which was not discussed at all in the first edition, but which has come into prominence since, is the question of possible intergenerational cycles of disadvantage – that is, whether deprivation in one generation can lead to problems in the next. The topic is an immense one and as it has recently been extensively reviewed in book form (Rutter and Madge, 1976) it will not be discussed here. However, one special aspect of the subject, the connections between experiences during childhood and later parenting behaviour during adult life, will be considered as part of the broader topic of influences on parenting. For years clinicians have been urging parents to deal with their children in this way or that but, until recently, very little attention was paid to the question of which types of experiences influence parenting behaviour. Five main variables have now come to the fore: the parents' own childhood experiences, events during the post-partum period, effects stemming from the characteristics of the child, the experience of having reared previous children, and the wider social environment.

### Childhood experiences and parenting behaviour

Several studies (see Rutter and Madge, 1976) have shown that people who were brought up in unhappy or disrupted homes are more likely to have illegitimate children, to become teenage mothers, to make an unhappy marriage and to divorce. Thus, Illsley and Thompson (1961) in their study of 3,000 Aberdeen women having their first baby found that those who had themselves been illegitimate or whose parents had divorced or separated were twice as likely as other women to have an illegitimate child or a pre-nuptial conception. Crellin *et al.* (1971) noted much the same in the National Child Development Study. Similarly, Wolkind *et al.* (1976) found that women who had been separated in childhood from one or both parents were more likely to have become pregnant in their teens, more likely to be unmarried when having their first child, and more likely to have psychiatric problems in early adult life. Moreover, a variety of studies (Waller and Hill, 1951; Langner and Michael, 1963; Jonsson, 1967; Gurin, Veroff and Feld, 1960) have shown that people whose parents were unhappily married are more likely themselves to show poor marital adjustment or to have marriages which end in divorce. Meier's (1965, 1966) follow-up study of former foster children indicated rates of marriage breakdown several times those in the general population.

Furthermore, a variety of investigations (see Spinetta and Rigler, 1972) have found that parents who batter their children tend to have had a seriously disturbed upbringing themselves, often associated with neglect, rejection or violence. This has been demonstrated in studies from a variety of countries, including England (e.g. Gibbens and Walker, 1956; Scott, 1973; Smith, 1975), Ireland (Lukianowicz, 1971) and the United States of America (see Steele and Pollock, 1968; Parke and Collmer, 1975). The links are quite strong, in that at least half and probably some three quarters of battering parents have experienced an unhappy, rejecting, cruel or violent upbringing. Even so, a substantial minority do not have this adverse background and a few seem to have had quite unexceptional childhoods. Also, it is necessary to recognize that the links are far stronger looking back than they are looking forward. That is to say, although more battering parents come from unhappy, affectionless and sometimes violent homes, it is likely that only a tiny minority of youngsters from such homes go on to physically abuse their children. Moreover, in that many battering parents show abnormalities of personality or emotional disorder, it remains uncertain how far the links concern these general problems and how far specific difficulties in parenting.

Clearly there are important links between childhood experiences and parenting behaviour, although further research is required to determine both the strength of the associations and the mechanisms involved.

Three studies should be particularly mentioned in this connection. Frommer and O'Shea (1973a and b) were the first workers to relate childhood experiences to direct measurement of patterns of parental care during the infancy period. They found that women reared in disrupted homes were more likely to prop up their two-month-old babies to feed themselves and more of the deprived mothers became pregnant again during the year after delivery.

Wolkind and his colleagues (Wolkind et al., 1977; Hall et al., 1979) have also studied the childhood antecedents of parenting patterns, as part of a prospective study of British-born mothers and their first-born babies in inner London. Detailed interview measures and sophisticated ethological-type techniques of observing mother–child interaction in the home were employed. They found that, compared with those from intact homes, mothers who as children had themselves experienced parental death, divorce or separation talked to their babies, touched them, and looked at them significantly less often. In addition, the mothers who came from a disrupted family were less likely to report that, at twenty weeks after birth, they saw their baby as a person. Thus, it appeared that a woman's experiences in childhood were associated with her behaviour as a mother.

Quinton and Rutter's (1980a and b) studies have focused more specifically on the nature of the childhood experiences likely to lead to difficulties in parenting. Parents who had had a child taken into the care of the local authority for the second time as a result of serious family difficulties were compared with a general population sample of roughly similar social status. The families with children in care had high rates of a wide range of psychosocial problems, so that it is evident that the findings apply only to parenting difficulties when they occur as part of multiple family, social and psychiatric disorders. It was found that parenting problems of this type and magnitude almost always arose in relation to a background of serious childhood adversity. A quarter of the mothers with children 'in care', as children, had themselves been taken away from their families into the care of the local authority (compared with seven per cent of controls); and two fifths had experienced separations through discord or rejection (compared with fourteen per cent of controls). Of course, in many cases, these adverse experiences in childhood were associated with mental disorders or criminality in the parents' parents and the intergenerational links could be genetic rather than experiential. However, while hereditary factors may well have played a part, further analyses of the pattern of association showed that the difference between the mothers with children in care and the control mothers applied to serious childhood adversities even in the absence of deviance or disorder in the grandparents, whereas the reverse did not apply. The implication is that personal experiences of an adverse kind were the crucial mediating variables. Moreover, it was evident that serious parenting problems in the context of widespread family difficulties rarely arose in the *absence* of such previous childhood adversities. Intergenerational continuities looking backwards were very strong. On the other hand, it was striking that childhood adversities were also quite common in the control group (although not as frequent as among the cases). Thus, it followed that there must be many individuals who experience severe deprivation in childhood but yet nevertheless become reasonably well-functioning adults. This important issue of resilience in the face of stress is considered in more detail below.

## Events in the post-partum period

A different type of 'deprivation' experience thought to influence parenting behaviour concerns events during the few days after giving birth. During the last decade, paediatricians have become increasingly aware of the importance of the neonatal period for the development of mother–infant ties and of maternal behaviour generally (Klaus and Kennell, 1976). Special attention, however, has come to focus on the suggestion that the damage stems from the separation of mother and new-born child. Klaus, Kennell, Leiderman and others (see Richards, 1978) have shown that a lack of contact in the first few hours after birth may have adverse effects on mothering during the subsequent months. Early physical contact seems to foster closer physical relationships and increased communication later. The findings are important but some of the claims concerning the crucial nature of those first hours after birth for the development of mother–infant bonding rather outrun the empirical evidence. Controversy largely centres on four issues: the persistence of the effects, which aspects of parenting are affected, the presence of a sensitive period, and the mechanics involved.

Rather long-lasting changes in mother–infant interaction were found by Klaus and Kennell (1976) in their groups of socially disadvantaged mothers and it was claimed that just a few hours of extra physical contact within the first few days after birth had effects on maternal behaviour which lasted for several years. However, not only have the findings from other investigations been rather different, but also Klaus and Kennell's claims of long-lasting effects rest on rather uncertain foundations even with respect to their own data. Thus, changes in maternal behaviour one year after birth were evident on maternal self-report and observational measures in only one of their seven standard situations (Kennell *et al.*, 1974). Similarly, Leiderman and Seashore (1975) found that mothers who had been separated from their infants in the neonatal period touched their children less at one year: but otherwise there were no significant differences between their separated and non-separated groups on questionnaire measures, blind interview assessments or systematic observations of mother–child interaction at home. Whiten (1977), too, found that the effects of neonatal separation on maternal behaviour were rather evanescent. De Chateau and Wiberg (1977a and b) found that primiparous mothers (i.e. those having their first baby) given extra contact in the neonatal period differed from primiparous mothers given routine care, but did not differ from multiparous mothers (i.e. those who had had previous babies) given routine care. Moreover, the Colorado group of investigators have not found that extended contact affected the later behaviour of either mothers (Svejda *et al.*, 1980) or fathers (Pannabecker and Emde, 1977). The balance of evidence suggests that separation of mother and child in the neonatal period may have effects on maternal behaviour which last a few months but that it is unusual for effects to persist for longer than that. It is not clear what factors predispose to a persistence of effects but it is noteworthy that long-term consequences in both prospective (Klaus and Kennell, 1976) and retrospective studies (Collingwood and Alberman, 1979) have generally applied to socially disadvantaged groups with many other problems. It seems unlikely that events in the neonatal period have an inevitable lasting impact on mother–child relationships, but if early stresses are combined with persisting adversity there may be enduring damage.

The next question is *which* aspects of parenting are affected by neonatal separation. Klaus and Kennell (1976) discuss their findings in terms of 'bonding' and 'attachment' but these terms are misleading in that the investigations have not included any specific measures of selective attachment and the analogy with the child's development of bonds is probably inappropriate (see Lozoff, pp. 84–5, in Klaus and Kennell, 1976). Both Richards (1978) and Leiderman (1980) point out that the main effects have been found with breast feeding, and with the extent of looking at and fondling the baby rather than with proximity-maintaining or caretaking responses. Moreover, although De Chateau and Wiberg (1977a and b) found differences according to the extent of neonatal contact *within* primiparous groups, they did not find any difference from multiparous women. It appears that experiences in the post-partum period may have had a *general* effect on parenting rather than any specific effects on bonding with a particular baby. Accordingly, it seems more accurate to consider the effects in terms of *style* of mother–infant interactions. The differences in style may sometimes have implications for the quality of parenting but this extrapolation involves inferences which have yet to be tested.

Hales *et al.* (1977) have suggested that the first few hours after birth constitute a sensitive period for the formation of affectional bonds between a mother and her infants. Klaus and Kennell (1976) follow the same argument, drawing parallels with animal data showing that in some species mothers will not accept their young if they are separated from them in the post-partum period. This line of reasoning is unsound on several different grounds. As already noted, the measures in humans do not assess bonding. Moreover, the notion that the early hours are critical is incompatible with the observations that fathers and adoptive parents both develop close ties to their children in spite of not having contact in the neonatal period (see e.g. Tizard, 1977). Of course, the immediate post-partum days are special for mothers both for psychosocial reasons (Richards, 1978) and perhaps also as a result of hormonal influences (Rosenblatt, 1975). It may be that ties develop most readily soon after birth but, nevertheless, it is clear that both mothers and fathers can, and commonly do, develop strong attachments to their children even in the absence of neonatal contact.

The last issue is how far neonatal mother–infant separation has effects on maternal behaviour as a result of *lack* of skin-to-skin contact in the hours after birth, and how far from hospitals *denying* mothers contact (Richards, 1978; Rutter, 1979a). Certainly, it may be accepted that the development of parent–infant relationships will be influenced by experiences in the neonatal period but it is dubious whether physical contact *as such* constitutes the crucial variable. The evidence on the mechanisms involved remains inconclusive but it seems likely that the damage comes in part from the effects on parental attitudes and feelings of being *prevented* from having access (as distinct from just not having contact); of the fears engendered by having a baby placed in special care; and of the restraints on spontaneous interactions which may stem from a hospital environment. Moreover, even this wider range of factors seems most likely to have an adverse effect on parent–child relationships largely when the neonatal separation concerns a mother from a deprived background and a child of low birth weight in need of special care (Collingwood and Alberman, 1979). Probably, it is not the sheer amount of physical contact between mother and infant which is crucial. Rather, mother–infant separation may be potentially damaging because of its meaning to the parents and because it forms part of a constellation of adversities in the mother, in the child, and in the events of the post-partum period.

It may be concluded that many of the theoretical implications drawn from studies of mother–infant interaction in the neonatal period have been premature, if not wrong. Also, claims on the high probability of persistent effects stemming solely from events in the first few hours after birth have not been substantiated. On the other hand, this field of research has undoubtedly been important in focusing attention on some of the possible influences on the early development of parent–child relationships, and in highlighting the fact that some hospital practices carry the potential of damaging parenting. Whatever the reservations about the more extravagant claims, there are ample grounds for concluding that experiences in the neonatal period may have at least short-term effects on parenting and that it is generally inadvisable for hospitals to prevent parent–infant contact in the neonatal period.

*Child characteristics*

The third influence on parenting comes from the child himself, as emphasized by Bell (1968, 1971 and 1974), Goldberg (1977), Lamb and Easterbrooks (1980) and others. For example, there is now considerable evidence that how adults speak to children is affected by the verbal skills of the children with whom they interact (Gardner, 1977; Pratt, Bumstead and Raynes, 1976; Siegel and Harkins, 1963; Snow and Ferguson, 1977; Spradlin and Rosenberg, 1964). Osofsky and O'Connell (1972) showed that experimental manipulation of children's dependency altered parental behaviour. Neonatal characteristics have also been found to influence parental responses (Brown and Bateman, 1978; Levy, 1958; Osofsky and Danzger, 1974).

The sex of the infant, too, may be important. It seems that parents, particularly fathers, play more roughly with boys than with girls and that this differential treatment begins in the first year of life; also parents tend to use harsher punishment with boys and find it more difficult to punish girls (Maccoby and Jacklin, 1980). Of course, it is difficult to determine how far these sex differences are a result of parents' views about boys and girls and how far a response to differences in the behavioural characteristics of young males and females. The importance of parental preconceptions was neatly shown by Smith and Lloyd (1978) when thirty-two primiparous mothers of five- to ten-month-old infants were asked to play with one of four 'actor babies' dressed and named as either a boy or girl. Maternal behaviour was significantly associated with the *perceived* sex of the baby but not with the biological sex of the actor baby or of the mother's own baby. On the other hand, it is likely that there are also effects on parenting which stem from sex differences in the infants' behaviour, in that differential treatment of male and female offspring has also been reported in sub-human primates. Thus, socially isolated monkeys tend to become generally rejecting and indifferent mothers but they are much more likely to physically abuse male infants (Ruppenthal *et al.*, 1976).

## The experience of bringing up children

The fourth influence on parenting comes from the very experience of bringing up children. Research findings, utilizing a variety of methodologies, have been consistent in showing that parents respond differently to their first born compared with the way they deal with later-born children (Clausen, 1966; Hilton, 1967: Jacobs and Moss, 1976; Lasko, 1954; Lewis and Kreitzberg, 1979; Rothbart, 1971; Thoman *et al.*, 1971). Parents tend to have a more intensive relationship with their first children, interacting with them more and showing more social, affectionate and caretaking behaviours. However, they are also more anxious and controlling. With later-born children they tend to be more relaxed, more consistent and less punitive, while at the same time talking to them less and giving them less attention. In part, these differences may reflect differences in the characteristics of the children, as both behavioural (Waldrop and Bell, 1966) and hormonal (Maccoby *et al.*, 1979) differences have been found between first-born and later-born neonates. However, it is unlikely that this constitutes the whole explanation as Thoman *et al.* (1971) found much less marked (and to some extent different) birth order differences in nurses' interaction with new-born babies, compared with mothers' interactions with their babies.

The influence of previous experience with infants on parenting behaviour is also demonstrated by the Wisconsin studies of rhesus monkeys subjected to appalling social isolation in early life. When adult they showed grossly abnormal sexual behaviour and were rejecting or indifferent parents of their first born. However, some became more maternal during the post-partum period and were much better mothers of their second and subsequent babies (Harlow and Suomi, 1971). It appears that later experiences with young monkeys can do something to ameliorate the damage done by early social isolation (Novak and Harlow, 1975; Suomi, Harlow and Novak, 1974).

*Social context*

It has also been found that parenting may be influenced both by the immediate social context and also by the wider social environment. The importance of the constraints imposed by the setting was discussed in chapter 9 in relation to the effects of day care. Parents are likely to behave differently according to the sort of home within which they have to bring up their children. Thus, Quinton and Rutter (1980b) found that parenting problems were more frequent in the presence of housing difficulties, even after account had been taken of the parents' background. Parent–child interaction may also be influenced by who else is present. This effect was evident, for example, in Clarke-Stewart's (1978) finding that mothers behaved differently with their fifteen- to thirty-month-old children according to whether or not the father was also in the room. The impact of the broader social milieu was indicated in Rutter and Quinton's (1977) general population studies of the families of ten-year-old children. Marital discord and maternal depression were both much more common among working-class women living in inner city areas, although it remains unclear why and how inner city life provides stresses on families and on parenting (see Rutter, 1980c). The potential strains of child-rearing for women of low social status were also evident in the London studies by Brown and his colleagues (1975). Cross-cultural data (Rohner, 1975; Werner, 1979) appear to suggest that mothers who are home alone all day with their children, without other adults who can share the tasks of child care, are more likely to become rejecting in their attitudes and behaviour. Causal inferences from such comparisons must necessarily be rather tentative but still there are good grounds for supposing that the ecological context does matter (Bronfenbrenner, 1979) and that the wider social environment does have an impact on parenting behaviour, even if the details of these effects remain obscure.

## Resilience in the presence of deprivation or disadvantage

The final issue to be discussed in this postscript is that of resilience, or why children do *not* succumb to deprivation or disadvantage.

All studies of deprived or disadvantaged children have noted wide variations in response. Even with the most terrible homes and the most stressful experiences some individuals come through unscathed and seem to have a stable healthy personality development (Rutter, 1979b). This is an old and well-established observation, but it is only in the last few years that we have begun to meet the challenge and ask why? What is different about the children who rise above the tide of disadvantage? What are the protective factors? What are the ameliorating circumstances? At the moment, very few answers are available to these questions. However, there has been a recent upsurge of interest in the problem and over the next decade this is likely to be a major growth area in the field of research into deprivation. Here there is space to consider modifying variables in relation to only one aspect of the subject. Family discord and disharmony have been selected as data are available from a series of epidemiological studies. Protective factors may be considered under six headings: multiplicity of stresses, changed circumstances, factors in the child, factors in the family, coping skills, and factors outside the home.

## Multiplicity of stresses

The first very striking finding is that *single* isolated chronic stresses carry no appreciable psychiatric risk. In a general population study of families of ten-year-olds, Rutter, Yule, Quinton, Rowlands, Yule and Berger (1975b) identified six family variables (including marital discord), all of which were strongly and significantly associated with child psychiatric disorder. Then families which had one, but only one, of these risk factors were separated out. None of these risk factors when they occurred in isolation was associated with disorders in the children; the risk was no higher than that for children without any family stresses. However, when any two stresses occurred together, the risk went up no less than *four*fold. With three and four concurrent stresses the risk went up several times further still. It is clear that the combination of chronic stresses provided very much more than an additive effect. There was an *interactive* effect such that the risk which attended several concurrent stresses was much more than the sum of the effects of the stresses considered individually. Brown *et al.* (1975) found much the same for vulnerability factors and depression in adults.

This effect by which the presence of one stress potentiates the damage caused by another has been noted in several other circumstances. For example, it was found that children from a chronically deprived home background were more likely to be adversely affected by recurrent admission to hospital (Quinton and Rutter, 1976). The same applies to the interaction of biological and social factors. Thus, over a decade ago, Drillien (1964) noticed that the effect of low birth weight on intelligence was most marked in children who also had the added disadvantage of poor social circumstances. Sameroff and Chandler (1975) have emphasized the same *interactive* effect with more recent data. This was also shown in the follow-up study of Kauai children (Werner *et al.*, 1971; Werner and Smith, 1977).

However, it is important to appreciate that there are also *transactional* effects whereby one stress (biological or social) actually increases the likelihood of occurrence of others. Thus, children from deprived homes were twice as likely to *have* recurrent admissions to hospital (Quinton and Rutter, 1976). The presence of chronic stresses increased the *rate of occurrence* of multiple acute stresses. This is an important issue, considered further below.

### Change in circumstances

The next issue concerns the effect of a change in family circumstances. To what extent are children better off if family stresses diminish or cease? The benefits of an improved environment in middle or late childhood were noted when discussing critical periods. The matter has been examined by studying children all of whom had been separated from their parents in early childhood as a result of family discord or family problems (Rutter, 1971a). Within this group of children, all of whom had experienced severe early stresses, those who were still in homes characterized by discord and disharmony were compared with those for whom things had improved and who were now in harmonious happy homes. It was evident that disorders were very much less frequent when discord had ceased. A change for the better in family circumstances was associated with a marked reduction in psychiatric risk for the child. This was also shown more directly in the observation that whether disorders in the children of divorcing parents diminished was related to whether divorce improved family relationships (Hetherington, Cox and Cox, 1978; Wallerstein and Kelly, 1980).

### Factors in the child

Factors in the child which are known to be important in modifying responses to deprivation or disadvantage include the child's sex, temperament, and genetic background.

It is well known that males are more vulnerable than females to all manner of physical stresses and hazards (see Rutter, 1970b). It now appears that to some extent this male susceptibility applies also to psychosocial stresses. This is most obvious with respect to family discord and disharmony which, in almost all studies, has been found to have a greater association with conduct disorders in boys than in girls. This sex difference was evident in British studies of the general population and of the children of mentally-ill parents (Rutter, 1970b; Wolkind and Rutter, 1973), and has been confirmed in American studies of child patient groups (Porter and O'Leary, 1980), of divorcing couples (Hetherington et al., 1979) and of the general population (Block et al., 1980) as well as in the Kauai longitudinal study (Werner and Smith, 1980). However, this greater vulnerability of the male does not apply to all forms of deprivation or disadvantage. Thus, it was not found in children who experienced an institutional upbringing (Wolkind, 1974). It should also be noted that the presence of overt brain damage has usually been found to equalize vulnerability between boys and girls (Rutter, 1977a; Rutter, Graham and Yule, 1970; Drillien et al., 1980). The reasons why boys appear more likely to respond adversely to parental discord remain obscure. It cannot be just a function of mothers retaining custody of the children following divorce (and hence that boys lack a same-sex role model whereas girls do not), as suggested by Whitehead (1979), because most investigators have found that the sex difference applies to unbroken discordant homes (Rutter, 1970b; Block et al., 1980; Porter and O'Leary, 1980; Werner and Smith, 1980) as well as to broken ones. However, the results need not necessarily mean an intrinsic sex difference in vulnerability to psychosocial stresses (although this remains a definite possibility). The findings could be due to a difference between boys and girls in the salience of the two parents, or to parents treating boys differently from girls during periods of conflict, or of girls having developed better coping skills (Block et al., 1980; Porter and O'Leary, 1980). Further research is needed to determine why being a girl seems to be protective when children are experiencing family discord.

The child's temperament is also important. Using interview measurement techniques based on the Thomas, Chess and Birch (1968) approach, it has been found that children who showed the features of low regularity, low malleability, negative mood and low fastidiousness were the ones most likely to develop a psychiatric disorder (Graham, Rutter and George, 1973). The presence of at least two of these adverse temperamental features increased the psychiatric risk during the next four years *threefold*. Part of the reason why temperamental adversity put the child at increased risk was to be found in the 'transactional' effect with parental criticism (Rutter, 1978b). Children with adverse temperamental features were twice as likely as other children to be the *target* of parental criticism. Thus, in discordant and quarrelsome homes, a child's temperament protected him or put him at risk by virtue of its influence on parent–child interaction. Even when there was marked disharmony in the home, the temperamentally easy child tended to escape much of the conflict.

The importance of temperamental features in modifying children's responses to deprivation was also strikingly shown by Werner and Smith (1980) in the Kauai longitudinal study. Children with a high-risk family background were compared according to whether or not they developed a psychosocial disorder. The 'resilient' high-risk children, who remained well in spite of the hazards they experienced, differed from those who succumbed in terms of contemporaneous temperamental ratings at both age one and two years. For example, the resilient children were more likely to be described by their mothers as affectionate, active, and calm.

The Isle of Wight and London epidemiological studies have shown the protective effect of good intelligence and above-average scholastic attainments (Rutter, 1979b). Whether this means that the intellectually more able children are constitutionally more resilient or whether it means that high self-esteem is protective remains uncertain.

Thirdly, there may be an heredity–environment interaction. This was suggested by the finding that the effects on the child of marital discord were most marked when the parent had a lifelong personality disorder (Rutter, 1971a). However, genetic and non-genetic factors are better differentiated by adoption studies. For example, Hutchings and Mednick (1974), using a cross-fostering design, showed that criminality in children was most common when *both* the biological *and* the adoptive father had a crime record. The rate was increased to a lesser extent if only the biological father was criminal but not at all if only the adoptive was. The implication is that genetic factors make a child more vulnerable to adverse environmental influences which have little impact on children who are not genetically susceptible. Crowe's (1974) data showed the same. Of course, as with all these leads on factors leading to vulnerability or invulnerability, the findings need to be replicated (particularly as the findings are based on small numbers with some of the differences falling short of statistical significance). However, all the pointers at the moment are in the direction of a fluid view of development in which hereditary and environmental influences not only interact but also *alter* each other in transactional fashion as growth proceeds (see Rutter, 1975).

## Factors in the family

Up to now almost all investigations of the family have concentrated on what goes wrong and almost no attention has been paid to positive or protective effects. However, there are a few leads. It has been found (Rutter, 1971a, 1979b) that a good relationship with one parent serves to protect children brought up in an otherwise discordant, unhappy home. Children with one good relationship were less likely to develop conduct disorders than other children in similar homes whose relationships with both parents were poor. The few relevant findings from other studies are also consistent with the protective effect of a good relationship with a parental figure (Conway, 1957; Pringle and Bossio, 1960; Pringle and Clifford, 1962; Wolkind, 1971). However, a recent prospective study of children's behaviour during the two years following parental divorce (Hetherington, Cox and Cox, 1979) has indicated that the relationship must be both a particularly good one and also one with a parent currently living with the child in order for these to be a significant buffering effect. Robins *et al.* (1975) found that black children living in broken homes of low social status were less likely to drop out of school if brought up by grandparents. In these circumstances, the extended family appeared to provide continuity and support in an otherwise unstable situation. Werner and Smith (1980) also found that resilient children in the Kauai longitudinal study tended to have better sources of emotional support both within and outside the family. In addition, resilience seemed to be fostered by a home which provided firm structure and clear rules. In a British study of multiple problem families, Wilson (1974) also found that strict and careful supervision of the children was associated with a reduced risk of delinquency. We may conclude that it is not only good relationships and readily available sources of emotional support which are likely to be protective at times of stress, but also that the translation of a caring attitude into a well-structured family environment with well-understood rules and effective supervision may be equally important. Interestingly, both features have been found to characterize well-functioning schools (Rutter *et al.*, 1979) as well as homes.

At the moment these findings provide no more than a few scattered pointers. The mechanisms involved are ill-understood and, in any case, are probably varied. What is important, however, is that even in the worst family circumstances it appears that a few 'good' factors can do much to balance the serious maladaptive and disruptive influences. *How* they do so remains to be determined.

## Coping skills

Lois Murphy (1962; Murphy and Moriarty, 1976) was one of the first people to emphasize the potential importance of children's positive coping strategies in dealing with challenges and threats. More recently the theme has been taken up by many other writers, as illustrated by the many volumes on the topic (e.g. Coelho *et al.*, 1974; Monat and Lazarus, 1977; Antonovsky, 1979). However, there are numerous conceptual and methodological problems which are inherent in the study of coping (Cohen and Lazarus, 1979) and adequate empirical demonstration of the effects of different coping strategies in childhood is still lacking. Intuitively, it seems likely that adaptation or maladaptation following stress or deprivation will be determined in part by the manner in which the individual responds to his hazardous circumstances. But is it a question of doing something active to deal with the threat, or is it crucial *which* coping strategy is employed? Are there generally effective or ineffective strategies or is the effectiveness specific to the individual or to the type of stress? These (and many other) basic questions have still to be answered. It seems obvious that some forms of response to deprivation will be unhelpful simply because they replace one problem with another. For example, see Quinton and Rutter's (1980a and b) retrospective study of mothers whose children had been taken 'into care' as a result of serious family problems; the mothers were not only more likely than controls to have come from discordant unhappy homes but also were more likely to have made an early marriage in their teens in order to escape from their plight. Not surprisingly, these marriages made only as an attempted solution to childhood problems frequently proved unsatisfactory and most failed. However, are there other coping strategies which foster resilience in the face of stress, and, if there are, *why* and *how* are they effective? It is not yet possible to draw any firm conclusions but research attention needs to be paid to the possibility of learned coping skills which may help protect a child against the stresses of a depriving or disadvantaged environment.

*Factors outside the home*

Lastly, there are protective factors outside the home. First, there is the impact of schooling. A study of London secondary schools showed that some were much more successful than others in helping children to develop normally without emotional or behavioural problems (Rutter, 1977b; Rutter *et al.*, 1975b; Rutter, Maughan, Mortimore and Ouston, 1979). Children from disadvantaged and discordant homes were less likely to develop problems if they attended better-functioning schools. For obvious reasons, this protective effect was most marked in relation to children's behaviour at school. However, it did seem that, to some extent, good experiences at school could mitigate stressful experiences within the home.

A variety of other investigations in other areas have similarly indicated that there are major differences between schools in rates of absenteeism, behavioural disturbance, delinquency and even employment after leaving (see Rutter *et al.*, 1979). Moreover, it has been shown that these differences are not artefacts of selective intake; they do indeed reflect a school influence. However, a well-functioning school is not primarily a matter of buildings, size or finance. Rather it is something about the school as a social institution. It appears that the crucial features include setting appropriately high expectations, good group management, effective feedback to the children with ample use of praise, the setting of good models of behaviour by the teachers, pleasant working conditions and giving pupils positions of trust and responsibility (Rutter *et al.*, 1979).

So far as other factors outside the home are concerned, the most obvious is the area in which families live. Much higher rates of psychiatric disorder have been found among families living in inner-city areas than among those living in small towns or in the countryside (Rutter, Cox, Tupling, Berger, Yule, 1975a). This finding has been recently replicated in Oslo (Lavik, 1977). It is important now to identify what stresses are involved in living in inner-city areas. However, it is at least as important to identify what makes some cities relatively free of these stress effects. Several investigations have found industrial towns and cities with quite low rates of disorder (Johnson, 1980; Rutter, 1967). We need to find out what makes them different.

In summary, on this topic of why children do *not* succumb to deprivation, it is beginning to be clear that ameliorating or protective factors can do much to aid normal development even in the worst circumstances. So far, knowledge on these factors is extremely limited, but if it could be increased it is likely that it would have very substantial policy, preventive and therapeutic implications.

# Conclusion

In conclusion, the last eight years have seen the continuing accumulation of evidence showing the importance of deprivation and disadvantage as influences on children's psychological development. Bowlby's (1951) original arguments on that score have been amply confirmed. However, as in 1972, it is now very clear that deprivation involves a most heterogeneous group of adversities which operate through several quite different psychological mechanisms. Thus, insofar as deprivation is a causal factor, the acute distress syndrome sometimes shown during admission to hospital or to a residential nursery is probably due in part to an interference with attachment behaviour and in part to the effects of a strange and frightening environment, with the disturbances after return home probably due in part to the adverse effects of separation on parent–child relationships; intellectual retardation is likely to be a function of a lack of adequate meaningful experiences; conduct disorders are in part a response to family discord and disturbed interpersonal relationships; and affectionless psychopathy may be a consequence of abnormal early bonding. New research has confirmed that, although an important stress, separation is not *the* crucial factor in most varieties of deprivation. Investigations have also demonstrated the importance of a child's relationship with people other than his mother. Most important of all there has been the repeated finding that many children are not damaged by deprivation.

The old issue of critical periods of development and the crucial importance of the early years has been reopened and re-examined. The evidence is unequivocal that experiences at *all* ages have an impact. However, it may be that the first few years do have a special importance for bond formation and social development.

New issues have also come to the fore in the last eight years. Those which are particularly likely to continue to influence our thinking and our practical policies are: firstly, a focus on the *reciprocal* nature of parent–child interaction and on the *process* by which parent–child relationships develop; secondly, a concern with the links between childhood experiences and parenting behaviour; thirdly, an appreciation of the importance of factors *outside* the home (both in terms of ecological influences on family functioning and also the crucial impact on child development of experiences at school); and fourthly, an attempt to study invulnerability and the factors which protect children and enable them to develop normally in spite of stress and disadvantage. The issue of 'maternal deprivation' continues to be a source of fruitful new findings, new concepts and new approaches.

# References

ACHESON, R. M. (1960), 'Effects of nutrition and disease on human growth', in J. M. Tanner (ed.), *Human Growth*, Pergamon.

AINSWORTH, M. D. (1962), 'The effects of maternal deprivation: a review of findings and controversy in the context of research strategy', in *Deprivation of Maternal Care: A Reassessment of its Effects*, World Health Organization, Geneva.

AINSWORTH, M. D. (1963), 'The development of infant–mother interaction among the Ganda', in B. M. Foss (ed.), *Determinants of Infant Behaviour*, vol. 2, Methuen.

AINSWORTH, M. D. (1964), 'Patterns of attachment behaviour shown by the infant in interaction with his mother', *Merrill-Palmer Q.*, vol. 10, pp. 51–8.

AINSWORTH, M. D. (1967), *Infancy in Uganda: Infant Care and the Growth of Attachment*, Johns Hopkins Press, Baltimore, Md.

AINSWORTH, M. D. (1969), 'Object relations, dependency and attachment: a theoretical review of the infant–mother relationship', *Child Devel.*, vol. 40, pp. 969–1025.

AINSWORTH, M. D. (1973), 'The development of infant–mother attachment', in B. M. Caldwell and H. N. Ricciuti (eds.), *Review of Child Development Research*, vol. 3, University of Chicago Press, Chicago.

AINSWORTH, M. D., and BELL, S. M. (1969), 'Some contemporary patterns of mother–infant interaction in the feeding situation', in A. Ambrose (ed.), *Stimulation in Early Infancy*, Academic Press, New York.

AINSWORTH, M. D., BELL, S. M., and STAYTON, D. J. (1974), 'Infant–mother attachment and social development: socialization as a product of reciprocal responsiveness to signals', in M. P. M. Richards (ed.), *The Integration of a Child into a Social World*, Cambridge University Press.

AINSWORTH, M. D., and WITTIG, B. A. (1969), 'Attachment and exploratory behaviour of one year olds in a strange situation', in B. M. Foss (ed.), *Determinants of Infant Behaviour*, vol. 4, Methuen.

ANDRY, R. G. (1960), *Delinquency and Parental Pathology*, Methuen.

ANTONOVSKY, A. (1979), *Health, Stress and Coping*, Jossey-Bass, San Francisco.

APLEY, J., DAVIES, J., DAVIS, D. R., SILK, B. (1971), 'Non-physical causes of dwarfism', *Proc. Roy. Soc. Med.*, vol. 64, pp. 135–8.

ARSENIAN, J. M. (1943), 'Young children in an insecure situation', *J. abnorm. soc. Psychol.*, vol. 38, pp. 225–49.

ASHER, E. J. (1935), 'The inadequacy of current intelligence tests for testing Kentucky mountain children', *J. genet. Psychol.*, vol. 46, pp. 480–86.

BACH, G. R. (1946), 'Father-fantasies and father-typing in father-separated children', *Child Devel.*, vol. 17, pp. 63–80.

BAERS, M. (1954), 'Women workers and home responsibilities', *Int. Lab. Rev.*, vol. 69, pp. 338–55.

BAKWIN, H. (1949), 'Emotional deprivation in infants', *J. Pediat.*, vol. 35, pp. 512–21.

BANDURA, A. (1969), 'Social-learning theory of identificatory processes', in D. A. Goslin (ed.), *Handbook of Socialization Theory and Research*, Rand McNally, New York.

BARNETT, S. A., and BURN, J. (1967), 'Early stimulation and maternal behaviour', *Nature*, vol. 213, pp. 150–52.

BARRACLOUGH, B., and NELSON, B. (1971), 'Marriage and suicide', paper presented at Annual Conference of Society for Psychosomatic Research, London, 1971.

BARRY, W. A. (1970), 'Marriage research and conflict: an integrative review', *Psychol. Bull.*, vol. 73, pp. 41–54.

BATESON, P. P. (1966), 'The characteristics and context of imprinting', *Biol. Rev.*, vol. 41, pp. 177–211.

BEAUMONT, W. (1833), *Experiment and Observations on the Gastric Juice and the Physiology of Digestion*, F. P. Allen, Plattsburg.

BEBBINGTON, P. (1980), 'Causal models and logical inference in epidemiological psychiatry', *Brit. J. Psychiat.*, vol. 136, pp. 317–25.

BECKER, W. C. (1964), 'Consequences of different kinds of parental discipline', in M. L. Hoffman and L. W. Hoffman (eds.), *Review of Child Development Research*, vol. 1, Russell Sage Foundation, New York.

BELL, R. Q. (1964), 'The effect on the family of a limitation in coping ability in a child: a research approach and a finding', *Merrill-Palmer Q.*, vol. 10, pp. 129–42.

BELL, R. Q. (1968), 'A reinterpretation of the direction of effects in studies of socialization', *Psychol. Rev.*, vol. 75, pp. 81–95.

BELL, R. Q. (1971), 'Stimulus control of parent or caretaker behaviour by offspring', *Devel. Psychol.*, vol. 4, pp. 63–72.

BELL, R. Q. (1974), 'Contributions of human infants to care-giving and social interaction', in M. Lewis and L. A. Rosenblum (eds.), *The Effects of the Infant on its Caregiver*, Wiley, New York.

BELL, R. W., and DENENBERG, V. H. (1963), 'The interrelationships of shock and critical periods in infancy as they affect adult learning and activity', *Anim. Behav.*, vol. 11, pp. 21–7.

BELL, S. M., and AINSWORTH, M. D. S. (1972), 'Infant crying and maternal responsiveness', *Child Devel.*, vol. 43, pp. 1171–1190.

BELSKY, J., and STEINBERG, L. D. (1978), 'The effects of day care: a critical review', *Child Devel.*, vol. 49, pp. 929–49.

BENDER, L. (1947), 'Psychopathic behavior disorders in children', in R. M. Linder and R. V. Seliger (eds.), *Handbook of Correctional Psychology*, Philosophical Library, New York.

BERGER, M., and PASSINGHAM, R. E. (1972), 'Early experience and other environmental factors: an overview', in H. J. Eysenck (ed.), *Handbook of Abnormal Psychology*, 2nd edn, Pitman.

BERNSTEIN, B. (1961), 'Social class and linguistic development: a theory of social learning', in A. H. Halsey, J. Floud and C. A. Anderson (eds.), *Education, Economy and Society*, Free Press.

BERNSTEIN, B. (1965), 'A socio-linguistic approach to social learning', in J. Gould (ed.), *Social Science Survey*, Penguin.

BERNSTEIN, B. (ed.) (1972), *Class, Codes and Control: Applied Studies towards a Sociology of Language*, Routledge & Kegan Paul.

BERNSTEIN, B., and YOUNG, D. (1967), 'Social class differences in conceptions of the uses of toys', *Sociology*, vol. 1. pp. 131–40.

BILLER, H. B. (1971), *Father, Child and Sex Role: Paternal Determinants of Personality Development*, Heath, Lexington.

BINGHAM, W. E., and GRIFFITHS, W. J. (1952), 'The effect of different environments during infancy on adult behaviour in the rat', *J. comp. physiol. Psychol.*, vol. 45, pp. 307–12.

BIRCH, H. G., and GUSSOW, J. D. (1970), *Disadvantaged Children: Health, Nutrition and School Failure*, Grune & Stratton.

BIRTCHNELL, J. (1969), 'The possible consequences of early parent death', *Brit. J. med. Psychol.*, vol. 42, pp. 1–12.

BLANCHARD, M., and MAIN, M. (1979), 'Avoidance of the attachment figure and social–emotional adjustment in day-care infants', *Devel. Psychol.*, vol. 15, pp. 445–6.

BLEHAR, M. C. (1974), 'Anxious attachment and defensive reactions associated with day care', *Child Devel.*, vol. 45, pp. 683–692.

BLEHAR, M. C., LIEBERMAN, A. F., and AINSWORTH, M. D. S. (1977), 'Early face-to-face interaction and its relation to later infant–mother attachment', *Child Devel.*, vol. 48, pp. 182–94.

BLOCK, J., BLOCK, J., and MORRISON, A. (1980), 'Parental agreement–disagreement on child-rearing orientations and gender-related personality correlates in children', *Child Devel.* (in press).

BOHMAN, M. (1970), *Adopted Children and Their Families: A Follow-Up Study of Adopted Children, Their Background, Environment and Adjustment*, Proprius, Stockholm.

BONIFACE, D., and GRAHAM, P. (1979), 'The three-year-old and his attachment to a special soft object', *J. Child Psychol. Psychiat.*, vol. 20, pp. 217–24.

BOWLBY, J. (1946), *Forty-Four Juvenile Thieves: Their Characters and Home-Life*, Baillère, Tindall & Cox.

BOWLBY, J. (1951), *Maternal Care and Mental Health*, World Health Organization, Geneva.

BOWLBY, J. (1958a), 'The nature of the child's tie to his mother', *Int. J. Psychoanal.*, vol. 39, pp. 350–73.

BOWLBY, J. (1958b), *Can I Leave My Baby?*, National Association for Mental Health.

BOWLBY, J. (1961), 'The Adolf Meyer lecture: childhood mourning and its implications for psychiatry', *Amer. J. Psychiat.*, vol. 188, pp. 481–97.

BOWLBY, J. (1962), 'Childhood bereavement and psychiatric illness', in D. Richter, J. M. Tanner, Lord Taylor and O. L. Zangwill (eds.), *Aspects of Psychiatric Research*, Oxford University Press.

BOWLBY, J. (1968), 'Effects on behaviour of disruption of an affectional bond', in J. D. Thoday and A. S. Parkes (eds.), *Genetic and Environmental Influences on Behaviour*, Oliver & Boyd.

BOWLBY, J. (1969), *Attachment and Loss: I. Attachment*, Hogarth Press.

BOWLBY, J. (1973), *Attachment and Loss: II. Separation, Anxiety and Anger*, Hogarth Press.

BOWLBY, J. (1980), *Attachment and Loss: III. Loss, Sadness and Depression*, Basic Books, New York.

BOWLBY, J., AINSWORTH, M. D., BOSTON, M., and ROSEN-

BLUTH, D. (1956), 'The effects of mother–child separation: a follow-up study', *Brit. J. med. Psychol.*, vol. 29, pp. 211–47.

BOWLBY, J., and PARKES, C. D. (1970), 'Separation and loss within the family', in E. J. Anthony and C. M. Koupernik (eds.), *The Child in His Family*, Wiley, London.

BRADLEY, R. H., and CALDWELL, B. M. (1976), 'Early home environment and changes in mental test performance in children from 6 to 36 months', *Devel. Psychol.*, vol. 12, pp. 93–7.

BRADLEY, R. H., CALDWELL, B. M., and ELARDO, R. (1979), 'Home environment and cognitive development in the first two years; a cross-lagged panel analysis', *Devel. Psychol.*, vol. 15, pp. 246–50.

BRANDIS, B., and HENDERSON, D. (1970), *Social Class, Language and Communication*, Routledge & Kegan Paul.

BRAZELTON, T. B., TRONICK, E., ADAMSON, L., ALS, H., and WEISE, S. (1975), 'Early mother–infant reciprocity', in R. Porter and M. O'Connor (eds.), *Parent–Infant Interaction*, Ciba Foundation Symposium 33 (new series), Associated Scientific Publishers, Amsterdam.

BRIDGER, W. H., and BIRNS, B. (1968), 'Experience and temperament in human neonates', in G. Newton and S. Levine (eds.), *Early Experience and Behavior*, C. C. Thomas, Springfield, Ill.

BRODBECK, A. J., and IRWIN, O. C. (1946), 'The speech behaviour of infants without families', *Child Devel.*, vol. 17, pp. 145–56.

BRONFENBRENNER, U. (1961), 'Some familial antecedents of responsibility and leadership in adolescents', in L. Petrullo and B. M. Bass (eds.), *Leadership and Interpersonal Behavior*, Holt, Rinehart & Winston, New York.

BRONFENBRENNER, U. (1968), 'Early deprivation in mammals: a cross-species analysis', in G. Newton and S. Levine (eds.), *Early Experience and Behavior*, C. C. Thomas, Springfield, Ill.

BRONFENBRENNER, U. (1974), 'Is early intervention effective? A report on the longitudinal evaluations of pre-school programmes', Office of Child Development, US Dept of Health, Education and Welfare, Bethesda, Md.

BRONFENBRENNER, U. (1979), *The Ecology of Human Development: experiments by nature and design*, Harvard University Press, Cambridge, Mass.

BROOKHART, J., and HOCK, E. (1976), 'The effects of experimental context and experiential background on infants' behavior toward their mothers and a stranger', *Child Devel.*, vol. 47, pp. 333–40.

BROSSARD, M. and DÉCARIE, T. G. (1971), 'The effects of three kinds of perceptual-social stimulation on the development of institutionalized infants: preliminary report of a longitudinal study', *Early child Devel. Care*, vol. 1, pp. 211–30.

BROWN, F. (1961), 'Depression and childhood bereavement', *J. ment. Sci.*, vol. 107, pp. 754–77.

BROWN, G. W., BHROLCHAIN, M. N., and HARRIS, T. (1975), 'Social class and psychiatric disturbance among women in an urban population', *Sociology*, vol. 9, pp. 225–54.

BROWN, G. W., and HARRIS, T. (1978), *Social Origins of Depression: A Study of Psychiatric Disorders in Women*, Tavistock Publications.

BROWN, G. W., and RUTTER, M. (1966), 'The measurement of family activities and relationships: a methodological study', *Hum. Rel.*, vol. 19, pp. 241–63.

BROWN, J. V., and BATEMAN, R. (1978), 'Relationships of human mothers with their infants during the first year of life: effects of prematurity', in R. W. Bell and W. P. Smotherman (eds.), *Maternal Influences and Early Behavior*, Spectrum, Holliswood, NY.

BROWN, R., CAZDEN, C., and BELLUGI-KLIMA, U. (1969), 'The child's grammar from I to III', in J. P. Hill (ed.), *Minnesota Symposia on Child Psychology*, vol. 2, University of Minnesota Press, Minneapolis.

BRUNER, J. (1980), *Under Five in Britain*, Grant McIntyre, London.

BRYANT, B., HARRIS, M., and NEWTON, D. (1980), *Children and Minders*, Grant McIntyre, London.

BUNCH, J. (1972), 'Recent bereavement in relation to suicide', *J. psychosom. Res.*, vol. 16, pp. 361–6.

BURCHINAL, L. G., and ROSSMAN, J. E. (1961), 'Relations among maternal employment indices and developmental characteristics of children', *Marr. fam. Living*, vol. 23, pp. 334–40.

BURLINGHAM, D., and FREUD, A. (1942), *Young Children in Wartime*, Allen & Unwin.

BURLINGHAM, D., and FREUD, A. (1944), *Infants without Families: The Case for and against Residential Nurseries*, Allen & Unwin.

CAIRNS, R. B. (1966a), 'Development, maintenance and extinction of social attachment behavior in sheep', *J. comp. physiol. Psychol.*, vol. 62, pp. 298–306.

CAIRNS, R. B. (1966b), 'The attachment behavior of mammals', *Psychol. Rev.*, vol. 73, pp. 409–26.

CAIRNS, R. B. (1972), 'Attachment and dependency: a psychobiological and social learning synthesis', in J. L. Gewirtz (ed.), *Attachment and Dependency*, Winston, Washington.

CAIRNS, R. B. (1977), 'Beyond social attachment: the dynamics of interactional development', in T. Alloway, P. Pliner and L. Krames (eds.), *Advances in the Study of Communication and Affect*, vol. 3, Plenum, New York.

CALDWELL, B. M. (1962), 'Mother–infant interaction in monomatric and polymatric families', *Amer. J. Orthopsychiat.*, vol. 32, pp. 340–41.

CALDWELL, B. M. (1964), 'The effects of infant care', in M. L. Hoffman and L. W. Hoffman (eds.), *Review of Child Development Research*, vol. 1, Russell Sage Foundation, New York.

CALDWELL, B. M. (1970), 'The effects of psychosocial deprivation on human development in infancy', *Merrill-Palmer Q.*, vol. 16, pp. 260–77.

CALDWELL, B. M., WRIGHT, C. M., HONIG, A. C., and TANNENBAUM, J. (1970), 'Infant day care and attachment', *Amer. J. Orthopsychiat.*, vol. 40, pp. 397–412.

CAPLAN, M. G., and DOUGLAS, V. I. (1969), 'Incidence of parental loss in children with depressed mood', *J. Child Psychol. Psychiat.*, vol. 10, pp. 225–32.

CARTWRIGHT, A., and JEFFREYS, M. (1958), 'Married women who work: their own and their children's health', *Brit. J. prev. soc. Med.*, vol. 12, pp. 159–71.

CASLER, L. (1961), 'Maternal deprivation: a critical review of the literature', *Monogr. Soc. Res. Child Devel.*, vol. 26, no. 2.

CASLER, L. (1965), 'The effects of supplementary verbal stimulation on a group of institutionalized infants', *J. Child Psychol. Psychiat.*, vol. 6, pp. 19–27.

CASLER, L. (1968), 'Perceptual deprivation in institutional settings', in G. Newton and S. Levine (eds.), *Early Experience and Behavior*, C. C. Thomas, Springfield, Ill.

CAZDEN, C. (1966), 'Subcultural differences in child language: an interdisciplinary review', *Merrill-Palmer Q.*, vol. 12, pp. 185–219.

CHOW, B. F., BLACKWELL, R. Q., BLACKWELL, B. N., HOU, T. Y., ANILANE, J. K., and SHERWIN, R. W. (1968), 'Maternal nutrition and metabolism of the offspring: studies in rats and man', *Amer. J. pub. Health*, vol. 58, pp. 668–77.

CLAIBORN, W. L. (1969), 'Expectancy effects in the classroom: a failure to replicate', *J. educ. Psychol.*, vol. 60, pp. 377–83.

CLARKE, A. D. B. (1968), 'Problems in assessing the later effects of early experience', in E. Miller (ed.), *Foundations of Child Psychiatry*, Pergamon.

CLARKE, A. D. B., CLARKE, A. M., and REIMAN, S. (1958), 'Cognitive and social changes in the feeble-minded: three further studies', *Brit. J. Psychol.*, vol. 49, pp. 144–57.

CLARKE, A. M., and CLARKE, A. D. B. (1976), *Early Experience: Myth and Evidence*, Open Books, London.

CLARKE-STEWART, K. A. (1973), 'Interactions between mothers and their young children: characteristics and consequences', *Monogr. Soc. Res. Child Devel.*, vol. 38, no. 153.

CLARKE-STEWART, K. A. (1978), 'And daddy makes three: the father's impact on mother and young child', *Child Devel.*, vol. 49, pp. 446–78.

CLARKE-STEWART, K. A., VANDER-STOEP, L. P., and KILLIAN, G. A. (1979), 'Analysis and replication of mother–child relations at two years of age', *Child Devel.*, vol. 50, pp. 777–93.

CLAUSEN, J. A. (1966), 'Family structure, socialization and personality', in L. W. Hoffman and M. Hoffman (eds.), *Rev. Child Devel. Res.*, vol. 2, Russell Sage Foundation, New York.

COATES, B., ANDERSON, E. P., and HARTUP, W. W. (1972), 'Interrelations in the attachment behavior of human infants', *Devel. Psychol.*, vol. 6, pp. 218–30.

COCHRAN, M. M. (1977), 'A comparison of group day and family child-rearing patterns in Sweden', *Child Devel.*, vol. 48, pp. 702–7.

COELHO, G. V., HAMBURG, D. A., and ADAMS, J. E. (eds.) (1974), *Coping and Adaptation*, Basic Books, New York.

COHEN, F., and LAZARUS, R. S. (1979), 'Coping with the stresses of illness', in G. C. Stone, F. Cohen, N. E. Adler, and associates, *Health Psychology – A Handbook*, Jossey-Bass, San Francisco, pp. 217–54.

COHEN, L. J. (1974), 'The operational definition of human attachment', *Psychol. Bull.*, vol. 81, pp. 107–217.

COHEN, L. J., and CAMPOS, J. J. (1974), 'Father, mother and stranger as elicitors of attachment behaviors in infancy', *Devel. Psychol.*, vol. 10, pp. 146–54.

COHEN, S. E. (1978), 'Maternal employment and mother–child interaction', *Merrill-Palmer Q.*, vol. 24, pp. 189–97.

COLLINGWOOD, J., and ALBERMAN, E. (1979), 'Separation at birth and the mother–infant relationship', *Devel. Med. Child Neurol.*, vol. 21, pp. 608–18.

CONDON, W. S., and SANDER, L. W. (1974), 'Speech: interactional participation and language acquisition', *Science*, vol. 183, pp. 99–101.

CONWAY, E. S. (1957), 'The institutional care of children: a case history', unpublished Ph.D. thesis, University of London.

COOPER, R. M., and ZUBEK, J. P. (1958), 'Effects of enriched and restricted early environments on the learning ability of bright and dull rats', *Canad. J. Psychol.*, vol. 12, pp. 159–64.

CORNELIUS, S., and DENNEY, N. (1975), 'Dependency in day-care and home-care children', *Devel. Psychol.*, vol. 11, pp. 575–82.

CORTER, C. M. (1973), 'A comparison of the mother's and a stranger's control over the behavior of infants', *Child Devel.*, vol. 44, pp. 705–13.

CORTER, C. M. (1974), 'Infant attachment', in B. Foss (ed.), *New Perspectives in Child Development*, Penguin, Harmondsworth.

COX, A., RUTTER, M., YULE, B., and QUINTON, D. (1977), 'Bias resulting from missing information: some epidemiological findings', *Brit. J. Prev. Soc. Med.*, vol. 31, pp. 131–6.

COX, F. N., and CAMPBELL, D. (1968), 'Young children in a new situation with and without their mothers', *Child Devel.*, vol. 39, pp. 123–31.

CRAIG, M. M., and GLICK, S. J. (1965), *A Manual of Procedures for Application of the Glueck Prediction Table*, University of London Press.

CRAVIOTO, J., DeLICARDIE, E. R., and BIRCH, H. G. (1966), 'Nutrition, growth and neurointegrative development: an experimental and ecologic study', *Pediatrics*, vol. 38 (suppl.), pp. 319–72.

CRELLIN, E., PRINGLE, M. L. K., and WEST, P. (1971), *Born Illegitimate: social and educational implications*, N.F.E.R., Slough.

CROOK, T., and ELIOT, J. (1980), 'Parental death during childhood and adult depression', *Psychol. Bull.*, vol. 87, pp. 252–9.

CROWE, R. R. (1974), 'An adoption study of antisocial personality', *Arch. gen. Psychiat.*, vol. 31, pp. 785–91.

CUMMINGS, F. M. (1980), 'Caretaker stability and day care', *Devel. Psychol.*, vol. 16, pp. 31–7.

CUMMINGS, S. T., BAYLEY, M. C., and RIE, H. E. (1966), 'Effects of the child's deficiency on the mother: a study of mothers of mentally retarded, chronically ill and neurotic children', *Amer. J. Orthopsychiat.*, vol. 36, pp. 595–608.

CURTISS, S. (1977), *Genie: A Psycholinguistic Study of a Modern-Day 'Wild Child'*, Academic Press, New York.

DARLINGTON, R. B., ROYCE, J. M., SNIPPER, A. S., MURRAY, H. W., and LAZAR, I. (1980), 'Pre-school programs and later school competence of children from low-income families', *Science*, vol. 208, pp. 202–4.

DAVENPORT, H. T., and WERRY, J. S. (1970), 'The effect of general anesthesia surgery and· hospitalization upon the behavior of children', *Amer. J. Orthopsychiat.*, vol. 40, pp. 806–824.

DAVENPORT, R. K., and ROGERS, C. M. (1968), 'Intellectual performance of differentially reared chimpanzees: 1. Delayed response', *Amer. J. ment. Def.*, vol. 72, pp. 674–80.

DAVENPORT, R. K., MENZEL, E. W., and ROGERS, C. M. (1961), 'Maternal care during infancy: its effect on weight gain and mortality in the chimpanzee', *Amer. J. Orthopsychiat.*, vol. 31, pp. 803–9.

DAVENPORT, R. K., MENZEL, E. W., and ROGERS, C. M. (1966), 'Effects of severe isolation on "normal" juvenile chimpanzees: health, weight gain and stereotyped behaviors', *Arch. gen. Psychiat.*, vol. 14, pp. 134–8.

DAVID, M., and APPELL, G. (1961), 'A study of nursing care and nurse–infant interaction: a report on the first half of an investigation', in B. M. Foss (ed.), *Determinants of Infant Behaviour*, vol. 1, Methuen.

DAVIS, K. (1947), 'Final note on a case of extreme isolation', *Amer. J. Sociol.*, vol. 52, pp. 432–7.

DAW, N. W., BERMAN, N. E. J., and ARIEL, M. (1978), 'Interaction of critical periods in visual cortex of kittens', *Science*, vol. 199, pp. 565–7.

DE CHATEAU, P., and WIBERG, B. (1977a and b), 'Long-term effect on mother–infant behaviour of extra contact during the first hour post partum: I. First observations at 36 hours; II. A follow-up at three months', *Acta Paediat. Scand.*, vol. 66, pp. 137–43 and 145–51.

DEFRIES, J. C. (1964), 'Prenatal maternal stress in mice: differential effects on behaviour', *J. Hered.*, vol. 55, pp. 289–295.

DEGROOT, A. D. (1951), 'War and the intelligence of youth', *J. Abn. Soc. Psychol.*, vol. 46, pp. 596–7.

DENENBERG, V. H. (1969), 'Animal studies of early experience: some principles which have implications for human development', in J. P. Hill (ed.), *Minnesota Symposia on Child Psychology*, vol. 3, University of Minnesota Press, Minneapolis.

DENENBERG, V. H., and KLINE, N. J. (1964), 'Stimulus intensity vs critical periods: a test of two hypotheses concerning infantile stimulation', *Canad. J. Psychol.*, vol. 18, pp. 1–5.

DENNIS, W. (1960), 'Causes of retardation among institutional children: Iran', *J. genet. Psychol.*, vol. 96, pp. 47–59.

DENNIS, W. (1973), *Children of the Crèche*, Appleton-Century-Crofts, New York.

DENNIS, W., and NAJARIAN, P. (1957), 'Infant development under environmental handicap', *Psychol. Monogr.*, vol. 71, pp. 1–13.

DEUTSCH, C. P. (1964), 'Auditory discrimination and learning: social factors', *Merrill-Palmer Q.*, vol. 10, pp. 277–96.

DEUTSCH, H. (1919), 'A two-year-old boy's first love comes to grief', reprinted (1959) in L. Jessner and E. Pavenstedt (eds.), *Dynamic Psychopathology in Childhood*, Grune & Stratton, New York.

DEUTSCH, M., KATZ, I., and JENSEN, A. (eds.) (1968), *Social Class, Race and Psychological Development*, Holt, Rinehart & Winston, New York.

DINNAGE, R., and PRINGLE, M. L. K. (1967a), *Residential Child Care: Facts and Fallacies*, Longman.

DINNAGE, R., and PRINGLE, M. L. K. (1967b), *Foster Home Care: Facts and Fallacies*, Longman.

DIXON, P. (1980), paper in preparation.

DOBBING, J. (1968), 'Vulnerable periods in developing brain', in A. N. Davison and J. Dobbing (eds.), *Applied Neurochemistry*, Blackwell.

DOBZHANSKY, T. (1967), 'On types, genotypes and genetic diversity in populations', in J. N. Spuhler (ed.), *Genetic Diversity and Human Behavior*, Aldine, Chicago.

DOLLARD, J., and MILLER, N. E. (1950), *Personality and Psychotherapy*, McGraw-Hill, New York.

DOUGLAS, J. W. B. (1960), 'Premature children at primary schools', *Brit. med. J.*, vol. 1, pp. 1008–13.

DOUGLAS, J. W. B. (1964), *The Home and the School*, MacGibbon & Kee.

DOUGLAS, J. W. B. (1970), 'Broken families and child behaviour', *J. Roy. Coll. Physns Lond.*, vol. 4, pp. 203–10.

DOUGLAS, J. W. B. (1973), 'Early disturbing events and later enuresis', in I. Kolvin, R. MacKeith and R. Meadow (eds.), *Bladder Control and Enuresis*, Clinics in Developmental Medicine Nos. 48/49, Heinemann/S I M P.

DOUGLAS, J. W. B. (1975), 'Early hospital admissions and later disturbances of behaviour and learning', *Devel. Med. Child Neurol.*, vol. 17, pp. 456–80.

## 230 References

DOUGLAS, J. W. B., and BLOMFIELD, J. M. (1958), *Children under Five*, Allen & Unwin.

DOUGLAS, J. W. B., ROSS, J. M., HAMMOND, W. A., and MULLIGAN, D. G. (1966), 'Delinquency and social class', *Brit. J. Criminol.*, vol. 6, pp. 294–302.

DOUGLAS, J. W. B., ROSS, J. M., and SIMPSON, H. R. (1968), *All Our Future: A Longitudinal Study of Secondary Education*, Peter Davies.

DOUGLAS, J. W. B., and TURNER, R. K. (1970), 'The association of anxiety provoking events in early childhood with enuresis', *Proc. Fifth Int. Sci. Meeting of Int. Epid. Assn*, Savremena Adinistracija, Belgrade.

DOYLE, A. B. (1975), 'Infant development in day care', *Devel. Psychol.*, vol. 11, pp. 655–6.

DREWE, E. A., ETTLINGER, G., MILNER, A. D., and PASSINGHAM, R. E. (1970), 'A comparative review of the results of neuropsychological research on man and monkey', *Cortex*, vol. 6, pp. 129–63.

DRILLIEN, C. M. (1964), *Growth and Development of the Prematurely Born Infant*, Livingstone, Edinburgh.

DRILLIEN, C. M., THOMSON, A. J. M., and BURGOYNE, K. (1980), 'Low birth-weight children at early school-age: a longitudinal study', *Devel. Med. Child Neurol.*, vol. 2, pp. 26–47.

DUNN, J. (1975), 'Consistency and change in styles of mothering', in R. Porter and M. O'Connor (eds.), *Parent–Infant Interaction*, Ciba Foundation Symposium 33 (new series), Associated Scientific Publishers, Amsterdam.

DUNN, J. (1980), 'Individual differences in temperament', in M. Rutter (ed.), *Scientific Foundations of Developmental Psychiatry*, Heinemann Medical.

DU PAN, M., and ROTH, S. (1955), 'The psychological development of a group of children brought up in a hospital type residential nursery', *J. Pediat.*, vol. 47, pp. 124–9.

EASTERBROOKS, M. A., and LAMB, M. E. (1979), 'The relationship between quality of infant–mother attachment and infant competence in initial encounters with peers', *Child Devel.*, vol. 50, pp. 380–87.

EATON, W. W. (1978), 'Life events, social supports, and psychiatric symptoms: a re-analysis of the New Haven data', *J. Health Soc. Behav.*, vol. 19, pp. 230–34.

ECKERMAN, C. O., WHATLEY, J. L., and KATZ, S. L. (1975), 'Growth of social play with peers during the second year of life', *Devel. Psychol.*, vol. 11, pp. 42–9.

ECKLAND, B., and KENT, D. P. (1968), 'Socialization and social structure', in *Perspectives on Human Deprivation: Biological, Psychological and Sociological*, US Department of Health, Education and Welfare, Washington, DC.

EISENBERG, L. (1967), 'Clinical considerations in the psychiatric evaluation of intelligence', in J. Zubin and G. A. Jervis (eds.), *Psychopathology of Mental Development*, Grune & Stratton.

EISENBERG, L. (1969), 'The social development of intelligence', in H. Freeman (ed.), *Progress in Mental Health*, Churchill.

ELARDO, R., BRADLEY, R. H., and CALDWELL, B. M. (1975), 'The relation of infants' home environment to mental test performance from 6 to 36 months: a longitudinal analysis', *Child Devel.*, vol. 46, pp. 71-6.

ENGEL, G. L., REICHSMAN, F., and SEGAL, H. (1956), 'A study of an infant with gastric fistula: I. Behavior and the rate of total hydrochloric acid secretion', *Psychosom. Med.*, vol. 18, pp. 374-98.

ETZEL, B. C., and GEWIRTZ, J. L. (1967), 'Experimental modification of caretaker-maintained high rate operant crying in a 6- and a 20-week old infant (infans tyrannotearus): extinction of crying with reinforcement of eye contact and smiling', *J. Exp. Child Psychol.*, vol. 5, pp. 303-13.

FABRICIUS, E. (1962), 'Some aspects of imprinting in birds', *Symp. Zool. Soc. Lond.*, vol. 8, pp. 139-48.

FAGIN, C. M. R. N. (1966), *The Effects of Maternal Attendance during Hospitalization on the Post-Hospital Behavior of Young Children: A Comparative Study*, F. A. Davis, Philadelphia.

FARRAN, D., and RAMEY, C. (1977), 'Infant day care and attachment behaviors toward mothers and teachers', *Child Devel.*, vol. 48, pp. 1112-16.

FAUST, O. A., JACKSON, K., CERMAK, E. G., BURTT, M. M., and WINKLEY, R. (1952), *Reducing Emotional Trauma in Hospitalized Children*, Albany Research Project, Albany, New York.

FERGUSON, B. F. (1979), 'Preparing young children for hospitalization', *Pediatrics*, vol. 64, pp. 656-64.

FERGUSON, T. (1966), *Children in Care - and After*, Oxford University Press.

FINKELSTEIN, N. W., DENT, C., GALLACHER, K., and RAMEY, C. T. (1978), 'Social behavior of infants and toddlers in a day-care environment', *Devel. Psychol.*, vol. 14, pp. 257-62.

FISCH, R. O., BILEK, M. K., DEINARD, A. S., and CHANG, P.-N. (1976), 'Growth, behavioral and psychologic measurements of adopted children: the influences of genetic and socio-economic factors in a prospective study', *J. Pediat.*, vol. 89, pp. 494–500.

FLOBTER, M. K., and GREENOUGH, W. T. (1979), 'Cerebellar plasticity: modification of Purkinje cell structure by differential rearing in monkeys', *Science*, vol. 206, pp. 227–9.

FOGELMAN, K. R., and GOLDSTEIN, H. (1976), 'Social factors associated with changes in educational attainment between 7 and 11 years of age', *Educ. Studies*, vol. 2, pp. 95–109.

FORGAYS, D. G., and FORGAYS, J. W. (1952), 'The nature of the effect of free-environmental experience in the rat', *J. comp. physiol. Psychol.*, vol. 45, pp. 322–8.

FORGUS, R. H. (1954), 'The effects of early perceptual learning on the behavioral organization of adult rats', *J. comp. physiol. Psychol.*, vol. 47, pp. 331–6.

FORGUS, R. H. (1955), 'Influence of early experience on maze-learning with and without visual cues', *Canad. J. Psychol.*, vol. 9, pp. 207–14.

FOX, M. W., and STELZNER, D. (1966), 'Approach/withdrawal variables in the development of social behaviour in the dog', *Anim. Behav.*, vol. 14, pp. 362–6.

FOX, N. (1977), 'Attachment of kibbutz infants to mother and metapelet', *Child. Devel.*, vol. 48, 1228–39.

FRANCIS, S. H. (1971), 'The effects of own-home and institution rearing on the behavioral development of normal and mongol children', *J. Child Psychol. Psychiat.*, vol. 12, pp. 173–90.

FREEBERG, N. E., and PAYNE, D. T. (1967), 'Parental influence on cognitive development in early childhood: a review', *Child Devel.*, vol. 38, pp. 65–87.

FREEDMAN, D. G. (1958), 'Constitutional and environmental interactions in rearing of four breeds of dog', *Science*, vol. 127, pp. 585–6.

FREEDMAN, D. G. (1965), 'Hereditary control of early social behaviour', in B. M. Foss (ed.), *Determinants of Infant Behaviour*, vol. 3, Methuen.

FREEDMAN, D. G., and KELLER, B. (1963), 'Inheritance of behaviour in infants', *Science*, vol. 140, pp. 196–8.

FREUD, A. (1946), *The Psycho-Analytical Treatment of Children*, Imago, London.

FREUD, A., and DANN, S. (1951), 'An experiment in group up-bringing', *Psychoanal. Stud. Child*, vol. 6, pp. 127–68.

FRIED, R., and MAYER, M. F. (1948), 'Socio-emotional factors accounting for growth failure in children living in an institution', *J. Pediat.*, vol. 33, pp. 444–56.

FRIEDLANDER, B. Z. (1971), 'Listening, language and the auditory environment: automated evaluation and intervention', in J. Hellmuth (ed.), *The Exceptional Infant: II. Studies in Abnormalities*, Brunner/Mazel, New York.

FROMMER, E. A., and O'SHEA, G. (1973a & b), 'Antenatal identification of women liable to have problems in managing their infants'; 'The importance of childhood experience in relation to problems of marriage and family-building', *Brit. J. Psychiat.*, vol. 123, pp. 149–56 and 157–60.

FURCHNER, C. S., and HARLOW, H. F. (1969), 'Preference for various surrogate surfaces among infant rhesus monkeys', *Psychonom. Sci.*, vol. 17, pp. 279–80.

GANZ, L. (1968), 'An analysis of generalization behavior in the stimulus-deprived organism', in G. Newton and S. Levine (eds.), *Early Experience and Behavior*, C. C. Thomas, Springfield, Ill.

GARBER, H., and HEBER, F. R. (1977), 'The Milwaukee project: indications of the effectiveness of early intervention in preventing mental retardation', in P. Mittler (ed.), *Research to Practice in Mental Retardation, 1. Care and Intervention*, University Park Press, Baltimore.

GARDNER, D. B., HAWKES, G. R., and BURCHINAL, L. G. (1961), 'Non-continuous mothering in infancy and development in later childhood', *Child Devel.*, vol. 32, pp. 225–34.

GARDNER, E. L., and GARDNER, E. B. (1970), 'Orientation of infant macaques to facially distinct surrogate mothers', *Devel. Psychol.*, vol. 3, pp. 409-10.

GARDNER, J. (1977), *Three aspects of childhood autism: Mother–child interactions, autonomic responsivity, and cognitive functioning* (unpublished Ph.D. thesis, University of Leicester).

GARDNER, R. A., and GARDNER, B. T. (1969), 'Teaching sign language to a chimpanzee', *Science*, vol. 165, pp. 664–72.

GARLAND, C., and WHITE, S. (1980), *Children and Day Nurseries*, Grant McIntyre, London.

GARROW, J. S., and PIKE, M. C. (1967), 'The long-term prognosis of severe infantile malnutrition', *Lancet*, vol. 1, pp. 1–4.

GARVIN, J. B., and SACKS, L. S. (1963), 'Growth potential of pre-school-aged children in institutional care: a positive approach to a negative condition', *Amer. J. Orthopsychiat.*, vol. 33, pp. 399–408.

GAVRON, H. (1966), *The Captive Wife*, Routledge & Kegan Paul.

GAW, F. (1925), 'A study of performance tests', *Brit. J. Psychol.*, vol. 15, pp. 374–92.

GEWIRTZ, J. L. (1961), 'A learning analysis of the effects of normal stimulation, privation and deprivation on the acquisition

## 234 References

of social motivation and attachment', in B. M. Foss (ed.), *Determinants of Infant Behaviour*, vol. 1, Methuen.

GEWIRTZ, J. L. (1968), 'The role of stimulation in models for child development', in L. L. Dittman (ed.), *Early Child Care: The New Perspectives*, Atherton Press, New York.

GEWIRTZ, J. L. (1969), 'Mechanisms of social learning: some roles of stimulation and behavior in early human development', in D. A. Goslin (ed.), *Handbook of Socialization Theory and Research*, Rand McNally, New York.

GEWIRTZ, J. L. (ed.) (1972a), *Attachment and Dependency*, Winston, Washington.

GEWIRTZ, J. L. (1972b), 'Attachment, dependence, and a distinction in terms of stimulus control', in J. L. Gewirtz (ed.), *Attachment and Dependency*, Winston, Washington.

GEWIRTZ, J. L., and BOYD, E. F. (1976), 'Mother–infant interaction and its study', in H. W. Reese (ed.), *Advances in Child Development and Behavior*, vol. 11, Academic Press, New York.

GEWIRTZ, J. L., and BOYD, E. F. (1977), 'Does maternal responding imply reduced infant crying?: a critique of the 1972 Bell and Ainsworth report', *Child Devel.*, vol. 48, pp. 1200–07.

GIBBENS, T. C. N., and WALKER, A. (1956), *Cruel Parents: case studies of prisoners convicted of violence towards children*, Institute for the Study and Treatment of Delinquency, London.

GIBSON, H. B. (1969), 'Early delinquency in relation to broken homes', *J. Child Psychol. Psychiat.*, vol. 10, pp. 195–204.

GLASS, H. B. (1954), 'The genetic aspects of adaptability', *Proc. Assn Res. Nerv. Ment. Dis.*, vol. 23, pp. 367–77.

GLUECK, S., and GLUECK, E. T. (1950), *Unravelling Juvenile Delinquency*, Commonwealth Fund, New York.

GLUECK, S., and GLUECK, E. T. (1962), *Family Environment and Delinquency*, Routledge & Kegan Paul.

GOLD, D., and ANDRES, D. (1978a), 'Relations between maternal employment and development of nursery school children', *Canad. J. Behav. Sci.*, vol. 10, pp. 116–29.

GOLD, D., and ANDRES, D. (1978b), 'Comparisons of adolescent children with employed and non-employed mothers', *Merrill-Palmer Q.*, vol. 24, pp. 243–54.

GOLDBERG, S. (1977), 'Social competence in infancy: a model of parent–infant interaction', *Merrill-Palmer Q.*, vol. 23, pp. 163–77.

GOLDBERGER, A. (1972), *Follow Up Notes on the Children from Bulldog Bank* (unpublished paper).

GOLDFARB, W. (1943a), 'The effects of early institutional care on adolescent personality', *J. Exper. Educ.*, vol. 12, pp. 106–29.

GOLDFARB, W. (1943b), 'Infant rearing and problem behavior', *Amer. J. Orthopsychiat.*, vol. 13, pp. 249–65.

GOLDFARB, W. (1945a), 'Psychological privation in infancy and subsequent adjustment', *Amer. J. Orthopsychiat.*, vol. 15, pp. 247–55.

GOLDFARB, W. (1945b), 'Effects of psychological deprivation in infancy and subsequent stimulation', *Amer. J. Psychiat.*, vol. 102, pp. 18–33.

GOLDFARB, W. (1947), 'Variations in adolescent adjustment of institutionally reared children', *Amer. J. Orthopsychiat.*, vol. 17, pp. 449–57.

GOLDFARB, W. (1955), 'Emotional and intellectual consequences of psychologic deprivation in infancy: a revaluation', in P. H. Hoch and J. Zubin (eds.), *Psychopathology of Childhood*, Grune & Stratton, New York.

GORDON, H. (1923), *Mental and Scholastic Tests among Retarded Children*, Board of Education.

GRAHAM, P., and GEORGE, S. (1972), 'Children's response to parental illness: individual differences', *J. Psychosom. Res.*, vol. 16, pp. 251–5.

GRAHAM, P., RUTTER, M., and GEORGE, S. (1973), 'Temperamental characteristics as predictors of behavior disorders in children', *Amer. J. Orthopsychiat.*, vol. 43, pp. 328–39.

GREGORY, I. (1965), 'Anterospective data following childhood loss of a parent', *Arch. gen. Psychiat.*, vol. 13, pp. 110–20.

GUITON, P. (1966), 'Early experience and sexual object choice in the brown leghorn', *Anim. Behav.*, vol. 14, pp. 534–8.

GURIN, G., VEROFF, J., and FELD, S. (1960), *Americans and their mental health: a nationwide interview survey*, Basic Books, New York.

HALES, D. J., LOZOFF, B., SOSA, R., and KENNELL, J. H. (1977), 'Defining the limits of the maternal sensitive period', *Devel. Med. Child Neurol.*, vol. 19, pp. 454–61.

HALL, F., PAWLBY, S. J., and WOLKIND, S. (1979), 'Early life experiences and later mothering behaviour: a study of mothers and their 20-week-old babies', in D. Shaffer and J. Dunn (eds.), *The First Years of Life: psychological and medical implications of early experience*, Wiley, Chichester and New York, pp. 153–174.

HANDEL, G. (ed.) (1968), *The Psychosocial Interior of the Family: A Source Book for the Study of Whole Families*, Allen & Unwin.

HARLOW, H. F. (1958), 'The nature of love', *Amer. Psychol.*, vol. 13, pp. 673–85.

HARLOW, H. F. (1961), 'The development of affectional patterns in infant monkeys', in B. M. Foss (ed.), *Determinants of Infant Behaviour*, vol. 1, Methuen.

HARLOW, H. F. (1963), 'The maternal affectional system', in B. M. Foss (ed.), *Determinants of Infant Behaviour*, vol. 2, Methuen.

HARLOW, H. F. (1969), 'Age-mate or peer affectional systems', in D. S. Lehrman, R. A. Hinde and E. Shaw (eds.), *Advances in the Study of Behavior*, vol. 2, Academic Press, New York.

HARLOW, H. F., and GRIFFIN, G. (1965), 'Induced mental and social deficits in rhesus monkeys', in S. F. Osler and R. E. Cooke (eds.), *The Biosocial Basis of Mental Retardation*, Johns Hopkins Press, Baltimore, Md.

HARLOW, H. F., and HARLOW, M. K. (1965), 'The affectional systems', in A. D. Schrier, H. F. Harlow and F. Stollnitz (eds.), *Behavior of Non-Human Primates*, vol. 2, Academic Press.

HARLOW, H. F., and HARLOW, M. K. (1969), 'Effects of various mother–infant relationships on rhesus monkey behaviours', in B. M. Foss (ed.), *Determinants of Infant Behaviour*, vol. 4, Methuen.

HARLOW, H. F., and HARLOW, M. K. (1970), 'Developmental aspects of emotional behavior', in P. Black (ed.), *Physiological Correlates of Emotion*, Academic Press, New York.

HARLOW, H. F., and HARLOW, M. K. (1971), 'Psychopathology in monkeys', in H. D. Kimmel (ed.), *Experimental Psychopathology*, Academic Press, New York.

HARLOW, H. F., and HARLOW, M. K. (1972), 'The affectional systems', in A. Schrier, H. F. Harlow and F. Stollnitz (eds.), *Behavior of Non-Human Primates*, vol. 2, Academic Press, New York.

HARLOW, H. F., SCHLITZ, K. A., and HARLOW, M. K. (1969), 'Effects of social isolation on the learning performance of rhesus monkeys', in *Proc. Second Int. Congr. Primatol., Atlanta, Georgia*, vol. 1, S. Karger.

HARLOW, H. F., and SUOMI, S. J. (1971), 'Social recovery by isolation reared monkeys', *Proc. Nat. Acad. Sci.*, vol. 68, pp. 1534–8.

HARLOW, H. F.. and ZIMMERMANN, R. R. (1959), 'Affectional responses in the infant monkey', *Science*, vol. 130, pp. 421–432.

HARNQVIST, K. (1968), 'Relative changes in intelligence from 13 to 18', *Scand. J. Psychol.*, vol. 9, pp. 50–82.

HARPER, L. V. (1971), 'The young as a source of stimuli controlling caretaker behaviour', *Devel. Psychol.*, vol. 4, pp. 73–88.

HARPER, P. A., and WIENER, G. (1965), '*Sequelae* of low birth weight', *Ann. Rev. Med.*, vol. 16, pp. 405–20.

HARTUP, W. W. (1979), 'Peer relations and the growth of social competence', in M. W. Kent and J. E. Rolf (eds.), *Primary Prevention of Psychopathology: 3. Social Competence in Children*, University Press of New England, Hanover, N H.

HARTUP, W. W. (1980), 'Peer relations and family relations: two social worlds', in M. Rutter (ed.), *Scientific Foundations of Developmental Psychiatry*, Heinemann Medical.

HAYWOOD, C. (1967), 'Experiential factors in intellectual development: the concept of dynamic intelligence', in J. Zubin and G. A. Jervis (eds.), *Psychopathology of Mental Development*, Grune & Stratton, New York.

HEARNSHAW, L. S. (1979), *Cyril Burt, Psychologist*, Cornell University Press, Ithaca.

HEATHERS, G. (1955), 'Emotional dependence and independence in nursery school play', *J. Genet. Psychol.*, vol. 87, pp. 37–57.

HEBB, D. O. (1949), *The Organization of Behavior*, Wiley.

HEBER, R. (1971), *Rehabilitation of Families at Risk for Mental Retardation: a progress report*, Rehabilitation Research and Training Center in Mental Retardation, Madison, Wisconsin.

HEBER, R. (1978), 'Sociocultural mental retardation – a longitudinal study', in D. Forgays (ed.), *Primary Prevention of Psychopathology: 2. Environmental Influences*, University Press of New England, Hanover, N H.

HEBER, R., and GARBER, H. (1974), *Progress report III: an experiment in the prevention of cultural-familial retardation*, Proceedings of the Third International Congress of the International Association of Scientific Studies in Mental Deficiency.

HEBER, R., GARBER, H., HARRINGTON, S., HOFFMAN, C., and FALENDER, C. (1972), *Rehabilitation of Families at Risk for Mental Retardation, December Progress Report*, University of Wisconsin, Madison.

HEIN, A., and HELD, R. (1967), 'Dissociation of the visual placing response into elicited and guided components', *Science*, vol. 158, pp. 390–92.

HEINICKE, C. M., FRIEDMAN, D., PRESCOTT, E., PUNCEL, C., and SALE, J. S. (1973), 'The organization of day care: considerations relating to the mental health of child and family', *Amer. J. Orthopsychiat.*, vol. 43, pp. 8–22.

HEINICKE, C. M., and WESTHEIMER, I. J. (1965), *Brief Separations*, Longman.

HELD, R., and BAUER, J. A. (1967), 'Visually guided reaching in infant monkeys after restricted rearing', *Science*, vol. 155, pp. 718–20.

HELD, R., and HEIN, A. (1963), 'Movement-produced stimulation in the development of visually guided behavior', *J. comp. physiol. Psychol.*, vol. 56, pp. 872–6.

HELFER, R. E., and KEMPE, C. H. (eds.) (1968), *The Battered Child*, University of Chicago Press, Chicago.

HENDERSON, N. D. (1964), 'Behavioral effects of manipulation during different stages in the development of mice', *J. comp. physiol. Psychol.*, vol. 57, pp. 284–9.

HERTZIG, M. E., BIRCH, H. G., THOMAS, A., and MENDEZ, O. A. (1968), 'Class and ethnic differences in the responsiveness of pre-school children to cognitive demands', *Monogr. Soc. Res. Child Devel.*, vol. 33, no. 117.

HESS, R. D. (1970), 'Social class and ethnic influences on socialization', in P. H. Mussen (ed.), *Carmichael's Manual of Child Psychology*, 3rd edn, Wiley, New York.

HESS, R. D., and SHIPMAN, V. C. (1965), 'Early experience and the socialization of cognitive modes in children', *Child Devel.*, vol. 36, pp. 869–86.

HESS, R. D., and SHIPMAN, V. C. (1967), 'Cognitive elements in maternal behavior', in J. P. Hill (ed.), *Minnesota Symposia on Child Psychology*, vol. 1, University of Minnesota Press.

HETHERINGTON, E. M., COX, M., and COX, R. (1978), 'The aftermath of divorce', in J. H. Stevens, Jr, and M. Matthews (eds.), *Mother–Child, Father–Child Relations*, Washington, DC: NAEYC.

HETHERINGTON, E. M., COX, M., and COX, R. (1979), 'Play and social interaction in children following divorce', *J. Soc. Issues*, vol. 35, pp. 26–49.

HILL, O. W. (1972), 'Childhood bereavement and adult psychiatric disturbance'. *J. psychosom. Res.*, vol. 16, pp. 357–60.

HILTON, I. (1967), 'Differences in the behavior of mothers to first-born and later-born children', *J. Pers. Soc. Psychol.*, vol. 7, pp. 282–90.

HINDE, R. A. (1970), *Animal Behavior*, 2nd edn, McGraw-Hill.

HINDE, R. A., and DAVIES, L. (1972), 'Removing infant rhesus from mother for 13 days compared with removing mother from infant', *J. Child Psychol. Psychiat.*, vol. 13, pp. 227–37.

HINDE, R. A., and McGINNIS, L. (1977), 'Some factors influencing the effect of temporary mother–infant separation: some experiments with rhesus monkeys', *Psychol. Med.*, vol. 7, pp. 197–212.

HINDE, R. A., and SPENCER-BOOTH, Y. (1967), 'The effect of social companions on mother–infant relations in rhesus monkeys', in D. Morris (ed.), *Primate Ethology*, Weidenfeld & Nicolson.

HINDE, R. A., and SPENCER-BOOTH, Y. (1970), 'Individual differences in the responses of rhesus monkeys to a period of separation from their mothers', *J. Child Psychol. Psychiat.*, vol. 11, pp. 159–76.

HINDE, R. A., and SPENCER-BOOTH, Y. (1971a), 'Towards understanding individual differences in rhesus mother–infant interaction', *Anim. Behav.*, vol. 19, pp. 165–73.

HINDE, R. A., and SPENCER-BOOTH, Y. (1971b), 'Effects of brief separation from mother on rhesus monkeys', *Science*, vol. 173, pp. 111–18.

HINDE, R. A., and STEVENSON-HINDE, J. (1976), 'Towards understanding relationships: dynamic stability', in P. P. G. Bateson and R. A. Hinde (eds.), *Growing Points in Ethology*, Cambridge University Press, pp. 451–80.

HOCK, E. (1978), 'Working and nonworking mothers with infants: perceptions of their careers, their infants' needs, and satisfaction with mothering', *Devel. Psychol.*, vol. 14, pp. 37–43.

HOFFMAN, H. S., and RATNER, A. M. (1973), 'A reinforcement model of imprinting: implications for socialization in monkeys and man', *Psychol. Rev.*, vol. 80, pp. 527–44.

HOFFMAN, L. W. (1963), 'Research findings on the effects of maternal employment on the child', in F. I. Nye and L. W. Hoffman (eds.), *The Employed Mother in America*, Rand McNally, New York.

HOFFMAN, L. W. (1974), 'Effects of maternal employment on the child – A review of the research', *Devel. Psychol.*, vol. 10, pp. 204–28.

HOFFMAN, L. W. (1979), 'Maternal employment: 1979', *Amer. Psychol.*, vol. 34, pp. 859–65.

HOROWITZ, F. D., and PADEN, L. Y. (1973), 'The effectiveness of environmental intervention programs', in B. M. Caldwell and H. N. Ricciuti (eds.), *Review of Child Development Research*, vol. 3, University of Chicago Press, Chicago.

HOWELLS, J. G. (1970), 'Fallacies in child care: I. That "separation" is synonymous with "deprivation"', *Acta Paedopsychiat.*, vol. 37, pp. 3–14.

HOWELLS, J. G., and LAYNG, J. (1955), 'Separation experiences and mental health: a statistical study', *Lancet*, vol. 2, pp. 285–8.

HUBEL, D. H., and WIESEL, T. N. (1965), 'Binocular interaction in striate cortex of kittens reared with artificial squint', *J. Neurophysiol.*, vol. 28, pp. 1041–59.

HUNT, J. McV. (1979), 'Psychological development: early experience', *Ann. Rev. Psychol.*, vol. 30, pp. 103–43.

HUSEN, T. (1951), 'The influence of schooling upon I Q', *Theoria*, vol. 17, pp. 61–8.

HUTCHINGS, B., and MEDNICK, S. A. (1974), 'Registered criminality in the adoptive and biological parents of registered male adoptees', in S. A. Mednick *et al.* (eds.), *Genetics, Environment and Psychopathology*, North-Holland, Amsterdam.

HYMOVITCH, B. (1952), 'The effects of experimental variations on problem solving in the rat', *J. comp. physiol. Psychol.*, vol. 45, pp. 313–21.

IGEL, G. J., and CALVIN, A. D. (1960), 'The development of affectional responses in infant dogs', *J. comp. physiol. Psychol.*, vol. 53, pp. 302–5.

ILLINGWORTH, R. S. (ed.) (1958), *Recent Advances in Cerebral Palsy*, Churchill, Edinburgh.

ILLINGWORTH, R. S., and HOLT, K. S. (1955), 'Children in hospital: some observations on their reactions with special reference to daily visiting', *Lancet*, vol. 2, pp. 1257–62.

ILLSLEY, R., and KINCAID, J. C. (1963), 'Social correlations of perinatal mortality', in N. R. Butler and D. G. Bonham (eds.), *Perinatal Mortality*, Livingstone, Edinburgh.

ILLSLEY, R., and THOMPSON, B. (1961), 'Women from broken homes', *Sociol. Rev.*, vol. 9, pp. 27–54.

IRVINE, E. E. (1966), 'Children in kibbutzim: thirteen years after', *J. child Psychol. Psychiat.*, vol. 7, pp. 167–78.

JACOBS, B. S., and MOSS, H. A. (1976), 'Birth order and sex of sibling as determinants of mother–infant interaction', *Child Devel.*, vol. 47, pp. 315–22.

JAMES-ROBERTS, I. (1979), 'Neurological plasticity, recovery from brain insult and child development', in H. W. Reese and L. P. Lipsitt (eds.), *Advances in Child Development and Behavior*, vol. 14, Academic Press, New York, pp. 253–319.

JENCKS, C., SMITH, M., ACLAND, H., BANE, M. J., COHEN, D., GINTIS, H., HEYNS, B., and MICHELSON, S. (1972), *Inequality: a reassessment of the effect of family and schooling in America*, Basic Books, New York.

JENSEN, A. R. (1969), 'How much can we boost I Q and scholastic achievement?', *Harv. educ. Rev.*, vol. 39, pp. 1–123.

JESSOR, R., and RICHARDSON, S. (1968), 'Psychosocial deprivation and personality development', in *Perspectives on Human Deprivation: Biological, Psychological and Sociological*, U S Department of Health, Education and Welfare, Washington, D C.

JOHNSON, M. C. (1980), 'Social adjustment of junior school children in a South Wales town' (submitted for publication).

JOLLY, H. (1969), 'Play is work, the role of play for sick and healthy children', *Lancet*, vol. 2, pp. 487–8.

JONES, H. E. (1954), 'The environment and mental development', in L. Carmichael (ed.), *Manual of Child Psychology*, Wiley.

JONSSON, G. (1967), 'Delinquent boys, their parents and grandparents', *Acta Psychiat. Scand.*, vol. 43, suppl. 195.

KADUSHIN, A. (1970), *Adopting Older Children*, Columbia University Press, New York.

KAGAN, J. (1965), 'Reflection-impulsivity and reading abiiity in primary grade children', *Child Devel.*, vol. 36, pp. 609–28.

KAGAN, J., KEARSLEY, R. B., and ZELAZO, P. R. (1978), *Infancy: Its Place in Human Development*, Harvard University Press, Cambridge, Mass.

KAUFMAN, I. C., and ROSENBLUM, L. A. (1969a), 'The waning of the mother–infant bond in two species of macaque', in B. M. Foss (ed.), *Determinants of Infant Behaviour*, vol. 4, Methuen.

KAUFMAN, I. C., and ROSENBLUM, L. A. (1969b), 'Effects of separation from mother on the emotional behaviour of infant monkeys', *Ann. New York Acad. Sci.*, vol. 159, pp. 681–95.

KENNELL, J. H., JERAULD, R., WOLFE, H., CHESTER, D., KREGER, N. C., McALPINE, W., STEFFA, N., and KLAUS, M. H. (1974), 'Maternal behaviour one year after early and extended post-partum contact', *Devel. Med. Child Neurol.*, vol. 16, pp. 172–9.

KERR, G. R., CHAMOVE, A. S., and HARLOW, H. F. (1969), 'Environmental deprivation: its effect on the growth of infant monkeys', *J. Pediat.*, vol. 75, pp. 833–7.

KING, R. D., and RAYNES, N. V. (1968), 'An operational measure of inmate management in residential institutions', *Soc. Sci. Med.*, vol. 2, pp. 41–53.

KING, R. D., RAYNES, N. V., and TIZARD, J. (1971), *Patterns of Residential Care: Sociological Studies in Institutions for Handicapped Children*, Routledge & Kegan Paul.

KIRK, S. A. (1958), *Early Education of the Mentally Retarded: An Experimental Study*, University of Illinois Press.

KISSEL, S. (1965), 'Stress-reducing properties of social stimuli', *J. Pers. Soc. Psychol.*, vol. 2, pp. 378–84.

KLACKENBERG, G. (1956), 'Studies in maternal deprivation in infants' homes', *Acta Pediat. (Stockholm)*, vol. 45, pp. 1–12.

KLAUS, M. H., and KENNELL, J. H. (1976), *Maternal–infant bonding: the impact of early separation or loss on family development*, C. V. Mosby, Saint Louis.

KLAUS, R. A., and GRAY, S. W. (1968), 'The Early Training Project for Disadvantaged Children: a report after five years', *Monogr. Soc. Res. Child Devel.*, vol. 33, no. 4.

KLINGHAMMER, E. (1967), 'Factors influencing choice of mate in altricial birds', in H. W. Stevenson, E. H. Hess and H. L. Rheingold (eds.), *Early Behavior: Comparative and Developmental Approaches*, Wiley, New York.

KLINGHAMMER, E., and HESS, E. H. (1964), 'Imprinting in an altricial bird: the blond ring dove', *Science*, vol. 146, pp. 265–6.

KOHEN-RAZ, R. (1968), 'Mental and motor development of kibbutz, institutionalized and home-reared infants in Israel', *Child Devel.*, vol. 39, pp. 489–504.

KOLUCHOVA, J. (1972), 'Severe deprivation in twins: a case study', *J. Child Psychol. Psychiat.*, vol. 13, pp. 107–14.

KOLUCHOVA, J. (1976), 'The further development of twins after severe and prolonged deprivation: a second report', *J. Child Psychol. Psychiat.*, vol. 17, pp. 181–8.

KORNER, A. F., CHUCK, B., and DONTCHOS, S. (1968), 'Organismic determinants of spontaneous oral behaviour in neonates', *Child Devel.*, vol. 39, pp. 1145–57.

KORNER, A. F., and GROBSTEIN, R. (1966), 'Visual alertness as related to soothing in neonates: implications for maternal stimulation at early deprivation', *Child Devel.*, vol. 37, pp. 867–76.

KOVACH, J. K., and HESS, E. H. (1963), 'Imprinting: effects of painful stimulation on the following response', *J. Comp. Physiol. Psychol.*, vol. 56, pp. 461–4.

KREITMAN, N., COLLINS, J., NELSON, B., and TROOP, J. (1970), 'Neurosis and marital interaction: I. Personality and symptoms', *Brit. J. Psychiat.*, vol. 117, pp. 33–46.

KUSHLIK, A. (1968), 'Social problems of mental subnormality', in E. Miller (ed.), *Foundations of Child Psychiatry*, Pergamon.

LAMB, M. E. (ed.) (1976), *The Role of the Father in Child Development*, Wiley, New York.

LAMB, M. E. (1977a), 'Father–infant and mother–infant inter-action in the first year of life', *Child Devel.*, vol. 48, pp. 167–181.

LAMB, M. E. (1977b), 'The development of mother–infant and father–infant attachments in the second year of life', *Devel. Psychol.*, vol. 13, pp. 637–48.

LAMB, M. E. (1978), 'Qualitative aspects of mother– and father–infant attachments', *Infant Behav. Devel.*, vol. 1, pp. 1–11.

LAMB, M. E., and STEVENSON, M. B. (1978), 'Father–infant relationships: their nature and importance', *Youth and Society*, vol. 9, pp. 277–98.

LAMB, M. E. (1979), 'The changing American family and its implications for infant social development: The sample case of maternal employment', in M. Lewis and L. A. Rosenblum (eds.), *The Social Network of the Developing Infant*, Wiley, New York.

LAMB, M. E., and EASTERBROOKS, M. A. (1980), 'Individual differences in parental sensitivity: some thoughts about origins, components and consequences', in M. E. Lamb and L. R. Sherrod (eds.), *Infant Social Cognition: empirical and theoretical considerations*, Lawrence Erlbaum, Hillsdale, NJ (in press).

LAMBERT, L., ESSEN, J., and HEAD, J. (1977), 'Variations in behaviour ratings of children who have been in care', *J. Child Psychol. Psychiat.*, vol. 18, pp. 335–46.

LANGNER, T. S., and MICHAEL, S. T. (1963), *Life Stress and Mental Health*, Collier-Macmillan, London.

LASKO, J. K. (1954), 'Parent behavior toward first and second children', *Genet. Psychol. Monogr.*, vol. 49, pp. 96–137.

LAVIK, N. (1977), 'Urban–rural differences in rates of disorder', in P. J. Graham (ed.), *Epidemiological Approaches in Child Psychiatry*, Academic Press, London.

LAWTON, D. (1968), *Social Class, Language and Education*, Rout-ledge & Kegan Paul.

LEE, E. S. (1951), 'Negro intelligence and selective migration: a Philadelphia test of the Klineberg hypothesis', *Amer. soc. Rev.*, vol. 16, pp. 227–33.

LEIDERMAN, P. H. (1981), 'Human mother to infant social bonding: is there a sensitive phase?', in G. Barlow, K. Immelmann, M. Main and L. Petrinovich (eds.), *Ethology and Child Development*, Cambridge University Press (in press).

LEIDERMAN, P. H., and LEIDERMAN, G. F. (1974), 'Affective and cognitive consequences of polymatric infant care in the East

African highlands', in A. Pick (ed.), *Minnesota Symposium in Psychology*, vol. 8, pp. 81–119, University of Minnesota Press, Minneapolis.

LEIDERMAN, P. H., and SEASHORE, M. J. (1975), 'Mother-infant neonatal separation: some delayed consequences', in R. Porter and M. O'Connor (eds.), *Parent–Infant Interaction*, Ciba Foundation Symposium 33 (new series), Associated Scientific Publishers, Amsterdam.

LENNEBERG, E. H. (1967), *Biological Foundations of Language*, Wiley, New York.

LEVINE, S. (1962), 'The effects of infantile experience on adult behavior', in A. J. Bachrach (ed.), *Experimental Foundations of Clinical Psychology*, Basic Books, New York.

LEVINE, S. (1969), 'An endocrine theory of infantile stimulation', in A. Ambrose (ed.), *Stimulation in Infancy*, Academic Press, London.

LEVINE, S., CHEVALIER, J. A., and KORCHIN, S. J. (1956), 'The effects of early shock and handling on later avoidance learning', *J. Pers.*, vol. 24, pp. 475–93.

LEVITIN, T. E. (1979), 'Children of divorce: an introduction', *J. Social Issues*, vol. 35, pp. 1–25.

LEVY, D. M. (1958), *Behavioral Analysis: Analysis of Clinical Observations of Behavior as Applied to Mother–Newborn Relationships*, C. C. Thomas, Springfield, Ill.

LEWIS, H. (1954), *Deprived Children*, Oxford University Press.

LEWIS, M., and KREITZBERG, V. S. (1979), 'Effects of birth order and spacing on mother–infant interactions', *Devel. Psychol.*, vol. 15, pp. 617–25.

LEWIS, M., and ROSENBLUM, L. A. (eds.) (1974), *The Effect of the Infant on Its Caregiver*, Wiley, New York.

LIDDELL, H. (1950), 'Some specific factors that modify tolerance for environmental stress', in *Life Stress and Bodily Disease*, Assoc. Res. Nerv. Ment. Dis., Williams & Wilkins, Baltimore, Md.

LIEBERMAN, A. F. (1977), 'Preschoolers' competence with a peer: relations with attachment and peer experience', *Child Devel.*, vol. 48, pp. 1277–87.

LINDSLEY, D., and RIESEN, A. (1968), 'Biological substrates of development and behavior', in *Perspectives on Human Deprivation: Biological, Psychological and Sociological*, U S Department of Health, Education and Welfare, Washington, D C.

LITTENBERG, R., TULKIN, S., and KAGAN, J. (1971), 'Cognitive components of separation anxiety', *Devel. Psychol.*, vol. 4, pp. 387-8.

LORENZ, K. Z. (1935), 'Der Kumpan in der Umwelt des Vogels', *J. Ornithol. Berlin*, vol. 83; reprinted in C. H. Schiller (ed.), *Instinctive Behaviour*, Methuen, 1957.

LORENZ, K. Z. (1937), 'The establishment of the instinct concept', in *Studies in Animal and Human Behaviour*, vol. I (trans. R. Martin), Methuen, London, 1970.

LUKIANOWICZ, N. (1971), 'Battered children', *Psychiatria Clinica* (Basel), vol. 4, pp. 257-80.

LYLE, J. G. (1959), 'The effect of an institutional environment upon the verbal development of imbecile children: I. Verbal intelligence', *J. ment. Defic. Res.*, vol. 3, pp. 122-8.

LYLE, J. G. (1960), 'The effect of an institutional environment upon the verbal development of imbecile children: III. The Brooklands residential family unit', *J. ment. Defic. Res.*, vol. 4, pp. 14-23.

LYNN, D., and SAWREY, W. L. (1959), 'The effects of father-absence on Norwegian boys and girls', *J. abnorm. soc. Psychol.*, vol. 59, pp. 258-62.

MAAS, H. S. (1963), 'The young adult adjustment of twenty wartime residential nursery children', *Child Welf.*, vol. 42, pp. 57-72.

McCALL, R. B., APPELBAUM, M. I., and HOGARTY, P. S. (1973), 'Developmental changes in mental performance', *Monogr. Soc. Res. Child Devel.*, vol. 38, no. 150.

McCANDLESS, B. R. (1964), 'Relation of environmental factors to intellectual functioning', in H. A. Stevens and R. Heber (eds.), *Mental Retardation: A Review of Research*, University of Chicago Press, Chicago.

MACCARTHY, D., and BOOTH, E. M. (1970), 'Parental rejection and stunting of growth', *J. psychosom. Res.*, vol. 14, pp. 259-65.

MACCARTHY, D., LINDSAY, M., and MORRIS, L. (1962), 'Children in hospital with mothers', *Lancet*, vol. 1, pp. 603-8.

McCLEARN, G. E. (1970), 'Genetic influences on behavior and development', in P. H. Mussen (ed.), *Carmichael's Manual of Child Psychology*, 3rd edn, Wiley, New York.

MACCOBY, E. E., DOERING, C. H., JACKLIN, C. N., KRAEMER, H., and MARKMAN, E. M. (1979), 'Concentrations of sex hormones in umbilical cord blood: their relation to sex and birth order of children', *Child Psychol.*, vol. 50, pp. 632-42.

MACCOBY, E. E., and FELDMAN, S. S. (1972), 'Mother-attachment and stranger reactions in the third year of life', *Monogr. Soc. Res. Child Devel.*, vol. 37, no. 146.

MACCOBY, E. E., and JACKLIN, C. N. (1980), 'Psychological sex differences', in M. Rutter (ed.), *Scientific Foundations of Developmental Psychiatry*, Heinemann Medical.

MACCOBY, E. E., and MASTERS, J. C. (1970), 'Attachment and dependency', in P. H. Mussen (ed.), *Carmichael's Manual of Child Psychology*, 3rd edn, Wiley.

McCORD, W., and McCORD, J. (1959), *The Origins of Crime: A New Evaluation of the Cambridge–Somerville Youth Study*, Columbia University Press, New York.

McCUTCHEON, B., and CALHOUN, K. S. (1976), 'Social and emotional adjustment of infants and toddlers to a day-care setting', *Amer. J. Orthopsychiat.*, vol. 46, pp. 104–8.

McDONALD, A. D. (1964), 'Intelligence in children of very low birth weight', *Brit. J. prev. soc. Med.*, vol. 18, pp. 59–74.

McDONALD, A. D. (1967), *Children of Very Low Birthweight*, Heinemann Medical.

McKINNEY, J. P., and KEELE, T. (1963), 'Effects of increased mothering on the behavior of severely retarded boys', *Amer. J. ment. Defic.*, vol. 67, pp. 556–62.

MACRAE, J. W., and HERBERT-JACKSON, E. (1976), 'Are behavioral effects of infant day-care program specific?', *Devel. Psychol.*, vol. 12, pp. 269–70.

MAPSTONE, E. (1969), 'Children in care', *Concern*, vol. 3, pp. 23–8.

MARANTZ, S. A., and MANSFIELD, A. F. (1977), 'Maternal employment and the development of sex-role stereotyping in five-to-eleven-year-old girls', *Child Devel.*, vol. 48, pp. 668–73.

MARCHANT, R., HOWLIN, P., YULE, W., and RUTTER, M. (1974), 'Graded change in the treatment of the behaviour of autistic children', *J. Child Psychol. Psychiat.*, vol. 15, pp. 221–8.

MARRIS, P. (1958), *Widows and Their Families*, Routledge & Kegan Paul.

MARSHALL, W. A. (1968), *Development of the Brain*, Oliver & Boyd, Edinburgh.

MASON, M. K. (1942), 'Learning to speak after six and one-half years of silence', *J. speech hear. Dis.*, vol. 7, pp. 295–304.

MASON, W. A. (1960), 'Socially mediated reduction in emotional responses of young rhesus monkeys', *J. abnorm. soc. Psychol.*, vol. 60, pp. 100–104.

MASON, W. A. (1967), 'Motivational aspects of social responsiveness in young chimpanzees', in H. W. Stevenson, E. H. Hess and H. L. Rheingold (eds.), *Early Behavior: Comparative and Developmental Approaches*, Wiley, New York.

MASON, W. A. (1968), 'Early social deprivation in the non-human primates: implications for human behavior', in D. C. Glass (ed.), *Environmental Influences*, Russell Sage Foundation, New York.

MASON, W. A., and BERKSON, G. (1975), 'Effects of maternal motility on the development of rocking and other behaviors in rhesus monkeys: a study with artificial mothers', *Devel. Psychobiol.*, vol. 8, pp. 197–211.

MASON, W. A., DAVENPORT, R. K., and MENZEL, E. W. (1968), 'Early experience and the social development of rhesus monkeys and chimpanzees', in G. Newton and S. Levine (eds.), *Early Experience and Behavior*, C. C. Thomas, Springfield, Ill.

MATAS, L., AREND, R. A., and SROUFE, L. A. (1978), 'Continuity of adaptation in the second year: the relationship between quality of attachment and later competence', *Child Devel.*, vol. 49, pp. 547–56.

MAYALL, B., and PETRIE, P. (1977), 'Minder, mother and child', *Studies in Education* (new series), vol. 5, University of London Institute of Education.

MEAD, M. (1962), 'A cultural anthropologist's approach to maternal deprivation', in *Deprivation of Maternal Care: A Reassessment of its Effects*, World Health Organization, Geneva.

MEIER, E. C. (1965), 'Current circumstances of former foster children', *Child Welfare*, vol. 44, pp. 196–206.

MEIER, E. C. (1966), 'Adults who were foster children', *Children*, vol. 13, pp. 16–22.

MEIER, G. W., and McGEE, R. K. (1959), 'A re-evaluation of the effect of early perceptual experience on discrimination performance during adulthood', *J. comp. physiol. Psychol.*, vol. 52, pp. 390–95.

MELZACK, R. (1965), 'Effects of early experience on behavior: experimental and conceptual considerations', in P. H. Hoch and J. Zubin (eds.), *Psychopathology of Perception*, Grune & Stratton, New York.

MELZACK, R., and SCOTT, T. H. (1957), 'The effects of early experience on the response to pain', *J. comp. physiol. Psychol.*, vol. 50, pp. 155–61.

MENZEL, E. W. (1964), 'Patterns of responsiveness in chimpanzees reared through infancy under conditions of environmental restrictions', *Psychol. Forsch.*, vol. 27, pp. 337–65.

Mićić, Z. (1962), 'Psychological stress in children in hospital', *Int. nurs. Rev.*, vol. 9, pp. 23–31.

Millar, S. (1968), *The Psychology of Play*, Penguin.

Miller, L. (1969), 'Child rearing in the kibbutz', in J. G. Howells (ed.), *Modern Perspectives in International Child Psychiatry*, Oliver & Boyd, Edinburgh.

Miller, R. E., Caul, W. E., and Mirsky, I. A. (1971), 'Patterns of eating and drinking in socially isolated rhesus monkeys', *Physiol. Behav.*, vol. 7, pp. 127–35.

Mineke, S., and Suomi, S. J. (1978), 'Social separation in monkeys', *Psychol. Bull.*, vol. 85, pp. 1376–1400.

Missakian, E. A. (1969), 'Effects of social deprivation on the development of patterns of social behavior', *Proc. Second Int. Congr. Primatol. Atlanta, Georgia*, vol. 2, S. Karger.

Monat, A., and Lazarus, R. S. (eds.) (1977), *Stress and Coping: an anthology*, Columbia University Press, New York.

Moore, T. W. (1963), 'Effects on the children', in S. Yudkin and A. Holme (eds.), *Working Mothers and Their Children*, Michael Joseph.

Moore, T. W. (1964), 'Children of full-time and part-time mothers', *Int. J. soc. Psychiat.*, special congress issue no. 2.

Moore, T. W. (1975), 'Exclusive early mothering and its alternatives: the outcome to adolescence', *Scand. J. Psychol.*, vol. 16, pp. 255–72.

Morgan, G. A., and Ricciuti, H. N. (1969), 'Infants' responses to strangers during the first year', in B. M. Foss (ed.), *Determinants of Infant Behaviour*, vol. 4, Methuen.

Moskowitz, D. S., Schwarz, J. C., and Corsini, D. A. (1977), 'Initiating day care at three years of age: effects on attachment', *Child Devel.*, vol. 48, pp. 1271–6.

Moss, H. A. (1967), 'Sex, age and state as determinants of mother–infant interaction', *Merrill-Palmer Q.*, vol. 13, pp. 19–36.

Murphy, L. B., and Moriarty, A. E. (1976), *Vulnerability, Coping and Growth from Infancy to Adolescence*, Yale University Press, New Haven, Conn.

Murphy, L. G., and associates (1962), *The Widening World of Childhood: paths toward mastery*, Basic Books, New York.

Naess, S. (1959), 'Mother–child separation and delinquency', *Brit. J. Delinq.*, vol. 10, pp. 22–35.

Naess, S. (1962), 'Mother-separation and delinquency: further evidence', *Brit. J. Criminol.*, vol. 2, pp. 361–74.

NEWBERRY, P., WEISSMAN, M. W., and MYERS, J. K. (1979), 'Working wives and housewives: do they differ in mental status and social adjustment?', *Amer. J. Orthopsychiat.*, vol. 49, pp. 282–91.

NISBET, J. D. (1953a), 'Family environment and intelligence', *Eugen. Rev.*, vol. 45, pp. 31–40.

NISBET, J. D. (1953b), *Family Environment: A Direct Effect of Family Size on Intelligence*, Eugenics Society.

NISSEN, H. W., CHOW, K. L., and SEMMES, J. (1951), 'Effects of restricted opportunity for tactual, kinesthetic and manipulative experience on the behavior of a chimpanzee', *Amer. J. Psychol.*, vol. 64, pp. 485–507.

NOVAK, M. A. (1979), 'Social recovery of monkeys isolated for the first year of life: II. Long term assessment', *Devel. Psychol.*, vol. 15, pp. 50–61.

NOVAK, M. A., and HARLOW, H. F. (1975), 'Social Recovery of monkeys isolated for the first year of life: I. Rehabilitation and therapy', *Devel. Psychol.*, vol. 11, pp. 453–65.

NUCKOLLS, K. B., CASSEL, J., and KAPLAN, B. H. (1972), 'Psychosocial assets, life crisis and the prognosis of pregnancy', *Amer. J. Epidemiol.*, vol. 95, pp. 431–41.

NYLANDER, I. (1960), 'Children of alcoholic fathers', *Acta Paediat.*, vol. 49, suppl. 121.

NYMAN, A. J. (1967), 'Problem solving in rats as a function of experience at different ages', *J. genet. Psychol.*, vol. 110, pp. 31–9.

OAKLEY, A. (1974), *Housewife*, Allen Lane, London; Penguin, Harmondsworth (1976).

O'CONNOR, N. (1956), 'The evidence for the permanently disturbing effects of mother–child separation', *Acta Psychol.*, vol. 12, pp. 174–91.

O'CONNOR, N. (1968), 'Children in restricted environments', in G. Newton and S. Levine (eds.), *Early Experience and Behavior*, C. C. Thomas, Springfield, Ill.

O'CONNOR, N., and FRANKS, C. M. (1960), 'Childhood upbringing and other environmental factors', in H. J. Eysenck (ed.), *Handbook of Abnormal Psychology*, Pitman.

OLEINICK, M. S., BAHN, A. K., EISENBERG, L., and LILIENFELD, A. M. (1966), 'Early socialization experiences and intra-familial environment', *Arch. gen. Psychiat.*, vol. 15, p. 344.

ORLANSKY, H. (1949), 'Infant care and personality', *Psychol. Bull.*, vol. 46, pp. 1–48.

OSOFSKY, J. D., and DANZGER, B. (1974), 'Relationships between neonatal characteristics and mother–infant interaction', *Devel. Psychol.*, vol. 10, pp. 124–30.

OSOFSKY, J. D., and O'CONNELL, E. J. (1972), 'Parent-child interaction: daughters' effects upon mothers' and fathers' behaviors', *Devel. Psychol.*, vol. 7, pp. 157–68.

OTTERSTRÖM, E. (1946), 'Delinquency and children from bad homes', *Acta Paediat. Scand.*, vol. 33, suppl. 5.

OYAMA, S. (1979), 'The concept of the sensitive period in developmental studies', *Merrill-Palmer Q.*, vol. 25, pp. 83–103.

PANNABECKER, B. J., and EMDE, R. N. (1977), 'The effects of extended father–newborn contact', in M. V. Batey (ed.), *Communicating Nursing Research*, vol. 10: *Optimizing environments for health; Nursing's unified perspective*, Western Interstate Commission for Higher Education, Boulder, Colorado.

PARKE, R. D., and COLLMER, C. W. (1975), 'Child abuse: an interdisciplinary analysis', in E. M. Hetherington (ed.), *Review of Child Development Research*, vol. 5, University of Chicago Press, Chicago.

PARKES, C. M. (1964), 'Recent bereavement as a cause of mental illness', *Brit. J. Psychiat.*, vol. 110, pp. 198–204.

PARKES, C. M. (1965), 'Bereavement and mental illness', *Brit. J. med. Psychol.*, vol. 38, pp. 1–26.

PASAMANICK, B., and KNOBLOCH, H. (1961), 'Epidemiologic studies on the complications of pregnancy and the birth process', in G. Caplan (ed.), *Prevention of Mental Disorder in Children*, Basic Books, New York.

PASSMAN, R. H. (1977), 'Providing attachment objects to facilitate learning and reduce distress: Effects of mothers and security blankets', *Devel. Psychol.*, vol. 13, pp. 25–8.

PASSMAN, R. H., and WEISBERG, P. (1975), 'Mothers and blankets as agents for promoting play and exploration by young children in a novel environment: the effects of social and nonsocial objects', *Devel. Psychol.*, vol. 11, pp. 170–77.

PATTERSON, F. G., BONVILLIAN, J. D., REYNOLDS, P. C., and MACCOBY, E. E. (1975), 'Mother and peer attachment under conditions of fear in rhesus monkeys (*Macaca mulatta*)', *Primates*, vol. 16, pp. 75–81.

PATTON, R. G., and GARDNER, L. I. (1963), *Growth Failure in Maternal Deprivation*, C. C. Thomas, Springfield, Ill.

PAYKEL, E. S., MYERS, J. K., DIENELT, M. N., KLERMAN, C. L., LINDETHAL, L. J., and PEPPER, M. P. (1969), 'Life events and depression: a controlled study', *Arch. Gen. Psychiat.*, vol. 21, pp. 753–60.

PAYKEL, E. S., EMMS, E. M., FLETCHER, J., and RASSABY, E. S. (1980), 'Life events and social support in puerperal depression', *Brit. J. Psychiat.*, vol. 136, pp. 339–46.

PETERSON, D. R., BECKER, W. C., HELLMER, C. A., SHOE-MAKER, D. J., and QUAY, H. C. (1959), 'Parental attitudes and child adjustment', *Child Devel.*, vol. 30, pp. 119–30.

PILLING, D., and PRINGLE, M. L. K. (1978), *Controversial Issues in Child Development*, Paul Elek, London.

PORTER, B., and O'LEARY, K. D. (1980), 'Marital discord and childhood behavior problems', *J. Abn. Child Psychol.*, vol. 8, pp. 287–95.

PORTNOY, F. C., and SIMMONS, C. H. (1978), 'Day care and attachment', *Child Devel.*, vol. 49, pp. 239–42.

POWELL, G. F., BRASEL, J. A., and BLIZZARD, R. M. (1967), 'Emotional deprivation and growth retardation simulating idiopathic hypopituitarism: I. Clinical evaluation of the syndrome', *New Eng. J. Med.*, vol. 276, pp. 1271–8.

POWELL, G. F., BRASEL, J. A., RAITI, S., and BLIZZARD, R. M. (1967), 'Emotional deprivation and growth retardation simulating idiopathic hypopituitarism: II. Endocrinologic evaluation of the syndrome', *New Eng. J. Med.*, vol. 276, pp. 1279–83.

POWER, M. J., ASH, P. M., SCHOENBERG, E., and SOREY, E. C. (1974), 'Delinquency and the family', *Brit. J. Soc. Work*, vol. 4, pp. 13–38.

PRATT, M. W., BUMSTEAD, D. C., and RAYNES, N. V. (1976), 'Attendant staff speech to the institutionalized retarded: language use as a measure of the quality of care', *J. Child Psychol. Psychiat.*, vol. 17, pp. 133–44.

PRECHTL, H. F. R. (1963), 'The mother–child interaction in babies with minimal brain damage', in B. M. Foss (ed.), *Determinants of Infant Behaviour*, vol. 2, Methuen.

PREMACK, D. (1971), 'Language in chimpanzee?', *Science*, vol. 172, pp. 808–22.

PRINGLE, M. L. K. (1976), 'Rights of adults or needs of children?', *Times Educational Supplement*, 23 July.

PRINGLE, M. L. K., and BOSSIO, V. (1958a), 'Intellectual, emotional and social development of deprived children', *Vita Humana*, vol. 1, pp. 66–92.

PRINGLE, M. L. K., and BOSSIO, V. (1958b), 'Language development and reading attainment of deprived children', *Vita Humana*, vol. 1, pp. 142–70.

PRINGLE, M. L. K., and BOSSIO, V. (1960), 'Early prolonged separations and emotional adjustment', *J. Child Psychol. Psychiat.*, vol. 1, pp. 37–48.

PRINGLE, M. L. K., and CLIFFORD, L. (1962), 'Conditions associated with emotional maladjustment among children in care', *Educ. Rev.*, vol. 14, pp. 112–23.

PRINGLE, M. L. K., and TANNER, M. (1958), 'The effects of early deprivation on speech development', *Lang. Speech*, vol. 1, pp. 269–87.

PROVENCE, S., and LIPTON, R. C. (1962), *Infants in Institutions*, International Universities Press, New York.

PRUGH, D. G., STAUB, E. M., SANDS, H. H., KIRSCHBAUM, R. L., and LENIHAN, E. A. (1953), 'A study of the emotional reactions of children and families to hospitalization and illness', *Amer. J. Orthopsychiat.*, vol. 23, pp. 70–106.

QUINTON, D., and RUTTER, M. (1976), 'Early hospital admissions and later disturbances of behaviour: An attempted replication of Douglas's findings', *Devel. Med. Child Neurol.*, vol. 18, pp. 447–59.

QUINTON, D., and RUTTER, M. (1980a), 'Parents with children in care: 1. Current circumstances and parenting skills', *J. Child Psychol. Psychiat.* (in press).

QUINTON, D., and RUTTER, M. (1980b), 'Parents with children in care: 2. Intergenerational continuities', *J. Child Psychol. Psychiat.* (in press).

RADLOFF, L. (1975), 'Sex differences in depression: The effects of occupation and marital status', *Sex Roles*, vol. 1, pp. 249–65.

RAJEKI, D. W., LAMB, M. E., and OBMASCHER, P. (1978), 'Toward a general theory of infantile attachment: a comparative review of aspects of the social bond', *Behav. Brain Sciences*, vol. 3, pp. 417–64.

RAPH, J. B., THOMAS, A., CHESS, S., and KORN, S. J. (1968), 'The influence of nursery school on social interactions', *Amer. J. Orthopsychiat.*, vol. 38, pp. 144–52.

RATHBUN, C., DI VIRGILIO, L., and WALDFOGEL, S. (1958), 'The restitutive process in children following radical separation from family and culture', *Amer. J. Orthopsychiat.*, vol. 28, pp. 408–15.

RATHBUN, C., MCLAUGHLIN, H., BENNETT, C., and GARLAND, J. A. (1965), 'Later adjustment of children following radical separation from family and culture', *Amer. J. Orthopsychiat.*, vol. 35, pp. 604–9.

REED, G., and LEIDERMAN, P. H. (1981), 'Age-related changes

in attachment behavior in polymatrically reared infants: the Kenyan Gusii', in T. Field, P. H. Leiderman *et al.* (eds.), *Culture and Infant Interaction*, Lawrence Erlbaum, New York.

RHEINGOLD, H. L. (1956), 'The modification of social responsiveness in institutional babies', *Monogr. Soc. Res. Child Devel.*, vol. 21, suppl. 63.

RHEINGOLD, H. L. (1960), 'The measurement of maternal care', *Child Devel.*, vol. 31, pp. 565–75.

RHEINGOLD, H. L. (1961), 'The effect of environmental stimulation upon social and exploratory behaviour in the human infant', in B. M. Foss (ed.), *Determinants of Infant Behaviour*, vol. 1, Methuen.

RHEINGOLD, H. L. (1963), *Maternal Behavior in Mammals*, Wiley, New York.

RHEINGOLD, H. L. (1969), 'The effect of a strange environment on the behaviour of infants', in B. M. Foss (ed.), *Determinants of Infant Behaviour*, vol. 4, Methuen.

RHEINGOLD, H. L., and BAYLEY, N. (1959), 'The later effects of an experimental modification of mothering', *Child Devel.*, vol. 30, pp. 363–72.

RHEINGOLD, H. L., and ECKERMAN, C. O. (1973), 'Fear of the stranger: a critical examination', in H. W. Reese (ed.), *Advances in Child Development and Behavior*, vol. VIII, Academic Press, New York.

RHEINGOLD, H. L., GEWIRTZ, J., and ROSS, H. (1959), 'Social conditioning of vocalizations in the infant', *J. comp. physiol. Psychol.*, vol. 52, pp. 68–73.

RHEINGOLD, H. L., and SAMUELS, H. R. (1969), 'Maintaining the positive behaviour of infants by increased stimulation', *Devel. Psychol.*, vol. 1, pp. 520–27.

RICCIUTI, H. (1974), 'Fear and development of social attachments in the first year of life', in M. Lewis and L. A. Rosenblum (eds.), *The Origins of Human Behavior: Fear*, Wiley, New York.

RICHARDS, M. P. M. (1978), 'Possible effects of early separation on later development of children – a review', in F. S. W. Brimblecombe, M. P. M. Richards and N. R. C. Robertson (eds.), *Separation and Special Care Baby Units*, Clinics in Developmental Medicine, no. 68, pp. 12–32, Heinemann/SIMP, London.

RIESEN, A. H. (1965), 'Effects of early deprivation of photic stimulation', in S. F. Osler and R. E. Cooke (eds.), *The Biosocial Basis of Mental Retardation*, Johns Hopkins Press, Baltimore.

RIESEN, A. H. (1975), *The Developmental Neuropsychology of Sensory Deprivation*, Academic Press, New York.

ROBERTSON, J. (1952), *A Two Year Old Goes to Hospital* (16 mm sound film with guidebook), Tavistock Child Development Research Unit.

ROBERTSON, J. (1958), *Going to Hospital with Mother* (16 mm sound film with guidebook), Tavistock Child Development Research Unit.

ROBERTSON, J. (ed.) (1962), *Hospitals and Children: A Parent's-Eye View*, Gollancz.

ROBERTSON, J., and BOWLBY, J. (1952), 'Responses of young children to separation from their mothers', *Courr. Cent. Int. Enf.*, vol. 2, pp. 131–42.

ROBERTSON, J., and ROBERTSON, J. (1967), *Young Children in Brief Separation: I. Kate, Aged Two Years Five Months in Fostercare for Twenty-Seven Days*, Tavistock Child Development Research Unit.

ROBERTSON, J., and ROBERTSON, J. (1968a), *Young Children in Brief Separation: II. Jane, Aged Seventeen Months in Fostercare for Ten Days*, Tavistock Child Development Research Unit.

ROBERTSON, J., and ROBERTSON, J. (1968b), *Young Children in Brief Separation: III. John, Aged Seventeen Months Nine Days in a Residential Nursery*, Tavistock Child Development Research Unit.

ROBERTSON, J., and ROBERTSON, J. (1971), 'Young children in brief separation: a fresh look', *Psychoanalytic Study of the Child*, vol. 26, pp. 264–315.

ROBERTSON, J., and ROBERTSON, J. (1977), 'Taking the side of the under-threes', *Australian Women's Weekly*, 20 July.

ROBINS, L. N. (1966), *Deviant Children Grown Up*, Williams & Wilkins, Baltimore.

ROBINS, L. N. (1970), 'The adult development of the antisocial child', *Seminar Psychiat.*, vol. 2, pp. 420–34.

ROBINS, L. N., WEST, P. A., and HERJANIC, B. L. (1975), 'Arrests and delinquency in two generations: a study of black urban families and their children', *J. Child Psychol. Psychiat.*, vol. 16, pp. 125–40.

ROBINSON, W. P., and RACKSTRAW, S. J. (1967), 'Variations in mother's answers to children's questions as a function of social class, verbal intelligence test scores and sex', *Sociology*, vol. 1, pp. 259–76.

ROE, A., and BURKS, B. (1945), *Adult Adjustment of Foster*

*Children of Alcoholic and Psychotic Parentage and the Influence of the Foster Home*, Yale University Alcoholic Studies.

ROGERS, C. M., and DAVENPORT, R. K. (1971), 'Intellectual performance of differentially reared chimpanzees: III. Oddity', *Amer. J. ment. Defic.*, vol. 75, pp. 526–30.

ROHNER, R. P. (1975), 'They love me, they love me not: a worldwide study of the effects of parental acceptance and rejection', Human Relations Area Files, Inc., New York.

ROOPNARINE, J. L., and LAMB, M. E. (1979), 'The effects of day care on attachment and exploratory behavior in a strange situation', *Merrill-Palmer Q.*, vol. 24, pp. 85–95.

ROSANOFF, A. J., HANDY, L. M., and PLESSET, I. R. (1941), *The Etiology of Child Behavior Difficulties, Juvenile Delinquency and Adult Criminality, with Special Reference to Their Occurrence in Twins*, Department of Institutions, Sacramento.

ROSE, R. J., HARRIS, E. L., CHRISTIAN, J. C., and NANCE, W. E. (1979), 'Genetic variance in non-verbal intelligence: data from the kinships of identical twins', *Science*, vol. 205, pp. 1153–1155.

ROSENBLATT, J. S. (1975), 'Prepartum and postpartum regulation of maternal behavior in the rat', in R. Porter and M. A. O'Connor (eds.), *Parent–Infant Interaction*, Ciba Foundation Symposium 33 (new series), Associated Scientific Publishers, Amsterdam.

ROSENBLUM, L. A. (1971a), 'Infant attachment in monkeys', in H. R. Schaffer (ed.), *The Origins of Human Social Relations*, Academic Press.

ROSENBLUM, L. A. (1971b), 'General discussion', in H. R. Schaffer (ed.), *The Origins of Human Social Relations*, Academic Press.

ROSENBLUM, L. A., and HARLOW, H. F. (1963), 'Approach–avoidance conflict in the mother-surrogate situation', *Psychol. Rep.*, vol. 12, pp. 83–5.

ROSENTHAL, M. K. (1973), 'Attachment and mother–infant interaction: some research impasses and a suggested change in orientation', *J. Child Psychol. Psychiat.*, vol. 14, pp. 201–7.

ROSENTHAL, R., and JACOBSON, L. F. (1968), *Pygmalion in the Classroom: Teacher Expectation and Pupils' Intellectual Development*, Holt, Rinehart & Winston, New York.

ROSENZWEIG, M. R., and BENNETT, E. L. (1977), 'Effects of environmental enrichment or impoverishment on learning and on brain values in rodents', in A. Oliviero (ed.), *Genetics,*

*Environment and Intelligence*, North-Holland, Amsterdam, pp. 163–96.

ROSENZWEIG, M. R., BENNETT, E. L., and DIAMOND, M. C. (1967), 'Effects of differential environments on brain anatomy and brain chemistry', in J. Zubin and G. A. Jervis (eds.), *Psychopathology of Mental Development*, Grune & Stratton.

ROSENZWEIG, M. R., KRECH, D., BENNETT, E. L., and DIAMOND, M. C. (1968), 'Modifying brain chemistry and anatomy by enrichment or impoverishment of experience', in G. Newton and S. Levine (eds.), *Early Experience and Behavior*, C. C. Thomas, Springfield, Ill.

ROSS, G., KAGAN, J., ZELAZO, P., and KOTELCHUCK, M. (1975), 'Separation protest in infants in home and laboratory', *Devel. Psychol.*, vol. 11, pp. 256–7.

ROSS, H. S., and GOLDMAN, B. D. (1977), 'Establishing new social relations in infancy', in T. Alloway, P. Pliner and L. Krames (eds.), *Advances in the Study of Communication and Affect: 3. Attachment Behavior*, Plenum, New York.

ROSS, J. M., and SIMPSON, H. R. (1971), 'The National Survey of Health and Development: II. Rate of school progress between 8 and 15 years and between 15 and 18 years', *Brit. J. educ. Psychol.*, vol. 41, pp. 125–35.

ROTHBART, M. K. (1971), 'Birth order and mother–child interaction in an achievement situation', *J. Pers. Soc. Psychol.*, vol. 17, pp. 113–20.

ROUDINESCO, J., and APPELL, G. (1950), 'Les répercussions de la stabilization hospitalière sur le développement psychomoteur des jeunes enfants', *Semaine des Hôpitaux de Paris*, vol. 26, pp. 2271–3. Abstract in R. Dinnage and M. L. K. Pringle, *Residential Child Care: Facts and Fallacies*, Longman, 1967.

ROUDINESCO, J., and APPELL, G. (1951), 'De certains répercussions de la carence de soins maternels et de la vie en collectivité sur les enfants de 1 à 4 ans', *Bulletins et Mémoires de la Société Médicale des Hôpitaux de Paris*, vol. 67, pp. 106–20. Abstract in R. Dinnage and M. L. K. Pringle, *Residential Child Care: Facts and Fallacies*, Longman, 1967.

ROWNTREE, G. (1955), 'Early childhood in broken families', *Pop. Stud.*, vol. 8, pp. 247–63.

ROY, A. (1978), 'Vulnerability factors and depression in women', *Brit. J. Psychiat.*, vol. 133, pp. 106–10.

RUBENSTEIN, J. L., and HOWES, C. (1976), 'The effect of peers on toddler interaction with mother and toys', *Child Devel.*, vol. 47, pp. 597–605.

RUBENSTEIN, J. L., and HOWES, C. (1979), 'Caregiving and infant behavior in day care and in homes', *Devel. Psychol.*, vol. 15, pp. 1–24.

RUBENSTEIN, J. L., PEDERSEN, F. A., and YARROW, L. J. (1977), 'What happens when mother is away: a comparison of mothers and substitute caregivers', *Devel. Psychol.*, vol. 13, pp. 529–30.

RUPPENTHAL, G. C., ARLING, G. L., HARLOW, H. F., SACKETT, G. P., and SUOMI, S. J. (1976), 'A 10-year perspective of motherless–mother monkey behavior', *J. Abn. Psychol.*, vol. 85, pp. 341–9.

RUTTER, M. (1966), *Children of Sick Parents: An Environmental and Psychiatric Study*, Oxford University Press.

RUTTER, M. (1967), 'A children's behaviour questionnaire for completion by teachers: preliminary findings', *J. Child Psychol. Psychiat.*, vol. 8, pp. 1–11.

RUTTER, M. (1970a), 'Autistic children: infancy to adulthood', *Seminars in Psychiatry*, vol. 2, pp. 435–50.

RUTTER, M. (1970b), 'Sex differences in children's responses to family stress', in E. J. Anthony and C. M. Koupernik (eds.), *The Child in His Family*, Wiley, New York.

RUTTER, M. (1971a), 'Parent–child separation: psychological effects on the children', *J. Child Psychol. Psychiat.*, vol. 12, pp. 233–60.

RUTTER, M. (1971b), 'Normal psychosexual development', *J. Child Psychol. Psychiat.*, vol. 11, pp. 259–83.

RUTTER, M. (1972a), 'Language retardation and psychological development', in M. Rutter and J. A. M. Martin (eds.), *Young Children with Delayed Speech*, Heinemann/SIMP, London.

RUTTER, M. (1972b), 'Maternal deprivation reconsidered', *J. psychosom. Res.*, vol. 16, pp. 241–50.

RUTTER, M. (1974), 'Dimensions of Parenthood: some myths and some suggestions', in Department of Health and Social Security Report: *The Family in Society: Dimensions of Parenthood*, HMSO, London.

RUTTER, M. (1975), *Helping Troubled Children*, Penguin, Harmondsworth; Plenum, New York, 1976.

RUTTER, M. (1977a), 'Brain damage syndromes in childhood: concepts and findings', *J. Child Psychol. Psychiat.*, vol. 18, pp. 1–21.

RUTTER, M. (1977b), 'Prospective studies to investigate behavioral change', in J. S. Strauss, H. M. Babigian and M. Roff (eds.), *The Origins and Course of Psychopathology*, Plenum, New York.

RUTTER, M. (1977c), 'Individual differences', in M. Rutter and L. Hersov (eds.), *Child Psychiatry: Modern Approaches*, Blackwell Scientific, Oxford.

RUTTER, M. (1977d), 'Separation, loss and family relationships', in M. Rutter and L. Hersov (eds.), *Child Psychiatry: Modern Aproaches*, Blackwell Scientific, Oxford.

RUTTER, M. (1978a), 'Early sources of security and competence', in J. S. Bruner and A. Garten (eds.), *Human Growth and Development*, Oxford University Press, London.

RUTTER, M. (1978b), 'Family, area and school influences in the genesis of conduct disorders', in L. Hersov, M. Berger and D. Shaffer (eds.), *Aggression and Antisocial Behaviour in Childhood and Adolescence* (J. Child Psychol. Psychiat. Monogr. Series no. 1), Pergamon, Oxford.

RUTTER, M. (1979a), 'Maternal deprivation, 1972–1978: new findings, new concepts, new approaches', *Child Devel.*, vol. 50, pp. 283–305.

RUTTER, M. (1979b), 'Protective factors in children's responses to stress and disadvantage', in M. W. Kent and J. E. Rolf (eds.), *Primary Prevention of Psychopathology: 3. Social Competence in Children*, University Press of New England, Hanover, NH.

RUTTER, M. (1979c), *Changing Youth in a Changing Society: Patterns of Adolescent Development and Disorder*, Nuffield Provincial Hospitals Trust, London (Harvard Univ. Press, Cambridge, Mass., 1980).

RUTTER, M. (1979d), 'Separation experiences: a new look at an old topic', *J. Pediat.*, vol. 95, pp. 147–54.

RUTTER, M. (1980a), 'Attachment and the development of social relationships', in M. Rutter (ed.), *Scientific Foundations of Developmental Psychiatry*, Heinemann Medical.

RUTTER, M. (1980b), 'Emotional development', in M. Rutter (ed.), *Scientific Foundations of Developmental Psychiatry*, Heinemann Medical.

RUTTER, M. (1980c), 'The city and the child', *Amer. J. Orthopsychiat.* (in press).

RUTTER, M. (1980d), 'Psychological *sequelae* of brain damage in childhood', *Amer. J. Psychiat.* (in press).

RUTTER, M. (1981), 'Social/emotional consequences of day care for pre-school children', *Amer. J. Orthopsychiat.* (in press).

RUTTER, M. (1980e), 'The long-term effects of early experience', *Devel. Med. Child Neurol.*, vol. 22, pp. 800–815.

RUTTER, M., BIRCH, H. G., THOMAS, A., and CHESS, S. (1964), 'Temperamental characteristics in infancy and the later development of behavioural disorders', *Brit. J. Psychiat.*, vol. 110, pp. 651–61.

RUTTER, M., and BROWN, G. W. (1966), 'The reliability and validity of measures of family life and relationships in families containing a psychiatric patient', *Soc. Psychiat.*, vol. 1, pp. 38–53.

RUTTER, M., COX, A., TUPLING, C., BERGER, M., and YULE, W. (1975), 'Attainment and adjustment in two geographical areas: I. The prevalence of psychiatric disorder', *Brit. J. Psychiat.*, vol. 126, pp. 493–509.

RUTTER, M., GRAHAM, P., and YULE, W. (1970), *A Neuropsychiatric Study in Childhood*, Heinemann.

RUTTER, M., KORN, S., and BIRCH, H. G. (1963), 'Genetic and environmental factors in the development of "primary reaction patterns"', *Brit. J. soc. clin. Psychol.*, vol. 2, pp. 161–73.

RUTTER, M., and MADGE, N. (1976), *Cycles of Disadvantage: a Review of Research*, Heinemann Educational, London.

RUTTER, M., MAUGHAN, B., MORTIMORE, P., and OUSTON, J. (1979), *15,000 Hours: Secondary Schools and their Effects on Children*, Open Books, London; Harvard University Press.

RUTTER, M., and MITTLER, P. (1972), 'Environmental influences on language development', in M. Rutter and J. A. M. Martin (eds.), *The Child with Delayed Speech*, Heinemann/ SIMP.

RUTTER, M., and QUINTON, D. (1977), 'Psychiatric disorder – ecological factors and concepts of causation', in H. McGurk (ed.), *Ecological Factors in Human Development*, North-Holland, Amsterdam.

RUTTER, M., TIZARD, J., and WHITMORE, K. (eds.) (1970), *Education, Health and Behaviour*, Longman.

RUTTER, M., YULE, B., QUINTON, D., ROWLANDS, O., YULE, W., and BERGER, M. (1975), 'Attainment and adjustment in two geographical areas: III. Some factors accounting for area differences', *Brit. J. Psychiat.*, vol. 126, pp. 520–33.

SACKETT, G. P. (1968), 'Abnormal behavior in laboratory-reared rhesus monkeys', in M. W. Fox (ed.), *Abnormal Behavior in Animals*, Saunders, New York.

SAINSBURY, P. (1971), 'Moving house and psychiatric morbidity', Paper presented at Annual Conference of Society for Psychosomatic Research, London, 1971.

SALZEN, E. A. (1978), 'Social attachment and a sense of security: a review', *Soc. Sci. Inf.*, vol. 17, pp. 555–627.

SAMEROFF, A. J., and CHANDLER, M. J. (1975), 'Reproductive risk and the continuum of caretaking casualty', in F. D. Horowitz (ed.), *Review of Child Development Research*, vol. 4, University of Chicago Press, Chicago.

SANDER, L. W. (1969), 'Comments on regulation and organization in the early infant–caretaker system', in R. J. Robinson (ed.), *Brain and Early Behaviour*, Academic Press, London.

SANDER, L. W., STECHLER, G., BURNS, P., and JULIA, H. (1970), 'Early mother–infant interaction and twenty-four-hour patterns of activity and sleep', *J. Amer. Acad. Child Psychiat.*, vol. 9, pp. 103–23.

SAYEGH, Y., and DENNIS, W. (1965), 'The effect of supplementary experiences upon the behavioural development of infants in institutions', *Child Devel.*, vol. 36, pp. 81–90.

SCARR, S. (1969), 'Social introversion–extraversion as a heritable response', *Child Devel.*, vol. 40, pp. 823–32.

SCARR, S., and WEINBERG, R. A. (1976), 'IQ test performance of black children adopted by white families', *Amer. Psychol.*, vol. 31, pp. 726–39.

SCARR, S., and WEINBERG, R. A. (1978), 'The influence of "family background" on intellectual attainment', *Amer. Sociol. Rev.*, vol. 43, pp. 674–92.

SCHAFFER, H. R. (1963), 'Some issues for research in the study of attachment behaviour', in B. M. Foss (ed.), *Determinants of Infant Behaviour*, vol. 2, Methuen.

SCHAFFER, H. R. (1965), 'Changes in developmental quotient under two conditions of maternal separation', *Brit. J. soc. clin. Psychol.*, vol. 4, pp. 39–46.

SCHAFFER, H. R. (1966), 'Activity level as a constitutional determinant of infantile reaction to deprivation', *Child Devel.*, vol. 37, pp. 595–602.

SCHAFFER, H. R. (1971), *The Growth of Sociability*, Penguin.

SCHAFFER, H. R., and CALLENDER, W. M. (1959), 'Psychological effects of hospitalization in infancy', *Pediatrics*, vol. 24, pp. 528–39.

SCHAFFER, H. R., and EMERSON, P. E. (1964), 'The development of social attachments in infancy', *Monogr. Soc. Res. Child Devel.*, vol. 29, no. 94.

SCHAFFER, H. R., and EMERSON, P. E. (1968), 'The effects of experimentally administered stimulation on developmental quotients of infants', *Brit. J. soc. clin. Psychol.*, vol. 7, pp. 61–7.

SCHIFF, M., DUYME, M., DUMARET, A., STEWART, J., TOMKIEWICZ, S., and FEINGOLD, J. (1978), 'Intellectual status of working-class children adopted early into upper-middle-class families', *Science*, vol. 200, pp. 1503–4.

SCHNEIRLA, T. A. (1965), 'Aspects of stimulation and organization in approach/withdrawal processes underlying vertebrate behavioral development', in D. S. Lehrman, R. A. Hinde and E. Shaw (eds.), *Advances in the Study of Behavior*, vol. I, Academic Press, New York and London.

SCHWARZ, J. C. (1972), 'Effects of peer familiarity on the behaviour of pre-schoolers in a novel situation', *J. Personality Soc. Psychol.*, vol. 24, pp. 276–84.

SCHWARZ, J. C., KROLICK, G., and STRICKLAND, R. G. (1973), 'Effects of early day experience on adjustment to a new environment', *Amer. J. Orthopsychiat.*, vol. 43, pp. 340–46.

SCHWARZ, J. C., STRICKLAND, R. G., and KROLICK, G. (1974), 'Infant day care: behavioral effects at pre-school age', *Devel. Psychol.*, vol. 10, pp. 502–6.

SCOTT, J. P. (1963), 'The process of primary socialization in canine and human infants', *Monogr. Soc. Res. Child Devel.*, vol. 28, no. 85.

SCOTT, J. P. (1971), 'Attachment and separation in dog and man: theoretical propositions', in H. R. Schaffer (ed.), *The Origins of Human Social Relations*, Academic Press, London.

SCOTT, J. P., and FULLER, J. L. (1965), *Genetics of the Social Behavior of the Dog*, University of Chicago Press, Chicago.

SCOTT, P. D. (1973), 'Fatal battered baby cases', *Medicine, Science and the Law*, vol. 13, pp. 197–206.

SCRIMSHAW, N. S., and GORDON, J. E. (1968), *Malnutrition, Learning and Behavior*, M I T Press, Lancaster.

SEARLE, L. V. (1949), 'The organization of hereditary maze-brightness and maze-dullness', *Genet. Psychol. Monogr.*, vol. 39, pp. 279–325.

SEARS, R. R. (1972), 'Attachment, dependency and frustration', in J. L. Gewirtz (ed.), *Attachment and Dependency*, Winston, Washington.

SEARS, R. R., PINTLER, M., and SEARS, P. S. (1946), 'Effect of father separation on preschool children's doll play aggression', *Child Devel.*, vol. 17, pp. 219–43.

SEAY, B., ALEXANDER, B. K., and HARLOW, H. F. (1964), 'Maternal behavior of socially deprived rhesus monkeys', *J. abnorm. soc. Psychol.*, vol. 69, pp. 345–54.

SEGALOWITZ, S. J., and GRUBER, F. A. (eds.) (1977), *Language Development and Neurological Theory*, Academic Press, New York.

SHARP, D., COLE, M., and LAVE, C. (1979), 'Education and cognitive development: the evidence from experimental research', *Monogr. Soc. Res. Child Devel.*, vol. 44, no. 178.

SHEPHERD, M., OPPENHEIM, B., and MITCHELL, S. (1971),

*Childhood Behaviour and Mental Health*, University of London Press.

SHIELDS, J. (1954), 'Personality differences and neurotic traits in normal twin schoolchildren', *Eugen. Rev.*, vol. 45, pp. 213–46.

SHIELDS, J. (1968), 'Psychiatric genetics', in M. Shepherd and D. L. Davies (eds.), *Studies in Psychiatry*, Oxford University Press.

SHIELDS, J. (1973), 'Heredity and psychological abnormality', in H. J. Eysenck (ed.), *Handbook of Abnormal Psychology* (2nd edn), Pitman, pp. 540–603.

SHIELDS, J. (1977), 'Polygenic influences', in M. Rutter and L. Hersov (eds.), *Child Psychiatry: Modern Approaches*, Blackwell Scientific, Oxford, pp. 22–46.

SHIELDS, J. (1980), 'Genetics and mental development', in M. Rutter (ed.), *Scientific Foundations of Developmental Psychiatry*, Heinemann Medical.

SIDOWSKI, J. B. (1970), 'Altruism, helplessness and distress: effects of physical restraint on the social and play behaviors of infant monkeys', *Proc. Seventy-Eighth Ann. Conv. Amer. Psychol. Assn.*

SIEGEL, A. E., and HAAS, M. B. (1963), 'The working mother: a review of research', *Child Devel.*, vol. 34, pp. 513–42.

SIEGEL, G. M., and HARKINS, J. P. (1963), 'Verbal behavior of adults in two conditions with institutionalized retarded children', *J. Speech and Hearing Disorders* (Monograph Supplement), vol. 10, pp. 39–47.

SILVER, H. K., and FINKELSTEIN, M. (1967), 'Deprivation dwarfism', *J. Pediat.*, vol. 70, pp. 317–24.

SKEELS, H. M. (1942), 'A study of the effects of differential stimulation on mentally retarded children: follow-up report', *Amer. J. ment. Def.*, vol. 46, pp. 340–50.

SKEELS, H. M. (1966), 'Adult status of children with contrasting early life experiences', *Monogr. Soc. Res. Child Devel.*, vol. 31, pp. 1–56.

SKEELS, H. M., and DYE, H. (1939), 'A study of the effects of differential stimulation on mentally retarded children', *Proc. Amer. Assn Ment. Def.*, vol. 44, pp. 114–36.

SKEELS, H. M., and FILLMORE, E. A. (1937), 'The mental development of children from underprivileged homes', *J. genet. Psychol.*, vol. 50, pp. 427–39.

SKEELS, H. M., and HARMS, I. (1948), 'Children with inferior social histories: their mental development in adoptive homes', *J. genet. Psychol.*, vol. 72, pp. 283–94.

SKEELS, H. M., UPDEGRAFF, R., WELLMAN, B. L., and WILLIAMS, H. M. (1938), 'A study of environmental stimulation: an orphanage preschool project', *Univ. Iowa Stud. child Welf.*, vol. 15, no. 4.

SKINNER, A. E., and CASTLE, R. L. (1969), *78 Battered Children: A Retrospective Study*, National Association for the Prevention of Cruelty to Children.

SKODAK, M., and SKEELS, H. M. (1949), 'A final follow-up study of one hundred adopted children', *J. genet. Psychol.*, vol. 75, pp. 85–125.

SLUCKIN, W. (1970), *Early Learning in Man and Animal*, Allen & Unwin.

SLUCKIN, W. (1973), *Imprinting and Early Learning* (2nd edn), Aldine Publishing Co., Chicago.

SMITH, C., and LLOYD, B. (1978), 'Maternal behavior and perceived sex of infant: revisited', *Child Devel.*, vol. 49, pp. 1263–5.

SMITH, S. M. (1975), *The Battered Child Syndrome*, Butterworth.

SNOW, C. E., and FERGUSON, C. A. (eds.) (1977), *Talking to Children: Language input and acquisition*, Cambridge University Press.

SNOW, C. E., and HOEFNAGEL-HOHLE, M. (1978), 'The critical period for language acquisition: evidence from second language learning', *Child Devel.*, vol. 49, pp. 1114–28.

SOLOMON, R. L., and CORBIT, J. D. (1974), 'An opponent-process theory of motivation: I. Temporal dynamics of affect', *Psychol. Rev.*, vol. 81, pp. 119–45.

SPELKE, E., ZELAZO, P., KAGAN, J., and KOTELCHUCK, M. (1973), 'Father interaction and separation protest', *Devel. Psychol.*, vol. 9, pp. 83–90.

SPENCER-BOOTH, Y. (1970), 'The relationships between mammalian young and conspecifics other than mothers and peers: a review', in D. S. Lehrman, R. A. Hinde, and E. Shaw (eds), *Advances in the Study of Behavior*, vol. 3, Academic Press, New York.

SPENCER-BOOTH, Y., and HINDE, R. A. (1971a), 'Effects of 6 days' separation from mother on 18 to 32-week-old rhesus monkeys', *Anim. Behav.*, vol. 19, pp. 174–91.

SPENCER-BOOTH, Y., and HINDE, R. A. (1971b), 'Effects of brief separations from mothers during infancy on behavior a review', in D. S. Lehrman, R. A. Hinde, and E. Shaw (eds.), *Psychiat.*, vol. 12, pp. 157–72.

SPINETTA, J. J., and RIGLER, D. (1972), 'The child-abusing parent: a psychological review', *Psychol. Bull.*, vol. 77, pp. 296–304.

SPIRO, M. E. (1958), *Children of the Kibbutz*, Oxford University Press.

SPITZ, R. A. (1946), 'Anaclitic depression', *Psychoanalytic Study of the Child*, vol. 2, pp. 313–42.

SPRADLIN, J. E., and ROSENBERG, S. (1964), 'Complexity of adult verbal behavior in a dyadic situation with retarded children', *J. Abn. Soc. Psychol.*, vol. 68, pp. 694–8.

SPROTT, W. J. H., JEPHCOTT, A. P., and CARTER, M. P. (1955), *The Social Background of Delinquency*, University of Nottingham.

SROUFE, L. A. (1977), 'Early Experience: evidence and myth', *Contemporary Psychology*, vol. 22, pp. 878–80.

SROUFE, L. A. (1979), 'The coherence of individual development: early care, attachment and subsequent developmental issues', *Amer. Psychol.*, vol. 34, pp. 834–41.

SROUFE, L. A., and WATERS, E. (1977), 'Attachment as an organizational construct', *Child Devel.*, vol. 48, pp. 1184–99.

STACEY, M., DEARDEN, R., PILL, R., and ROBINSON, D. (1970), *Hospitals, Children and Their Families: The Report of a Pilot Study*, Routledge & Kegan Paul.

STALLINGS, J., and PORTER, A. (1980), *National Day Care Home Study: Observation Component*, Final Report to Dept of Health, Education and Welfare, Washington, D C.

STARR, R. H. (1971), 'Cognitive development in infancy: assessment, acceleration and actualization', *Merrill-Palmer Q.*, vol. 17, pp. 153–86.

STAYTON, D. J., and AINSWORTH, M. D. S. (1973), 'Individual differences in infant response to brief, everyday separations as related to other infant and maternal behaviors', *Devel. Psychol.*, vol. 9, pp. 213–25.

STAYTON, D. J., AINSWORTH, M. D. S., and MAIN, M. B. (1973), 'Development of separation behavior in the first year of life: protest, following, and greeting', *Devel. Psychol.*, vol. 9, pp. 213–25.

STEDMAN, D. J., and EICHORN, D. H. (1964), 'A comparison of the growth and development of institutionalized and home-reared mongoloids during infancy and early childhood', *Amer. J. ment. Def.*, vol. 69, pp. 391–401.

STEELE, B. F., and POLLOCK, C. B. (1968), 'A psychiatric study of parents who abuse infants and small children', in R. E. Helfer and C. H. Kempe (eds.), *The Battered Child*, University of Chicago Press.

STEIN, D. G., ROSEN, J. J., and BUTTERS, N. (eds.) (1974), *Plasticity and recovery of functions in the central nervous system*, Academic Press, New York.

STEIN, Z. A., and KASSAB, H. (1970), 'Nutrition', in J. Wortis (ed.), *Mental Retardation*, vol. 2, Grune & Stratton, New York.

STEIN, Z. A., and SUSSER, M. (1966), 'Nocturnal enuresis as a phenomenon of institutions', *Devel. Med. child Neurol.*, vol. 8, pp. 677–85.

STEIN, Z. A., and SUSSER, M. (1967), 'The social dimensions of a symptom', *Soc. Sci. Med.*, vol. 1, pp. 183–201.

STEIN, Z. A., and SUSSER, M. (1970), 'Mutability of intelligence and epidemiology of mild mental retardation', *Rev. educ. Res.*, vol. 40, pp. 29–67.

STEINSCHNEIDER, A. (1967), 'Developmental psychophysiology', in Y. Brackbill (ed.), *Infancy and Early Childhood*, Free Press.

STERN, D., JAFFE, J., BEEBE, B., and BENNETT, S. L. (1975), 'Vocalizing in unison and in alternation: two modes of communication within the mother-infant dyad', *Annals of the New York Academy of Sciences*, vol. 263, pp. 89–100.

STEVENS, A. (1975), *Attachment and Polymatric Rearing. A study of attachment formation, separation anxiety and fear of strangers in infants reared by multiple mothering in an institutional setting* (unpublished D M thesis, University of Oxford). ford).

STEVENSON, H. W., PARKER, T., WILKINSON, A., BONNE-VAUX, B., and GONZALES, M. (1978), 'Schooling, environment and cognitive development: A cross-cultural study', *Monogr. Soc. Res. Child Devel.*, vol. 43, no. 175.

STEVENSON, I. (1957), 'Is the human personality more plastic in infancy and childhood?', *Amer. J. Psychiat.*, vol. 114, pp. 152–61.

STOLZ, L. M. (1960), 'Effects of maternal employment on children: evidence for research', *Child Devel.*, vol. 31, pp. 749–82.

STOLZ, L. M., *et al.* (1954), *Father Relations of War-Born Children*, Stanford University Press, Stanford, Calif.

SUOMI, S. J. (1977), 'Adult male-infant interactions among monkeys living in nuclear families', *Child Devel.*, vol. 48, pp. 1255–70.

SUOMI, S. J., HARLOW, H. F., and DOMEK, C. J. (1970), 'Effect of repetitive infant-infant separation of young monkeys', *J.*

*abnorm. Psychol.*, vol. 76, pp. 161–72.

SUOMI, S. J., HARLOW, H. F., and NOVAK, M. A. (1974), 'Reversal of social deficits produced by isolation rearing in monkeys', *J. Hum. Evol.*, vol. 3, pp. 527–34.

SVEJDA, M. J., CAMPOS, J. J., and EMDE, R. N. (1980), 'Mother-infant "bonding": failure to generalize', *Child Devel.* (in press).

TAIT, C. D., and HODGES, E. F. (1962), *Delinquents: Their Families and the Community*, C. C. Thomas, Springfield, Ill.

TALBOT, N. B., SOBEL, E. H., BURKE, B. S., LINDEMANN, E., and KAUFMAN, S. B. (1947), 'Dwarfism in healthy children: its possible relation to emotional, nutritional and endocrine disturbances', *New Eng. J. Med.*, vol. 236, pp. 783–93.

THEIS, S. VAN S. (1924), *How Foster Children Turn Out*, State Charities Aid Association, New York.

THOMAN, E. B., BARNETT, C. R., and LEIDERMAN, P. H. (1971), 'Feeding behaviors of newborn infants as a function of parity of the mother', *Child Devel.*, vol. 42, pp. 1471–83.

THOMAN, E. B., TURNER, A. M., LEIDERMAN, P. H., and BARNETT, C. R. (1970), 'Neonate–mother interaction: effects of parity on feeding behavior', *Child Devel.*, vol. 41, pp. 1103–11.

THOMAS, A., CHESS, S., and BIRCH, H. G. (1968), *Temperament and Behaviour Disorders in Children*, University of London Press.

THOMAS, A., CHESS, S., BIRCH, H. G., HERTZIG, M., and KORN, S. (1963), *Behavioural Individuality in Early Childhood*, University of London Press.

THOMPSON, W. R., and GRUSEC, J. (1970), 'Studies of early experience', in P. H. Mussen (ed.), *Carmichael's Manual of Child Psychology*, 3rd edn, Wiley, New York.

THOMPSON, W. R., and HERON, W. (1954), 'The effects of restricting early experience on the problem-solving capacity of dogs', *Canad. J. Psychol.*, vol. 8, pp. 17–31.

THOMPSON, W. R., and MELZACK, R. (1956), 'Early environment', *Sci. Amer.*, vol. 194, pp. 38–42.

THOMPSON, W. R., and OLIAN, S. (1961), 'Some effects on offspring behaviour of maternal adrenalin injection during pregnancy in three inbred mouse strains', *Psychol. Rep.*, vol. 8, pp. 87–90.

TIZARD, B. (1971), 'Environmental effects on language development: a study of residential nurseries', paper read at Annual Conference of the British Psychological Society, June 1971, University of Exeter.

TIZARD, B. (1977), *Adoption: A Second Chance*, Open Books, London.

TIZARD, B., COOPERMAN, O., JOSEPH, A., and TIZARD, J. (1972), 'Environmental effects on language development: a study of young children in long-stay residential nurseries', *Child Devel.*, vol. 43, pp. 337–58.

TIZARD, B., and HODGES, J. (1978), 'The effect of early institutional rearing on the development of eight-year-old children', *J. Child Psychol. Psychiat.*, vol. 19, pp. 99–118.

TIZARD, B., and JOSEPH, A. (1970), 'Cognitive development of young children in residential care: a study of children aged 24 months', *J. Child Psychol. Psychiat.*, vol. 11, pp. 177–86.

TIZARD, B., and REES, J. (1974), 'A comparison of the effects of adoption, restoration to the natural mother, and continued institutionalization on the cognitive development of four-year-old children', *Child Devel.*, vol. 45, pp. 92–9.

TIZARD, J. (1964), *Community Services for the Mentally Handicapped*, Oxford University Press.

TIZARD, J. (1969), 'The role of social institutions in the causation, prevention and alleviation of mental retardation', in C. Haywood (ed.), *Socio-Cultural Aspects of Mental Retardation*, Academic Press.

TIZARD, J., and TIZARD, B. (1971), 'The social development of two-year-old children in residential nurseries', in H. R. Schaffer (ed.), *The Origins of Human Social Relations*, Academic Press.

TIZARD, J., and TIZARD, B. (1972), 'The institution as an environment for development', in M. P. M. Richards (ed.), *The Integration of a Child into a Social World*, Cambridge University Press.

TODD, G. A., and PALMER, B. (1968), 'Social reinforcement of infant babbling', *Child Devel.*, vol. 39, pp. 591–6.

TRACY, R. L., LAMB, M. E., and AINSWORTH, M. D. S. (1976), 'Infant approach behavior as related to attachment', *Child Devel.*, vol. 47, pp. 571–8.

TRASLER, G. (1960), *In Place of Parents: A Study of Foster Care*, Routledge & Kegan Paul.

TURNER, C. H., DAVENPORT, R. K., and ROGERS, C. M. (1969), 'The effect of early deprivation on the social behavior of adolescent chimpanzees', *Amer. J. Psychiat.*, vol. 125, pp. 1531–6.

UCKO, L. E. (1965), 'A comparative study of asphyxiated and non-asphyxiated boys from birth to five years', *Devel. Med. child Neurol.*, vol. 7, pp. 643–57.

URSIN, H., BAADE, E., and LEVINE, S. (1978), *Psychobiology of Stress: A Study of Coping Men*, Academic Press, New York.

VANDELL, D. L. (1979), 'Effects of a playgroup experience on mother–son and father–son interactions', *Devel. Psychol.*, vol. 15, pp. 379–85.

VERNON, D. T. A., FOLEY, J. M., and SCHULMAN, J. L. (1967), 'Effect of mother–child separation and birth order on young children's responses to two potentially stressful experiences', *J. Person. soc. Psychol.*, vol. 5, pp. 162–74.

VERNON, D. T. A., FOLEY, J. M., SIPOWICZ, R. R., and SCHULMAN, J. L. (1965), *The Psychological Responses of Children to Hospitalization and Illness*, C. C. Thomas.

VERNON, P. E. (1969), *Intelligence and Cultural Environment*, Methuen.

VOGEL, S. R., BROVERMAN, I. K., BROVERMAN, D. M., CLARKSON, F. E., and ROSENKRANTS, P. S. (1970), 'Maternal employment and perception of sex roles among college students', *Devel. Psychol.*, vol. 3, pp. 384–91.

WALDROP, M., and BELL, R. Q. (1966), 'Effects of family size and density on newborn characteristics', *Amer. J. Orthopsychiat.*, vol. 36, pp. 544–50.

WALLER, W. W., and HILL, R. (1951), *The Family: a dynamic interpretation*, Dryden, New York.

WALLERSTEIN, J. S., and KELLY, J. B. (1980), *Surviving the Breakup: How Children and Parents Cope with Divorce*, Basic Books, New York; Grant McIntyre, London.

WALTERS, R. H., and PARKE, R. D. (1965), 'The role of the distance receptors in the development of social responsiveness', in L. P. Lipsitt and C. C. Spiker (eds.), *Advances in Child Development and Behavior*, vol. 2, Academic Press, New York.

WARDLE, C. J. (1961), 'Two generations of broken homes in the genesis of conduct and behaviour disorders in childhood', *Brit. med. J.*, vol. 2, pp. 349–54.

WASZ-HÖCKERT, O., LIND, J., VUORENKOSKI, V., PARTANEN, T., and VALANNE, E. (1968), *The Infant Cry: A Spectrographic and Auditory Analysis* (Clinics in Developmental Medicine, no. 29), Heinemann/SIMP, London.

WATERS, E., WIPPMAN, J., and SROUFE, L. A. (1979), 'Attachment, positive affect, and competence in the peer group: two studies in construct validation', *Child Devel.*, vol. 50, pp. 821–9.

WATSON, P. (1970), 'How race affects IQ', *New Soc.*, 16 July, pp. 103–4.

WEINBERG, J., and LEVINE, S. (1977), 'Early handling influences on behavioral and physiological responses during active avoidance', *Devel. Psychobiol.*, vol. 10, pp. 161–9.

WEISBERG, P. (1963), 'Social and nonsocial conditioning of infant vocalizations', *Child Devel.*, vol. 34, pp. 377–88.

WERNER, E. E. (1979), *Cross-Cultural Child Development: a view from the planet earth*, Brooks/Cole, Monterey, California.

WERNER, E. E., BIERMAN, J. M., and FRENCH, F. E. (1971), *The Children of Kauai: a longitudinal study from the prenatal period to age 10*, Univ. Press of Hawaii, Honolulu.

WERNER, E. E., and SMITH, R. S. (1977), *Kauai's Children Come of Age*, Univ. Press of Hawaii, Honolulu.

WERNER, E. E., and SMITH, R. S. (1980), *Vulnerable, But Invincible: a longitudinal study of resilient children and youth*, McGraw-Hill, New York.

WEST, D. J. (1969), *Present Conduct and Future Delinquency*, Heinemann.

WEST, D. J., and FARRINGTON, D. P. (1973), *Who Becomes Delinquent?*, Heinemann Educational.

WEST, D. J., and FARRINGTON, D. P. (1977), *The Delinquent Way of Life*, Heinemann Educational, London.

WHEELER, L. R. (1942), 'A comparative study of the intelligence of East Tennessee mountain children', *J. educ. Psychol.*, vol. 33, pp. 321–34.

WHITE, B. L. (1967), 'An experimental approach to the effects of experience on early human behavior', in J. P. Hill (ed.), *Minnesota Symposia on Child Psychology*, vol. 1, University of Minnesota Press, Minneapolis.

WHITE, B. L. (1971), *Human Infants: Experience and Psychological Development*, Prentice-Hall, Englewood Cliffs, N.J.

WHITEHEAD, L. (1979), 'Sex differences in children's responses to family stress: a re-evaluation', *J. Child Psychol. Psychiat.*, vol. 20, pp. 247–54.

WHITEN, A. (1977), 'Assessing the effects of perinatal events on the success of the mother–infant relationship', in H. R. Schaffer (ed.), *Studies in Mother–Infant Interaction*, Academic Press, London.

WHITTEN, C. F., PETTIT, M. G., and FISCHHOFF, J. (1969), 'Evidence that growth failure from maternal deprivation is secondary to undereating', *J. Amer. Med. Assn*, vol. 209, pp. 1675–82.

WHO EXPERT COMMITTEE ON MENTAL HEALTH (1951), *Report on the Second Session 1951*, World Health Organization, Geneva.

WIDDOWSON, E. M. (1951), 'Mental contentment and physical growth', *Lancet*, vol. 1, pp. 1316–18.

WIESEL, T. N., and HUBEL, D. H. (1963), 'Single cell responses in striate cortex of kittens deprived of vision in one eye', *J. Neurophysiol.*, vol. 26, pp. 1003–17.

WIESEL, T. N., and HUBEL, D. H. (1965a), 'Comparison of the effects of unilateral and bilateral eye closure on cortical unit responses in kittens', *J. Neurophysiol.*, vol. 28, pp. 1029–40.

WIESEL, T. N., and HUBEL, D. H. (1965b), 'Extent of recovery from the effects of visual deprivation in kittens', *J. Neurophysiol.*, vol. 28, pp. 1060–72.

WILCOX, B. M., STAFF, P., and ROMAINE, M. F. (1980), 'A comparison of individual and multiple assignment of caregivers to infants in day care', *Merrill-Palmer Q.*, vol. 26, pp. 53–62.

WILLERMAN, L. (1979), 'Effects of families on intellectual development', *Amer. Psychol.*, vol. 34, pp. 923–9.

WILSON, H. (1974), 'Parenting in poverty', *Brit. J. Soc. Work*, vol. 4, pp. 241–54.

WINETT, R. A., FUCHS, W. L., MOFFATT, S. A., and NERVIANO, V. J. (1977), 'A cross-sectional study of children and their families in different child-care environments: some data and conclusions', *J. Comm. Psychol.*, vol. 5, pp. 149–59.

WINICK, M., MEYER, K. K., and HARRIS, R. C. (1975), 'Malnutrition and environmental enrichment by early adoption', *Science*, vol. 190, pp. 1173–5.

WOLFER, J. A., and VISINTAINER, M. A. (1979), 'Pre-hospital psychological preparation for tonsillectomy patients: effects on children's and parents' adjustment', *Pediatrics*, vol. 64, pp. 646–55.

WOLFF, P. H. (1969), 'The natural history of crying and other vocalizations in early infancy', in B. M. Foss (ed.), *Determinants of Infant Behaviour*, vol. 4, Methuen.

WOLFF, S., and ACTON, W. P. (1968), 'Characteristics of parents of disturbed children', *Brit. J. Psychiat.*, vol. 114, pp. 593–61.

WOLFHEIM, J. H., JENSEN, G. D., and BOBBITT, R. A. (1970), 'Effects of group environment on the mother–infant relationship in pig-tailed monkeys (*Macaca nemestrina*)', *Primates*, vol. 11, pp. 119–24.

WOLKIND, S. N. (1974), 'The components of "affectionless psychopathy" in institutionalized children', *J. Child Psychol. Psychiat.*, vol. 15, pp. 215–20.

WOLKIND, S. N., HALL, F., and PAWLBY, S. J. (1977), 'Individual differences in mothering behaviour: a combined epidemiological and observational approach', in P. Graham (ed.), *Epidemiological Approaches in Child Psychiatry*, Academic Press, London.

WOLKIND, S. N., KRUK, S., and CHAVES, L. P. (1976), 'Childhood separation experiences and psychosocial status in primiparous women: preliminary findings', *Brit. J. Psychiat.*, vol. 128, pp. 391–6.

WOLKIND, S. N., and RUTTER, M. (1973), 'Children who have been "in care" – an epidemiological study', *J. Child Psychol. Psychiat.*, vol. 14, pp. 97–105.

WOODS, P. J., RUCKELSHAUS, S. I., and BOWLING, D. M. (1960), 'Some effects of "free" and "restricted" environmental rearing conditions upon adult behavior in the rat', *Psychol. Rep.*, vol. 6, pp. 191–200.

WOOTTON, B. (1959), *Social Science and Social Pathology*, Allen & Unwin.

WOOTTON, B. (1962), 'A social scientist's approach to maternal deprivation', in *Deprivation of Maternal Care: A Reassessment of its Effects*, World Health Organization, Geneva.

WORTIS, H. (1970), 'Poverty and retardation: social aspects', in J. Wortis (ed.), *Mental Retardation*, vol. 1, Grune & Stratton.

WYNNE, J., and HULL, D. (1977), 'Why are children admitted to hospital?', *Brit. Med. J.*, vol. 2, p. 1140.

YANDO, R. M., and KAGAN, J. (1968), 'The effects of teacher tempo on the child', *Child Devel.*, vol. 39, pp. 27–34.

YARROW, L. J. (1961), 'Maternal deprivation: toward an empirical and conceptual re-evaluation', *Psychol. Bull.*, vol. 58, pp. 459–90.

YARROW, L. J. (1963), 'Research in dimensions of early maternal care', *Merrill-Palmer Q.*, vol. 9, pp. 101–14.

YARROW, L. J. (1964), 'Separation from parents during early childhood', in M. L. Hoffman and L. W. Hoffman (eds.), *Review of Child Development Research*, vol. 1, Russell Sage Foundation, New York.

YARROW, L. J. (1968), 'The crucial nature of early experience', in D. C. Glass (ed.), *Environmental Influences*, Russell Sage Foundation, New York.

YARROW, M. R., SCOTT, P., DE LOEUW, L., and HERNIG, C.

(1962), 'Child rearing in families of working and non-working mothers', *Sociometry*, vol. 25, pp. 122–40.

YUDKIN, S., and HOLME, A. (1963), *Working Mothers and Their Children*, Michael Joseph.

YULE, W., and RAYNES, N. V. (1972), 'Behavioural characteristics of children in residential care in relation to indices of separation', *J. Child Psychol. Psychiat.*, vol. 13, pp. 249–58.

ZIGLER, E. (1966), 'Mental retardation: current issues and approaches', in M. L. Hoffman and L. W. Hoffman (eds.), *Review of Child Development Research*, vol. 2, Russell Sage Foundation, New York.

# Author Index

# Subject Index